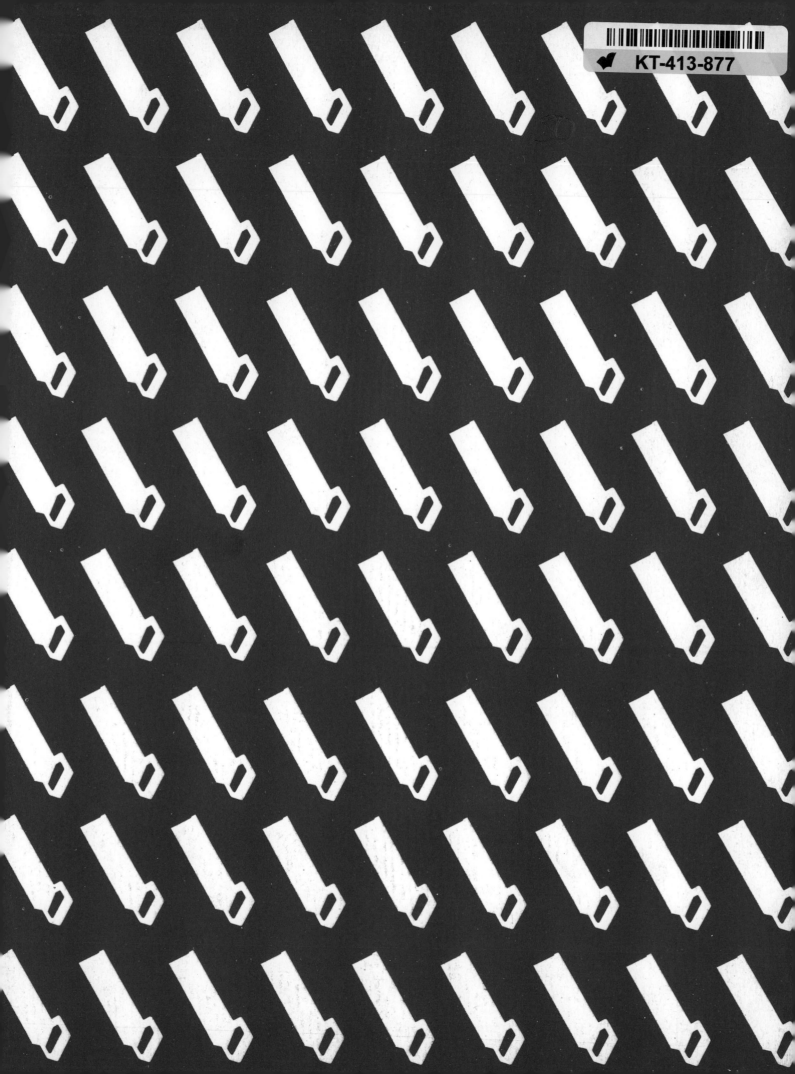

THE DIY
TOOL GUIDE

How to choose, use and care for
your tools and equipment

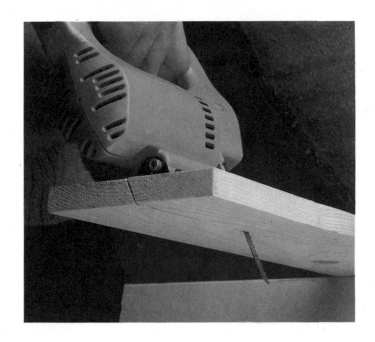

THE DIY TOOL GUIDE

How to choose, use and care for your tools and equipment

Edited by Rick Ball

ORBIS PUBLISHING·London

Acknowledgments

Advertising Arts pp 51 (artwork), 53 (artwork); *Arka Graphics* pp 110–111; *Bingham, Graham* pp 43–44; *Emmerich (Berlon) Ltd* pp 86–87 (photos); *Evans, Calvin* p 62 (artwork); *Fleury, Eugene* pp 25–26 (artwork), 39 (artwork), 45–49, 123; *Hayward Art Group* pp 16–17 (artwork), 85, 102–106, 108–109; *Meekums, Barry* p 64; *Orbis Publishing Ltd* pp 82, 116; *Orbis/Dudley Reed* p 101; *Orbis/Langham Studios* pp 10–12, 14–17 (photos), 28–29, 32–33 (photos), 56–59 (photos), 64 (inset), 66, 112–113; *Orbis/Peter Pugh Cook* pp 12 (workbenches), 21–23 (photos); *Orbis/John Rawlings Studio* pp 88, 96 (photo); *Orbis/Terry Trott* pp 18–20, 25–27 (photos), 34–42, 50–55 (photos), 60–63 (photos), 67–77, 79–81, 104 (photo), 120–121, 124–125; *Orbis Verlag* p 6; *Studio Briggs* pp 84, 86–87; *Venner Artists* pp 1, 22–24 (artwork), 33 (artwork), 89–101, 122; *Weller, Peter* pp 60–61 (artwork); *Whitehead, Garry* pp 56–57 (artwork), 118–119.

First published in Great Britain by Orbis Publishing
Limited: London 1980
© Orbis Publishing Limited 1980

Printed in Czechoslovakia
ISBN: 0 85613 224 1
50120

Contents

Introduction

Doing the job yourself saves money, but before the handyman begins counting the financial benefits of DIY, he must dig deep in his pocket to buy the best tools he can afford. There's absolutely no point in trying to skimp on a tool kit. The old saying which tells us 'you get what you pay for' is nowhere truer than in the tool shop. Cheap tools may be adequate for those limiting their DIY efforts to fixing the odd shelf, but their working life is almost invariably brief.

Most of us learn the lesson the hard way. Confronted by the high cost of quality tools in the specialist shops, we have all been tempted by those bargain tool offers on the market stall. I suspect those who succumbed to the temptation and bought a cheap tool will nurse a sneaking sympathy for the proverbial bad workman who blamed his latest bodge on bad tools. The poor quality of any cheap and cheerful screwdriver will soon show through, making good work impossible and forcing us to relegate it to such humble duties as opening paint tins, while we swear never again to fall for false economy.

Another lesson many of us have learned the hard way is that tools should be used only for the jobs they were designed to do, and no more. The unsavoury alternative to tool care is irreparable damage to a pricey tool. How many of us have bought good tools only to fall into such traps as opening a stubborn paint tin with the nearest screwdriver, thereby ruining an excellent tool, or prised out an awkward tack with a handy but expensive chisel?

The high cost of good tools means that only the very wealthy are in a position to walk into a tool shop and buy a complete instant tool kit. Most of us are obliged to buy our tools one by one, slowly building up a good range of versatile tools as each one becomes crucial for our next project.

This brings us to the problem of which tools to buy first. Clearly there are certain absolutely indispensable tools, such as a hammer, screwdriver and saw, without which few jobs are possible. But which hammer, which type of saw? *The DIY Tool Guide* has been devised to help answer those questions, by providing a completely independent and impartial analysis of the tools on the market, outlining their function and providing illustrated instructions on the most efficient methods of using them.

It is worth stressing at this point that the best way to handle tools is also the safest. Careless handling of a good sharp chisel or saw can put a premature end to your career in DIY. Safety first is even more essential where power tools are con-cerned. The twin threats of electricity and a rapidly spinning circular saw blade should breed caution in the home handyman.

Both during use and in storage, elementary precautions will avoid accidents with cutting tools. Storing chisels loose and unprotected in a deep tool box, where you rummage regularly in search of an elusive spanner or wall plug, can result in unpleasant cuts. For this reason, proper storage is vital. It is doubly vital if you want to protect your financial investment as well as your health. Even the best quality tools can be easily damaged by collision with their neighbours in the tool box. It may be hard to believe, but provision of proper storage for tools is a sensible first step in the process of building a proper range of tools. It can also save you many frustrating hours otherwise wasted in hunting the tool you need through a chaos of boxes.

While such considerations as safety and storage are fundamental, the main function of this book remains the clear and unbiased presentation of basic information and technical data on the tools needed by the home handyman starting out on a home improvement campaign. Beginning with th elements of a basic tool kit, we proceed to examine the individual tools one by one. We also show the array of tools needed for such specific jobs as laying concrete and bricklaying, which the more adventurous will certainly wish to tackle during fine weather. Indeed, we hope that, spurred on by an improved knowledge of tools, many thousands will be encouraged to expand their DIY horizons, realising that behind the mystique of tools lie simple principles which the average handyman – or woman – can master.

Our only concern is that, if you buy all the tools described in *The DIY Tool Guide*, your pocket will be reeling from shock. We therefore extend some practical sympathy by showing you how you can use your basic tools to create some more, such as the excellent home-made sash cramp project, a real money saver. Of course, only the rash or rich would buy an expensive tool for a one-off job, but luckily the solution to this problem is growing easier day by day, as tool hire shops spread around the country. In the interests of economy, we include an appendix on the range of tools available through hire. Our survey is rounded off by a handy guide to metric/Imperial conversion, completing a book which we believe will be a unique and invaluable addition to any tool kit.

The basic tool kit

In an emergency, most households can muster a collection of basic tools, accumulated over the years and scattered in odd drawers and cupboards throughout the house. Few of us will therefore have to build up a tool kit completely from scratch. However, if the DIY bug bites, we begin to question the adequacy of our old tools. When we are seized by the DIY enthusiast's compulsion to expand the contents of the tool box, it is easy to waste large sums of money buying sophisticated, expensive but unsuitable tools, where simpler alternatives would have been both cheaper and more appropriate.

To prevent such costly mistakes, the following pages illustrate and explain the elements of a good, versatile basic tool kit. The total cost of all these items would make even the keenest handyman pale, but there is no need to buy everything at once. Besides the handyman's well-tried ploy of dropping heavy hints about presents at birthdays and Christmas, *The DIY Tool Guide's* hints can be followed for making some of your own basic tools. We have included simple tips for creating ingenious money-saving substitute tools, for example a bradawl and nail punch.

Some may be surprised to find that the electric drill is given pride of place in the basic tool kit, a judgement which may not meet with approval among the traditional craftsmen. However, we include this modern addition to the handyman's aids for both practical and psychological reasons. The jobs an electric drill can handle are all within the scope of older mechanical tools, but anyone who has attempted to drill even the smallest hole through a concrete lintel without the help of a power tool will no doubt agree that the electric drill can save enormous expenditure of time, effort and frustration making the initial expenditure of money well worth while.

Learning to use new tools consumes enough time and energy without labouring under the additional burden of blistered hands!

Our basic tool kit also gives space to a workbench. Without insisting on the absolute necessity for such an item, the versatile mobile bench illustrated is a good companion for the do-it-yourselfer, although the more adventurous will perhaps be tempted to make the admirable workbench featured later in the book. Life is of course possible without any special bench, but the principle we have followed is simple: if it makes the job easier, it is worth considering.

The tools chosen for the basic tool kit are all the products of reputable manufacturers, who can offer valuable after-sales service to the handyman. We do not, of course, suggest that these are the only reliable tools on the market, but we would insist on the value of choosing good names. This is a particularly good guideline for the newcomer to DIY whose lack of familiarity with the tools will make informed choice difficult.

The important items in the basic tool kit are analysed in more detail in the section of *The DIY Tool Guide* devoted to individual tools, where the many variations on each theme are described and illustrated. Before any purchasing decisions are taken, this section of the book will provide the background information needed for an informed choice, allowing the reader to select, at his, or her, ease, that elusive right tool for the job.

Special projects, such as laying concrete, need special and occasionally unfamiliar tools. For this reason, the tool analysis is followed by an examination of the tools required to lay concrete or bricks.

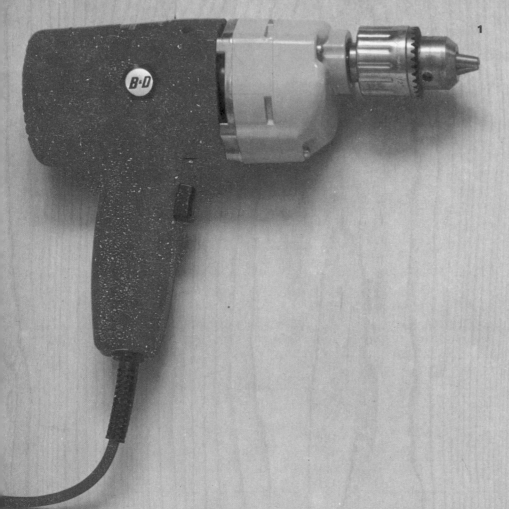

Most of the jobs tackled by the DIY novice involve simple techniques such as screwing fitments to walls, making shelves, laying floor coverings and so on. And you do not need a vast range of tools to take care of these everyday tasks.

The tools shown here and on the following pages are all useful but you do not have to buy all of them at once. So if you already have an electric drill you can get by without a hand one. A cross pein hammer and veneer tenon saw are not essential, while a vice will keep you going until you invest in a proper workbench. And you can always hire specialist tools (or if you are lucky borrow them from friends) as and when the need arises.

As your experience grows you will learn how to get the best out of your existing tools, when to make do with substitutes and when to acquire new ones. Top quality tools are expensive and it is a temptation to balance your budget by going for cheaper ones. But this policy usually proves more expensive in the long run and our advice is to buy the very best tools you can afford and to maintain them well.

1 Electric drill Go for a two-speed model which has a 12mm ($\frac{1}{2}$in) capacity chuck and also incorporates a hammer action. When drilling into different materials – wood, metal and so on – speeds from slow to fast are needed and variable speed facility allows for this. The 12mm ($\frac{1}{2}$in) chuck will enable you to bore large diameter holes and the hammer action to drill into really hard materials, such as the concrete lintel above a window to fix a curtain rail. (Black & Decker D720H 12mm/$\frac{1}{2}$in two-speed drill plus hammer action)

2 Hand drill (wheel brace) and countersink bit You can drill holes with it in a variety of materials using wood or masonry twist drills. It is usually supplied with a removable handle so you can work in tight corners often inaccessible to a power drill. Countersink bits make a neat, perfectly round recess for countersunk screws. (Stanley double pinion open gear hand drill 803, three-jaw chuck, chuck capacity 0–8mm/0–$\frac{5}{16}$in, countersink bit 137, 12mm/$\frac{1}{2}$in)

3 Steel measuring tape A 3m (10ft) length will be enough to cover all normal measuring jobs. Dual markings enable you to work in metric or Imperial units. Plastic window at top of case gives instant, accurate measures of internal recesses, drawer interiors. (Stanley Top Sight rule, 3m/10ft)

4 Combination square Version illustrated incorporates inside/outside try square (for measuring angles), straight-edge/marking edge, depth gauge, mitre square, small spirit level, scriber, protractor and screw gauge for screws Nos 4–12. The stock slides along a 305mm (12in) steel rule and can be locked in anywhere along it. (Stanley DIY combination square 46–150)

5 Try square Simpler alternative to combination, 229mm (9in) blade. (Stanley try square 19)

6 Cutting knife Multi-blade 127mm (5$\frac{1}{4}$in) long tool with range of blades to tackle cutting of materials from laminate to vinyl. (Stanley trimming knife 199A including five blades, blade guard, plus 5194 laminate blade)

7 Steel (cabinet) scraper This type gives a fine finish to hardwood surfaces, veneers and laminate edgings, shaving rather than scraping the surface.

4

5

6

7

8

9   10   11

12

13

STANLEY
No. 19
9in-23cm

SANDVIK
324 13 TEETH / 14 POINTS
12½/320MM
SWEDISH QUALITY STEEL SANDVIK AB SWEDEN

14

2000

SANDVIK AB • SWEDEN

Swedish Quality Steel • Super-Cut • Hard-Point

SANDVIK
22" / 550 mm
7 TEETH / 8 POINTS

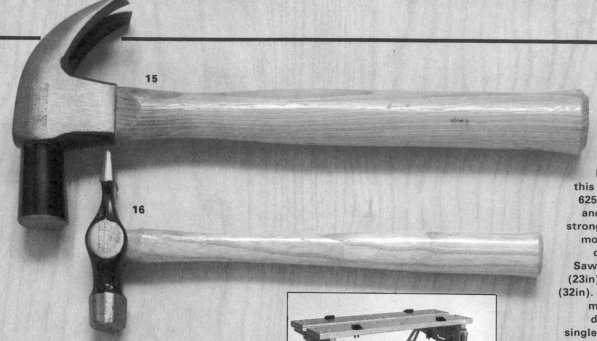

15

16

A workbench is likely to be the costliest item of your tool kit and we recommend this dual-height Workmate 625 (below). It is versatile and easy to carry and has strong vice jaws for holding most work pieces, from a door to a piece of pipe. Sawhorse height is 585mm (23in), bench height 813mm (32in). Cheaper self-assembly models available are the dual-height 600 and the single-height 400 (Black and Decker Workmate WM 625)

You can make your own by cutting up an old piece of saw steel into a square; file each edge square and you will have four working edges on each side. (Sandvik 474 scraper)

8 Block plane For a range of trimming jobs a model such as the one illustrated is most useful. The depth of cut is adjustable for coarse or fine work, including plastics. If you progress to more sophisticated woodwork you can buy a smoothing plane later. (Stanley $60\frac{1}{2}$ low angle, adjustable block plane, 152mm/6in length)

9 Bradawl Essential for marking timber and other soft materials prior to drilling. It is pressed into the surface to provide an accurate guide for the drill bit. You can use a small worn screwdriver instead; file the blade to a chisel edge.

17

18   19

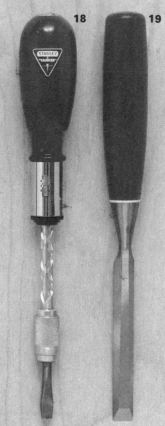

10 Nail punch For sinking pin and nail heads below the surface of timber without the hammer head bruising the work. You could start off with a 152mm (6in) nail with the point blunted.

11 Plumb bob Essential for establishing true verticals. You can make one yourself by tying a weight to a length of string.

12 Hacksaw A smaller type such as the one illustrated is useful for cutting through metal, sawing through rusty nuts, bolts, screws and nails. (Eclipse Junior 675)

13 Veneer tenon saw A fine tooth saw for small jobs where the larger panel saw with its coarser tooth setting would be impractical. Ideal for laminates, mitring and dowelling, it does not have the hard spine (back) common to most traditional tenon saws and offers greater cutting scope. (Sandvik hard point 324)

14 Panel saw Although there is a vast range of saws, each designed to do different work, the panel saw will cope with most straightforward sawing jobs. It is worth buying a hardpoint version as it will last longer than a conventional saw before the teeth blunt. 550mm (22in) long with seven teeth (eight points) per 25mm (1in). (Sandvik 2000 Supercut hardpoint handsaw)

15 Claw hammer Dual purpose type, one side of the head for normal banging, the other shaped like a claw for extracting nails. 680g (24oz). (Stanley Jobmaster 90)

16 Warrington cross pein hammer For driving home small nails and pins, either side of the head can be used. The cross pein (narrow rectangular side) is useful when working in confined spaces or where the size of nail head restricts normal holding. 225g (8oz). (Stanley WO)

17 General purpose flat file Select a file that is coarse cut on one side for rough filing and fine cut on the other for smoothing and finishing metal. Apart from keeping your scraper sharp, this file will help in a variety of smoothing jobs. (Stubs FB246T dual-cut handyman's file)

18 Yankee screwdriver Range of interchangeable bits makes this several screwdrivers in one, coping with various screws from electrical equipment sizes right up to large No 12s, including Pozidriv screws with cross slot heads. Its pump action makes work easier. You can also make pilot holes with it. (Stanley Yankee Handyman 133H 245mm/$9\frac{5}{8}$in spiral ratchet screwdriver, 6mm/$\frac{1}{4}$in slotted bit)

19 Bevel edge chisel Basically intended for light work, this sloping-side chisel can reach into tight corners. With a plastic-handled type you can use a hammer without fear of the handle breaking. Start with a 12mm ($\frac{1}{2}$in) size, adding 6mm ($\frac{1}{4}$in) and 25mm (1in) sizes as you need them. (Stanley 5002 series)

Tools one by one

The right tool for a particular job soon pays for itself in saved time, but the benefits don't end there. Possession of the correct tool makes accurate work easier and prevents the over-hasty handyman misusing and possibly ruining another expensive item in the tool box. It is all too easy to damage a quality tool by using it in the wrong situation. A simple example will illustrate the point. A perfectly serviceable twist drill, capable of cutting rapidly through wood, is soon blunted by any attempt to force it through masonry, while the specially designed tip of the masonry bit will make little impact on hardwood, merely becoming overheated.

A further example illustrates the benefits brought by a versatile tool kit. Most handymen possess a couple of screwdrivers, perhaps the most abused of all tools, but special jobs need special screwdrivers. To attempt any electrical work without a properly insulated screwdriver is clearly to risk far more than the price of a new screwdriver, but the handyman may be less aware of the merits of the many screwdrivers specially adapted to such difficult tasks as reaching awkward screws in tight corners, where the general purpose screwdriver cannot be properly deployed without causing damage to either the screw or the tip of the screwdriver blade. With the right screwdriver, you can work quickly, safely and in the most inaccessible spots, where you might have thought it impossible to drive the screw successfully.

The tools we have already shown in the basic tool kit have been chosen because of their outstanding versatility or their absolute necessity, but on occasion a particular job may demand a particular tool. The following pages contain an illustrated breakdown of such tools, one by one, explaining what each variation on the basic tool will do and how to get the best out of it. Even the most experienced handyman should find some useful new time-saving hints among the more fundamental details designed for the newcomer to DIY. When a job demands a new tool, *The DIY Tool Guide* should help you pinpoint the right tool. Armed with this information, you can enter the often confusing world of the tool shop with confidence. You will know the right questions to ask, and that will almost certainly guarantee good service.

We do not suggest that every handyman needs every tool we mention, but we believe that every handyman's work will be improved by the possession of the right tool for the job he is undertaking. This information is not always readily available in a particular shop, where some of the more unusual tools – whose names are unlikely to be familiar to the novice – may be out of stock. A leisurely look at the relevant pages of *The DIY Tool Guide* will not only identify the tool but also give you the name of the tool and, in most cases, the name of the manufacturer. If any difficulties are experienced in locating the tool in your local shops, contact the manufacturer for the address of your nearest stockist.

Sometimes a shortage of time or money means delaying purchase of a new tool. We therefore continue our money-saving policy of suggesting easy ways in which some tools can be improved when money is tight, or in those irritating moments at the weekend when a job is held up by the absence of a vital tool when the shops are closed. For example, there is the cunning home-made level using a remarkably inexpensive piece of transparent pipe, such as the home brewer will almost certainly have among his equipment. Not only is this method cheap and easy, it is 100 per cent accurate, its accuracy guaranteed by nature itself, and it can do one job which an expensive spirit level cannot do – it can go round corners. We don't normally recommend cutting corners, but if necessary, *The DIY Tool Guide* will tell you how it's done!

Hammers

In many household tool kits there is just one hammer to tackle all the jobs, from driving in a small panel pin to hitting a chisel. When a comparatively modest outlay will bring you an excellent kit of hammers offering a lifetime's service it is a pity to stick with just one type for every job.

Hammers are sold according to the weight of the head and the extensive range available enables you to choose the right weight for your strength. Buy a good quality, well-balanced hammer with a forged steel head since the cheaper cast heads tend to shatter. The striking face should be domed with slightly chamfered edges so if you hit a nail at a slight angle it should still go in straight.

There are six main types of hammer: claw, Warrington cross pein, pin, club, ball pein and wood mallet – this last often associated just with banging in cricket stumps or tent pegs.

Claw hammer

Available in various weights from 455–680g (16–24oz), the claw hammer is used mainly for heavier woodwork (fence building or other constructional work). It is dual purpose; one side of the head is for banging, while the other side is shaped to a long curved claw tapering to a fine 'V' for removing nails and pins. You will not then need a pair of pincers to withdraw badly knocked-in nails. Claw hammers come with steel or wood shafts; the steel shaft is stronger, but its rubber or leather handle grip becomes slippery if your hands sweat. If this happens, wipe the rubber with a wet rag to to remove any grease.

To extract nails Hook the claw of the hammer round the nail and work the handle in a lever action. Keep the handle as upright as possible and remove the nail with a series of pulls. If extracting a long nail, slip a block of wood under the hammer head once you have partly withdrawn the nail. This will increase the leverage and help the nail come out more easily; it will also protect the surface of the work from bruising.

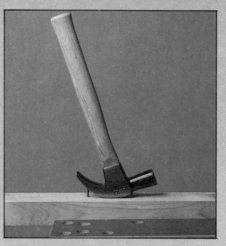

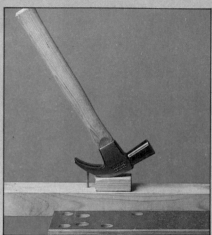

Left Employ the full weight of the hammer by holding it near the end, keeping the wrist straight
Below left Use a claw hammer to extract nails. Hook the claw round the nail and use the handle like a lever, keeping the hammer as upright as possible
Below For extra leverage when extracting a long nail, place a block of wood under the hammer head once the nail is partly withdrawn
Below right A club hammer and a bolster chisel combine to cut brick
Right A mallet and chisel make good working partners

1 Steel shaft claw hammer. **2** Wood shaft claw. **3** Pin hammer. **4** Ball pein hammer. **5** Warrington cross pein. **6** Club hammer. **7** Wood mallet

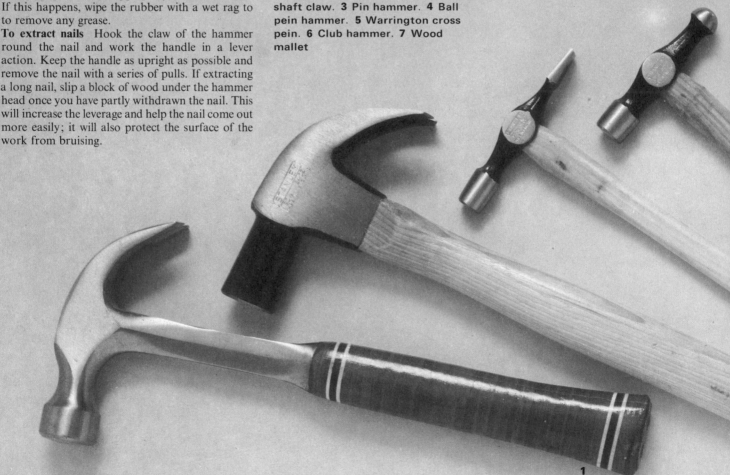

Warrington cross pein hammer

A good all-round woodworking hammer available in weights from 170–455g (6–16oz). It has a flat wedge shape (the pein) on one side of the head for starting small nails and panel pins. A good quality type will have a handle made of ash which is a tough, flexible wood capable of withstanding continual jarring.

Pin hammer

The lightest of the Warrington hammers, available in 100 or 115g (3½ or 4oz) weights, this is used on fine pins which would bend under the weight of heavier hammers. It is ideal for woodworking involving panel pins, such as picture framing.

Club hammer

Mainly used with a bolster chisel to cut bricks and paving stones and for masonry jobs and light demolition work. Club hammers are sold in 1135, 1360 and 1815g (2½, 3 and 4lb) weights, the heaviest being ideal for structural building work. Hold the club hammer about halfway up the handle for maximum efficiency with the minimum of effort.

Ball pein hammer

This type of hammer has a hardened steel face which is not easily damaged and is therefore ideal for metalwork and for driving in masonry nails. One side of the head, formed in the shape of a round knob, is specially designed for hitting rivets or for beating metal. It is available in a range of weights from 155–1135g (4oz–2½lb).

Mallet

Usually made of beech, the mallet is used with wood handle chisels or gouges which would be damaged by a steel hammer. The handle slots into the head and is unlikely to work loose since the head tends to tighten onto the handle with use. Mallets are sold according to the size of the striking face of the head, which is usually between 100–150mm (4–6in).

Using a hammer

Hold the handle near the end, not in the middle (except with a club hammer), so you use the full weight of the hammer. Always keep your eye on the nail head and tap it gently until the nail grips. Then strike it with increasing firmness, keeping the handle at right-angles to the nail.

Always keep the striking face of the hammer clean by rubbing it occasionally with emery paper – grease on the face can cause the hammer to slip, resulting in damage to the work surface or possibly injuring your fingers.

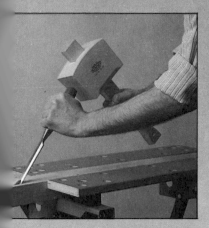

2   3   4   5   6   7

Screwdrivers

It is crucial the tip of your screwdriver blade fits perfectly inside the screw head; you must therefore have a range of screwdrivers to use with the various screw sizes.

Matching screwdriver to screw
If your screwdriver is too small it will tear up the screw head and its own tip could also be damaged; if it is too large it will damage the surface of the work on the final few turns especially if the screw is to be countersunk. The most commonly used screw sizes range from Nos 4–14 and the following chart shows you what width of screw-driver to use for each gauge.

Screw gauge	Tip width
No 4	5mm ($\frac{3}{16}$in)
No 6	5mm ($\frac{3}{16}$in)
No 8	6mm ($\frac{1}{4}$in)
No 10	8mm ($\frac{5}{16}$in)
No 12	9mm ($\frac{3}{8}$in)
No 14	9mm ($\frac{3}{8}$in)

You will need a full range of screwdrivers for use with both slotted and Supadriv (which are now replacing Pozidriv) cross slot screws or a special Yankee type with interchangeable blades.
Yankee A useful screwdriver that houses a comprehensive range of interchangeable bits giving choice of blade sizes (including Pozidriv). It has the added advantage of a pump action mechanism to make certain types of work quicker.
Ratchet Has a device which prevents the screwdriver being turned in more than one direction at a time. Because of this, you do not have to release your grip on the handle when inserting or withdrawing a screw.
Pozidriver This type of screwdriver is available in various sizes and blade lengths and must be used with Supadriv or Pozidriv screws. Once again make sure you have the right size point for the screw being used. With this type the screwdriver tip holds the screw in place, whether in the vertical or near horizontal position, which is especially useful when inserting screws in awkward places.
Phillips Although similar to the Pozidriver this is designed for use with the old type Phillips screws which have a differently shaped slot in the head. Always use a Phillips screwdriver for Phillips screws and a Pozidriver for Supadriv or Pozidriv screws. If you use either type of screwdriver on the wrong screw you will damage the screw head and possibly the point of your screwdriver.
In tight corners If you are working in a really tight corner and you cannot manoeuvre a normal screwdriver, use a stubby one which has a very short blade. This type is available for both modern screw

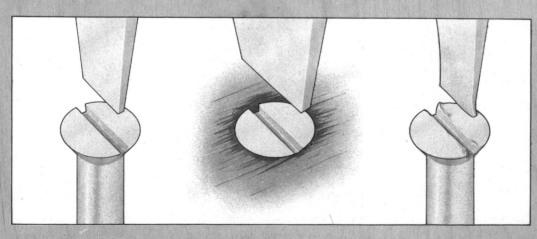

Far left The tip of the screwdriver blade must fit perfectly inside the screw head
Centre If the tip is too big it will damage the surrounding timber on the last few turns
Left If too small, it will damage the screw head

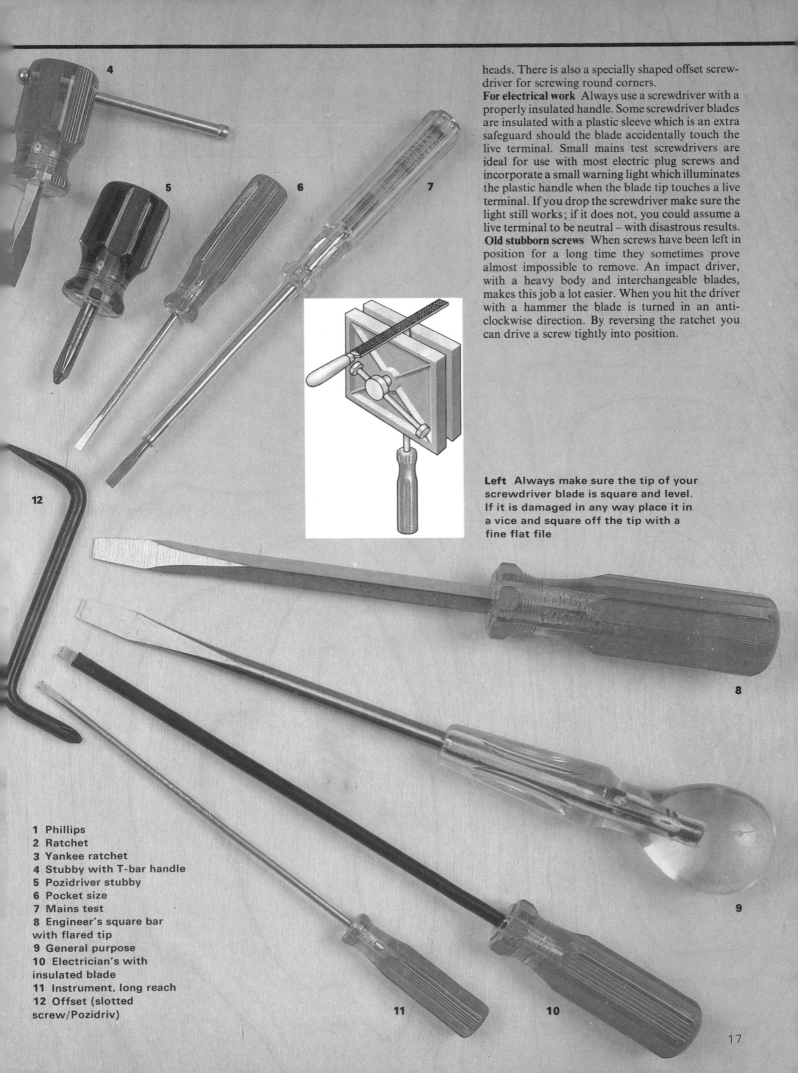

heads. There is also a specially shaped offset screwdriver for screwing round corners.

For electrical work Always use a screwdriver with a properly insulated handle. Some screwdriver blades are insulated with a plastic sleeve which is an extra safeguard should the blade accidentally touch the live terminal. Small mains test screwdrivers are ideal for use with most electric plug screws and incorporate a small warning light which illuminates the plastic handle when the blade tip touches a live terminal. If you drop the screwdriver make sure the light still works; if it does not, you could assume a live terminal to be neutral – with disastrous results.

Old stubborn screws When screws have been left in position for a long time they sometimes prove almost impossible to remove. An impact driver, with a heavy body and interchangeable blades, makes this job a lot easier. When you hit the driver with a hammer the blade is turned in an anti-clockwise direction. By reversing the ratchet you can drive a screw tightly into position.

Left Always make sure the tip of your screwdriver blade is square and level. If it is damaged in any way place it in a vice and square off the tip with a fine flat file

1 Phillips
2 Ratchet
3 Yankee ratchet
4 Stubby with T-bar handle
5 Pozidriver stubby
6 Pocket size
7 Mains test
8 Engineer's square bar
with flared tip
9 General purpose
10 Electrician's with
insulated blade
11 Instrument, long reach
12 Offset (slotted
screw/Pozidriv)

Squares and measures

When you are working with wood you will only achieve the perfect result if your measurements are accurate. And not only distances are crucial; angles and levels must be correct or your finished job will not only look untidy and unprofessional, but it may not fit together properly.

There are a variety of tools for checking your work is accurate and some you can improvise on or make up yourself.

Try square
This tool is essential if you are to saw a square end across a length of timber or if you want to check if a section of timber is square. It is available in three standard blade sizes – 152, 229 and 305mm (6, 9 and 12in). The tempered steel blade is locked firmly into the stock (handle) to form a perfect right-angle. Traditionally a wood stock was riveted to the blade, but now moulded plastic is used as an alternative.

A perfect try square will guarantee a 90 degree angle along both the inside and outside edges of the blade and you can easily check the accuracy of the right-angle. Lay the stock close against the straight edge of a piece of timber and mark a pencil line along the outer edge of the blade across the timber. Turn the try square over so the stock lies close to the timber but pointing the other way. If the blade is still parallel with the pencil line, your try square is accurate.

Combination square
This versatile tool, made from strong die-cast metal, provides both the inside and outside 90 degree angles of the try square and also a straight-edge/marking edge, depth gauge, adjustable mitre square, spirit level and scriber. You can buy a combination square that includes a protractor for 35–90 degree angles and a screw gauge for Nos 4–12 screws.

Sliding bevel
Available in various sizes, this tool adjusts to form any angle. The blade is easily held in position with a simple finger-tight lock.

Folding rule
Boxwood rule traditionally used by the carpenter. This folding type is available in 610 or 914mm (24 or 36in) lengths (when fully extended).

Steel tape
The retractable steel measuring tape is now the most popular for both the professional and the home handyman and is available in either metric or Imperial, or both. The range of lengths is 2–5m (6–16ft) and widths 6–19mm ($\frac{1}{4}$–$\frac{3}{4}$in). We recommend you buy one that has a sliding thumb lock and both metric and Imperial measurements on the tape unless you are completely at ease working with the metric system.

Top sight This version, with a window at the top of the case, is particularly handy since you can read it easily when measuring into recesses. The most useful size, which is light in weight, is the 3m (10ft) long, 12mm ($\frac{1}{2}$in) wide tape.

For measuring tapes of 3m (10ft) long or more we recommend you buy the 19mm ($\frac{3}{4}$in) wide type, since this is more rigid when measuring over longer distances.

Long measure
The building measuring tape is essential for outside work when building, or setting out your garden. Available in lengths ranging from 10–30m (33–100ft), a useful working size is the 20m (66ft) one. It is made of either steel or cloth; although cloth tapes are quite satisfactory for long distances, avoid using this type for small carpentry jobs where precision is vital.

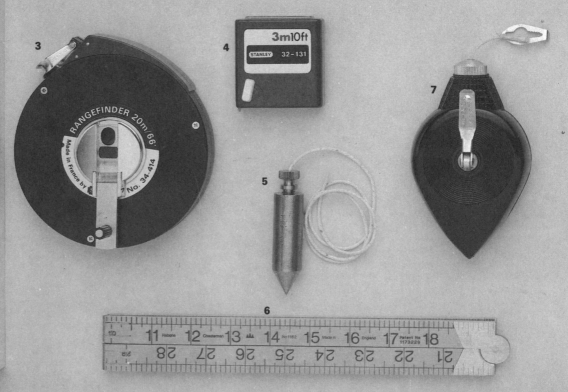

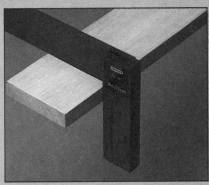

Rigid steel rule
Used for measuring metalwork, this rule is usually supplied in 305, 610 or 1000mm (12, 24 or 39in) lengths. It is also useful as a straight-edge or as a guide when using a laminate-cutter or cutting knife.

Lines and levels
When starting most structural projects and fitments, you must either form a true vertical or find a perfectly level surface. Specialist tools are available, although you will achieve a satisfactory result with some simple improvisation.

Plumb line
The accuracy of the vertical line is important, particularly when setting up shelf support rails and vertical sides of wardrobes and door frames and when hanging wall coverings. The force of gravity will ensure that any weight suspended from a string line will, if kept still, hang in a true vertical line – the plumb line. Although easy to make yourself with string and a balanced weight, a plumb bob is inexpensive and guarantees the correct shape weight necessary to reduce swing when suspended.

Once the string line is perfectly still, the exact vertical can be transferred in pencil onto the surface behind. An easy way to do this is to mark the position of the top and bottom of this line with crosses, remove the plumb line and join up the crosses using a pencil and straight-edge.

An alternative is a chalk line reel. The line is housed in a canister containing powdered chalk

Top left & right Checking try square is accurate. **Above** To square across timber, place blade of try square flat on surface and draw pencil line along outer edge of blade. Follow this line round other three faces; if final line fails to meet first, timber is not square. **Above right** If adjoining timber edges are not flush with edges of try square, wood is not square. **Right** Using try square to find true horizontal line

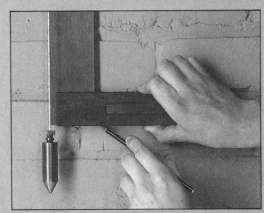

1 Rigid steel rule to measure metalwork
2 Spirit level to check level surfaces
3 Retractable steel measuring tape
4 Top sight steel measuring tape
5 Plumb bob for true verticals
6 Folding boxwood rule
7 Chalk line reel to mark verticals
8 Sliding bevel to mark accurate angles
9 Multi-purpose combination square
10 Simple try square to check right-angles

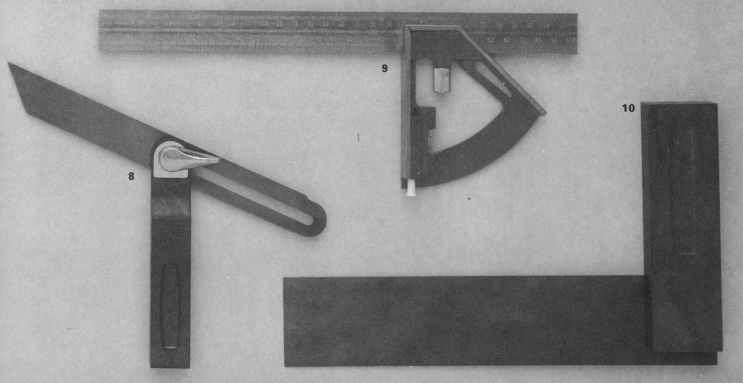

which coats the line each time it is extended. When the bob at the end of the line is stationary the line is held taut and plucked. A vertical chalk line is left on the wall which can easily be removed after use.

Spirit level

Level surfaces are crucial in a lot of DIY work and are usually checked with a spirit level. The longer the level, the more accurate it will be, since it covers a greater measuring length. If you have a small spirit level, use it placed on a longer straight piece of timber.

The spirit level has, set in the centre of its length, a capsule containing liquid and a bubble. Two lines are marked on the centre of the capsule the same distance apart as the length of the bubble. When checking, the surface is level if the bubble sits exactly inside the two lines.

To check whether a spirit level is accurate, place it on a flat surface. The bubble should rest in exactly the same position when the level is reversed through 180 degrees; if it moves, take the level to your tool merchant for adjustment.

Home-made levels

A good spirit level can be quite expensive to buy. If your budget is limited, there are several ways you can improvise by making your own levels.

Using a try square You will get an accurate horizontal line by using a 90 degree angle set against a true vertical line. Mark your vertical line with a plumb line and weight (as already described) and set the outside edge of your try square blade flush against it. Mark a pencil line along the outer edge of the stock. Turn the try square over with the outside edge flush against the vertical line on the other side and again mark a pencil line along the stock. This will give you a true horizontal line.

Using a pointer or plumb line You can check whether a surface is level or not by hanging either a pointer or a plumb line on a specially marked T-shaped joint. Make the joint by screwing a long piece of hardwood midway along a shorter piece, checking with a try square that they meet at right-angles and the bottom edges of each piece are flush. Mark a line accurately down the centre of the upright and then drill two holes big enough to take small lengths of dowel, one near the top of the upright and one two-thirds the way down. Make a balanced pointer by chamfering one end of a thin piece of timber and drill a hole slightly bigger than the dowel in the centre of the other end. Insert the lower dowel to hang the pointer and the top dowel to hang the plumb line. You must saw a groove in the exposed end of the top dowel to insert the plumb line. Where the plumb bob hangs, cut out a square hole so the line rests near the upright. Mark out the square, drill holes in each corner and cut out with a coping saw. Lay the 'T' joint on the surface to be checked; the surface is level if the arrow or bob aligns with the marked vertical line on the upright.

Using transparent pipe Water, like all other liquids, always finds its own level. You can use it as an accurate measure by attaching a section of transparent pipe to each end of an ordinary hose-pipe (or use a full length of transparent pipe). Put the pipe in a U-shaped position and fill with water until it overflows, ensuring there is no air in the pipe. By raising or lowering either end of the pipe the water will move up or down. The water level at either end indicates true horizontal.

Left Check whether surface is level by hanging pointer on specially made T-shaped joint. Upright should be about 900mm (or 3ft) high and base about 600mm (or 2ft) long. Put pointer over 9mm ($\frac{3}{8}$in) dowel 19mm ($\frac{3}{4}$in) long, half of which should be inserted in upright. Lay base of 'T' joint on surface, which is level if arrow aligns with marked vertical on upright
Centre left Alternatively use plumb line, which will align with marked vertical if surface is level
Below left To find true horizontal using glass and water, mark chosen height from surface on which glass stands at several points round glass. Fill with water up to marked line; if water level coincides with line, then surface is level
Below If surface is not level, water will not align with mark on glass
Bottom Water level at either end of transparent pipe indicates true horizontal

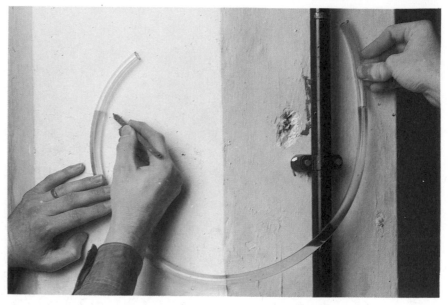

Handsaws for timber

To work efficiently with wood you must have more than that single saw used for all jobs. 1 Veneer tenon saw (Sandvik hardpoint 324). 2 Traditional tenon saw (Spear & Jackson R52 Spearior). 3 Panel saw (Sandvik 2000 Supercut hardpoint handsaw). 4 Teflon-coated panel saw (Spear & Jackson G104 Black Prince). 5 Rip saw (Spear & Jackson R189 Medallion). 6 Bow saw (Marples M2400 Twine strained beechwood). 7 Coping saw (Eclipse 7CP). 8 Pad saw

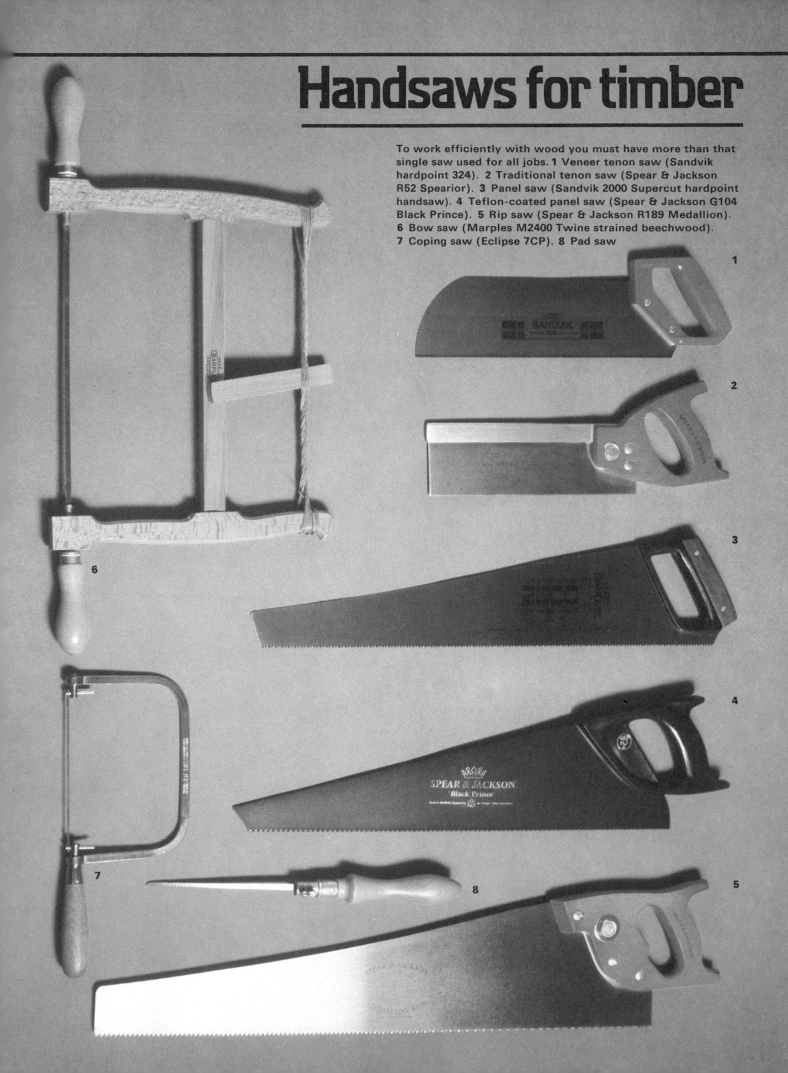

A saw blade consists of a series of teeth bent out on alternate sides of the blade. This formation is called the set and enables the sawdust and chips of wood to be carried away in the gullets between the teeth to prevent clogging. It also makes the saw cut (or kerf) slightly wider than the blade so the blade slips through without jamming and can be turned fractionally if it goes off the cutting line.

Saws are sold according to point number, which is always one more than the number of teeth per 25mm (1in). The more teeth there are the slower and finer the cut; a 14 point saw has 13 teeth per 25mm and cuts slower but more finely than one with ten teeth per 25mm.

Most handsaws are available with hardpoint teeth for extra wear. These will take a long time to blunt but cannot be sharpened: they have to be guillotined off and new teeth cut into the remaining blade, preferably by the manufacturer. You can then sharpen these new teeth as it becomes necessary.

Made of steel, some blades have a non-stick coating (such as Teflon) which helps prevent jamming and rusting. Handles are usually plastic or wood, the latter being not as strong as plastic but more comfortable to use over long periods.

Hang up the saw after use. Keep a blade guard over the teeth to protect the cutting edge and always oil an uncoated blade after use, remembering to wipe it clean before beginning fresh work. If an uncoated blade starts to rust, clean it with steel wool dipped in rust remover or white spirit. Wipe with an oil-soaked cloth after treatment. Remember never to use abrasives on Teflon-coated blades.

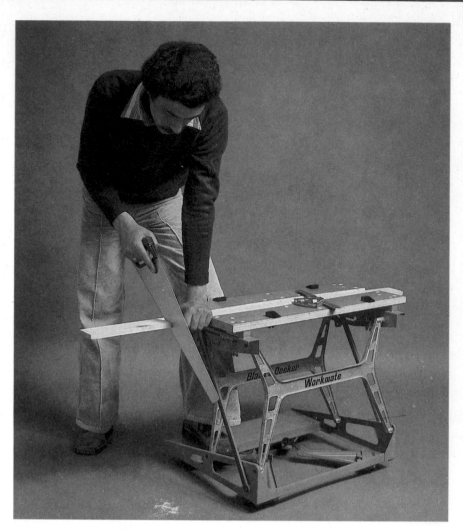

Panel saw
The best type of all-round handsaw for cutting large timber to size. For general work we recommend an 8 point saw with a 550mm (22in) blade. The panel saw has cross-cut teeth for cutting across the grain: the tooth angle is the same on both sides of the point and the saw cuts equally well on the push and pull strokes. It will also cut with the grain (rip-sawing), but this is hard work on boards more than 25mm (1in) thick.

Rip saw
Designed specifically for cutting timber fast with the grain, this type is worth buying only if you have a lot of board-ripping to do. It is generally 4 or 5 point and the teeth resemble a series of chisels: one side is angled much more steeply than the other and the saw cuts only on the down stroke, when the chisel edges are driven into the wood.

To use a panel or rip saw Grip the handle with your index finger pointing along the blade. Support the timber in a vice (a bench vice if you have one) or on

Above right Keep saw at 45 degree angle to wood when cross-cutting
Above, far right Saw at 60 degree angle when ripping (cutting with grain)
Right Types of teeth: **1** Chisel-like teeth of rip saw. **2** Cross-cut teeth of panel saw. **3** Tenon saw teeth for cutting with and across grain
Far right Always saw on waste side of cutting line, not on line itself, or wood will be undersize. **Inset** Guide initial cut towards you with your free thumb; don't push saw forward with thumb close to line

Types of saw teeth

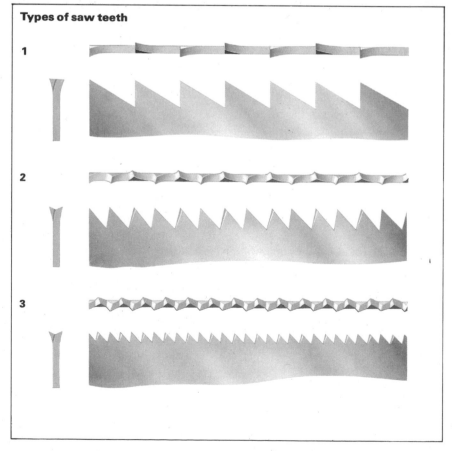

1

2

3

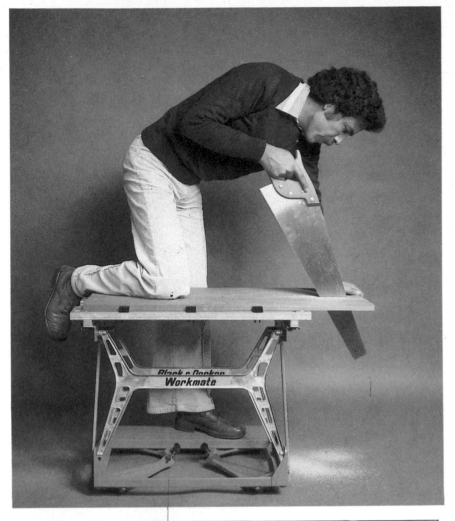

trestles or chairs, and use your knee and free hand to steady the wood. Start the cut by firmly drawing back the blade, holding it square to the wood at a shallow angle. Use your free thumb to guide the initial cut towards you; never push the saw forward with your thumb close to the cutting line as the saw may jump and hit the thumb. Keep your shoulder behind the line of the saw.

Always saw on the waste side of the cutting line; if you saw on the line the wood would be undersize when filed or planed smooth. Scribble arrows on the waste side of the line to remind you on which side to saw.

Saw steadily and rhythmically, using the full length of the blade and applying light pressure only on the downward stroke. Keep the blade at about 45 degrees to the wood when cross-cutting and at about 60 degrees when rip-cutting. Always let the saw do the work. When you near the end of the cut, support the waste end to prevent it tearing away from the main piece. When cutting across the grain, always have the waste end overhanging the trestle or the saw will jam. If the saw jams, remove it and lubricate the blade by rubbing it with a candle.

Tenon saw

For cutting joints and all fine and accurate work, both with and across the grain. The blade is rectangular and has a spine (or back) which gives you more control when cutting small pieces of wood. For all-round use we recommend a 15 point saw with a 250 or 300mm (10 or 12in) blade. Hold the tenon saw as you would the panel saw, with your index finger pointing along the blade to steady it. Always use the full length of the blade.

Small veneer-type tenon saw

Similar to the tenon saw, but without the spine, this enables you to make a fine cut at a deeper angle in sheet material such as thin plywood or veneer.

Specialist saws

Although the saws mentioned above will cope with basic woodworking jobs, you will need specialist saws for more intricate work.

Bow saw

Consisting of a narrow blade stretched in a wood frame, this type is used for cutting curves in timber more than 12mm ($\frac{1}{2}$in) thick.

Coping saw

A smaller version of the bow saw, to use on thinner wood, this has an adjustable blade fixed in a steel frame.

Both of these saws can cut only as far into the timber as the distance between the blade and the saw frame. To cut a hole in the middle of a piece of wood you must first drill a pilot hole through which to thread the saw blade. You can then fix the blade to the frame and begin sawing. Take care not to force the blade as it will wander from the cutting line and may break.

Pad (or keyhole) saw

This saw overcomes the problems of frame size presented by the bow and coping saws since it has a narrow blade clamped to a handle at one end only. It is invaluable for cutting holes in the middle of large panels. Again you will have to drill a pilot hole to insert the blade before you can begin sawing.

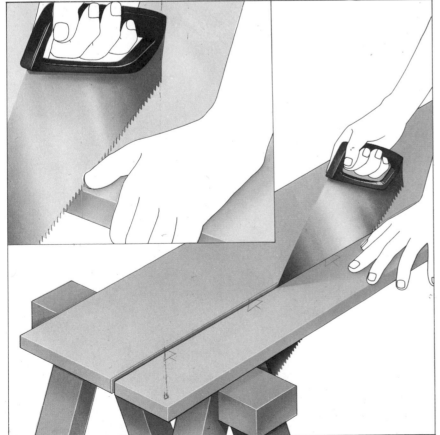

Right way to saw

1 Bow saw carefully if it is not cutting square to wood
2 If saw wanders from cutting line, turn handle slightly to twist blade along its length
3 To prevent saw wandering, clamp timber batten on cutting line and saw against this
4 If trimming thin slice off end of timber, clamp scrap wood to overhang main piece, mark cutting line round both pieces of wood and saw through both together
5 Hold saw cut open with narrow edges when ripping (cutting with grain)
6 To ensure small sections of wood are cut square, use tenon saw with bench hook, a wood board with strip of timber fixed to both ends on opposite sides (one on top and one underneath – see detail) and cut shorter than board to accommodate saw. Butt one end of bench hook against edge of workbench, holding workpiece steady against other end.
Make a bench hook by screwing straight and square-cut pieces of wood to piece of hardwood about 250 × 230 × 18mm (10 × 9 × ¾in)

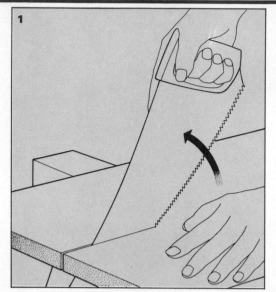

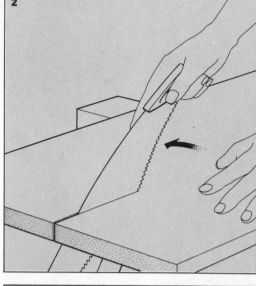

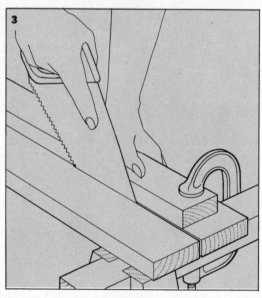

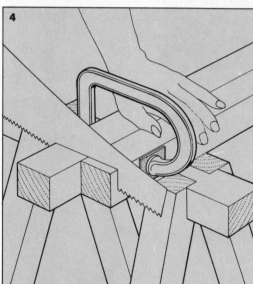

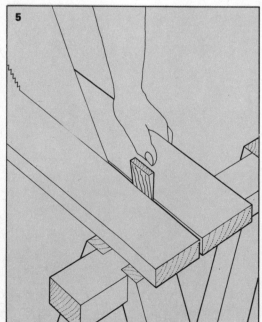

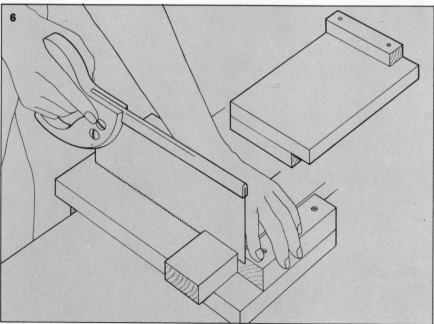

Braces and hand drills

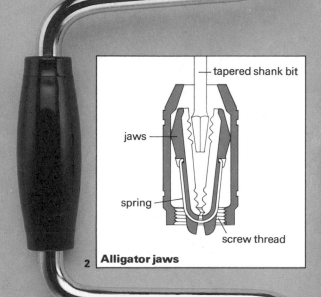

Alligator jaws

Labels on diagram: tapered shank bit, jaws, spring, screw thread

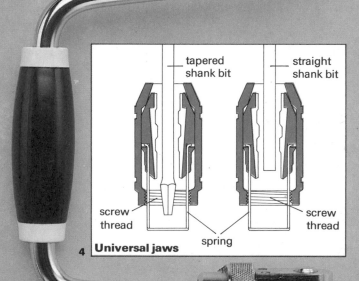

Universal jaws

Labels on diagram: tapered shank bit, straight shank bit, screw thread, spring, screw thread

Braces and hand drills are a valuable addition to any tool kit. Although slower than power drills, they are more easily controlled and enable you to work in tight corners and where there is no electricity to run a power drill. They are particularly suitable for intricate work.

Swing brace

Often called a carpenter's or bit brace, this is particularly good for quick drilling of accurate holes in wood. The swing brace is measured by the diameter of the circle formed by the grip and sizes are 200–350mm (8–14in), the most popular for general work being 250mm (10in). You can get a fixed brace or one with a ratchet action. The ratchet type is more useful since you can drill a hole by working the grip backwards and forwards through 90 degrees rather than through 360 – a real advantage when working in confined spaces. The ratchet can be locked in a clockwise or anti-clockwise direction or so it moves through 360 degrees, like the fixed brace. The type of jaws fitted to the brace is important since the jaws determine what sort of bits can be used: Universal jaws will take both tapered and straight shanked bits, while Alligator jaws will take only bits which have a tapered shank.

1 Fixed swing brace
2 Alligator jaws
3 Swing brace with ratchet action
4 Universal jaws
5 Joist brace

25

There are small braces available for specialist jobs. These include the electrician's brace, which has a diameter, or sweep, of only 150mm (5⅞in), and the joist brace, which has a short drilling shaft with Universal jaws and is fitted with a long side arm which turns the shaft.

Using the swing brace When drilling through wood, ensure a clean hole and prevent the face of the timber breaking away by marking the position of the hole with a bradawl or nail punch. Place the point of the bit in this mark and turn the brace gently to drive the bit into the wood. When it starts to appear on the other side, withdraw the bit by turning the brace handle in the opposite direction. Complete the drilling by turning the wood round and placing the bit in the hole you made from the other side. If you cannot drill from both sides or if the timber is too thin, clamp a

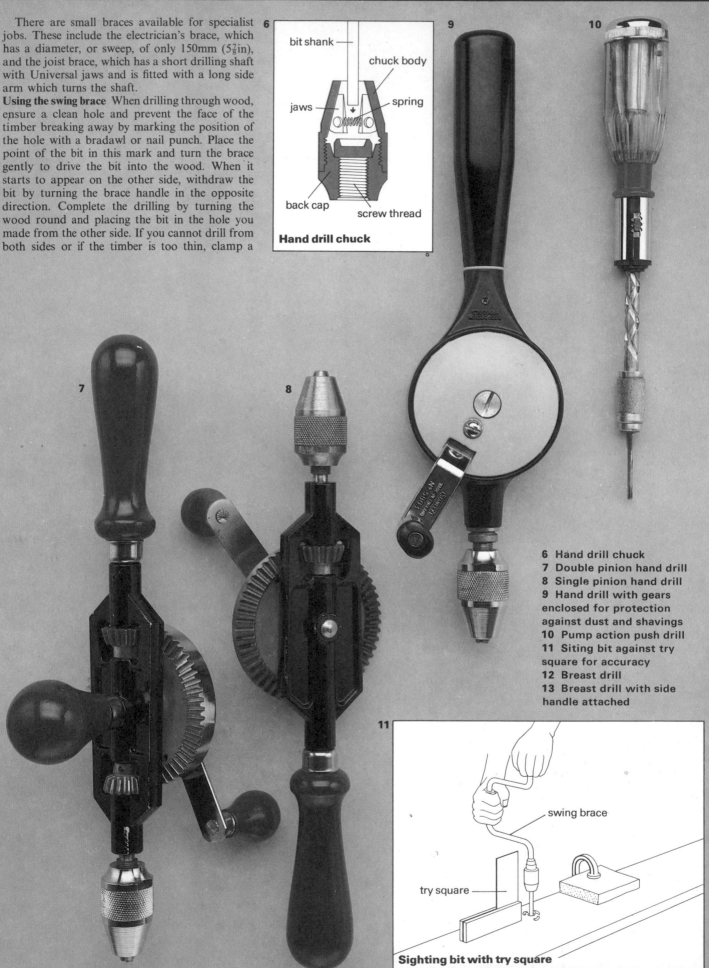

6 Hand drill chuck

bit shank
chuck body
jaws
spring
back cap
screw thread

Hand drill chuck

6 Hand drill chuck
7 Double pinion hand drill
8 Single pinion hand drill
9 Hand drill with gears enclosed for protection against dust and shavings
10 Pump action push drill
11 Siting bit against try square for accuracy
12 Breast drill
13 Breast drill with side handle attached

swing brace

try square

Sighting bit with try square

piece of scrap wood behind the point where you want the hole and drill right through into this.

If you are drilling to a fixed depth, fit the bit with a depth stop; either buy a special rubber collar or wrap round a piece of adhesive tape. Drilling holes squarely with a swing brace may prove difficult at first, so sight the bit against a try square to ensure accuracy.

Hand drill or wheel brace

This can be used with wood or masonry twist drills to make holes of up to 8mm ($\frac{5}{16}$in) diameter in a variety of materials. Single pinion hand drills are available, but better quality types have two pinions: the second pinion balances the gear wheels so the cogs meet perfectly. You can get hand drills where the gears are enclosed to protect them from dust and shavings.

An additional side handle is supplied with most models. This is detachable and should be used when more pressure and control are needed. With the side-handle removed, you can work in tight corners which may be inaccessible with a power drill.
Using the wheel brace Turn the handle at a constant speed, but not too fast. Small twist drills tend to clog quickly so withdraw the bit frequently to clear the waste. To withdraw the drill, keep turning the handle in the same direction and pull the drill away from the work. For normal work grip the main handle in your fist; when more pressure is needed, press the main handle into your body and grip the side handle to keep the brace straight as you use the turning handle.

Hand drills need very little maintenance apart from keeping the gears free of dust and occasionally giving the drill a light oiling. After a great deal of use the jaws may become worn and fail to grip the bit securely; but replacements are easily fitted. Twist the chuck as if opening the jaws and remove it from the brace. Hold the body of the chuck in a vice, unscrew the back cap, remove the chuck from the vice and take out the jaws. Squeeze the new jaws together and push them into the chuck, refit the back cap and screw the cap back onto the brace.

Breast drill

Used for heavy drilling jobs, the breast drill has two speeds, the slower one being used for tough materials such as masonry and steel. A breast pad is fitted at the top of the drill shaft so you can put your full weight behind the drill; the pad is adjustable for either horizontal or vertical drilling. A detachable side handle is also a standard feature.

The chuck of the breast drill will take any bit up to 12mm ($\frac{1}{2}$in) with parallel-sided shanks. It will also take bits up to 25mm (1in) with turned down shanks. Like the hand drill, various types are available, including one with completely enclosed working parts.

Push drill

A pump action drill which you use with only one hand. It is ideal for light work, such as making pilot holes (especially for hinges where you can hold the hinge in place with one hand and use the drill with the other), and for drilling small holes in thin plywood and mouldings. Interchangeable drill points are available from 1.6 to 4.4mm ($\frac{1}{16}$–$\frac{11}{64}$in).

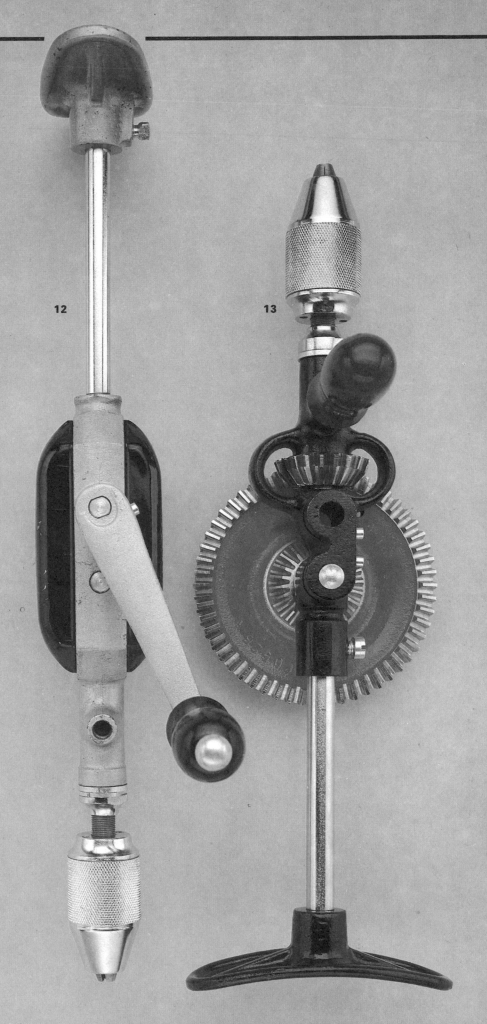

12

13

Drill bits

Drilling accurately into wood will be made easy if you use the right equipment. A whole range of bits is available for use with swing braces, hand drills (sometimes known as wheel braces) and electric drills, although swing brace and drill bits are often not interchangeable because of the type of fitting. Each bit is specially shaped to do a specific job, so it is important to check which one you need for the work in hand. Bits are available in a range of sizes, with width measurements in both metric and Imperial.

Auger bits

Used specifically for drilling into wood, the most common auger bits have a clearly defined spiral so the waste is cleared rapidly from the hole when drilling. Auger bits with tapered ends must be used exclusively with a swing brace fitted with Alligator type jaws. Straight shank bits can be used with a swing brace fitted with Universal jaws. Two types of auger bit are used with the brace, the Jennings and solid centre pattern bits.

Jennings pattern The most common type, this is particularly suitable for drilling deep holes since the long spiral keeps the hole straight.

Solid centre pattern Although this is not as accurate as the Jennings pattern, it has a slightly faster drilling action.

Twist bits

Often referred to as twist drills, twist bits are the most common drilling tools used by the handyman with either a hand or electric drill. You can buy them individually or in sets; the usual sizes are 0.8–6mm ($\frac{1}{32}$–$\frac{1}{4}$in). Designed for drilling small holes, they do tend to clog quickly so when drilling deep holes (especially in hardwood) the bits should be withdrawn regularly to remove the waste.

Warning Take particular care when using the smallest sizes since these bits are thin and brittle. Always hold the drill square to the work and apply only light pressure when drilling.

Specialist bits

Depending on the type of work and material used, special purpose bits are available, some for use with a brace and some for use with a hand drill or an electric drill.

Expansive bit Suitable for drilling into softwood, it has an adjustable cutting head so you can drill different size holes into wood at least 13mm ($\frac{1}{2}$in) thick. However it is difficult to keep straight when drilling deep holes.

Forstner bit Ideal for accurate drilling of flat-bottomed holes. But you will have to apply a lot of pressure when using it.

Centre bit Its use should be restricted to drilling through plywood. Unlike the spiral twist auger bits, this type of head is inclined to wander off course when drilling deep holes.

Countersink bit Different patterns are available for drilling with a brace or hand or electric drill. Its cutting edge funnels out the surface of wood to take the head of a countersunk screw. Once the cutting edge of this bit has worn down you will have to replace it.

Screwdriver bit For use with a brace or hand or electric drill. You must use a multi-speed electric drill since you have to work at very low speeds.

Dowel bit This bit, which drills flat-bottomed holes into wood, must be used with an electric drill at full speed. It tends to be difficult to control since it drills quickly without the accuracy of an auger bit.

Flatbit Popular for use with electric drills, it is suitable for drilling wider holes in wood. Take care, particularly when working with hardwood, because the bit tends to overheat and blacken along the cutting edge. This indicates the steel has lost its temper and the cutting edge is ruined. Keep the bit as cool as possible by using it only in short bursts. It is easy to sharpen and as long as the cutting face is kept sharp, there is little risk of this bit overheating quickly, therefore making it ideal for deep drilling into wood.

Screw sink bit Available in sets, this type is multi-purpose since it drills a pilot hole of the correct diameter for the screw and countersinks for the head of the screw in one drilling operation.

Hole saw bit Useful when making large holes in thin gauge material such as plywood. Different diameter holes can be drilled by changing the ring saw around the centre pilot drill.

Spear point bit Used at slow speed for drilling glass. The point should be continually lubricated with turpentine or white spirit during drilling.

Yankee drilling point bit Special small drilling bit available for use with the push drill and Yankee pump action screwdriver. This is ideal for making small holes.

Heavy duty bits

These are designed for drilling into hard materials such as masonry, brick and concrete, because they have specially treated cutting edges.

Masonry drill This type of twist drill, used at slow speed, is suitable for drilling into masonry and brickwork. It has a tungsten carbide cutting edge which must be resharpened by the manufacturer.

Percussion drill Looks like the masonry drill and also has a tungsten carbide cutting edge. It is designed for use with a percussion or hammer drill for boring into concrete. Always use it at a slow speed. The cutting edge will have to be resharpened by the manufacturer.

1 Twist drill
2 Masonry drill
3 Percussion drill
4 Countersink bit
5 Hand screwdriver bit
6 Hand dowel bit
7 Centre bit
8 Forstner bit
9 Flat bit
10 Auger bit, Jennings pattern
11 Auger bit, solid centre
12 Expansive bit
13 Yankee drilling point
14 Screw sink bit
15 Hole saw bit
16 Spear point bit
Opposite Sharpening a Jennings pattern auger bit with a needle file

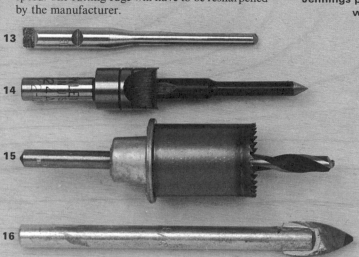

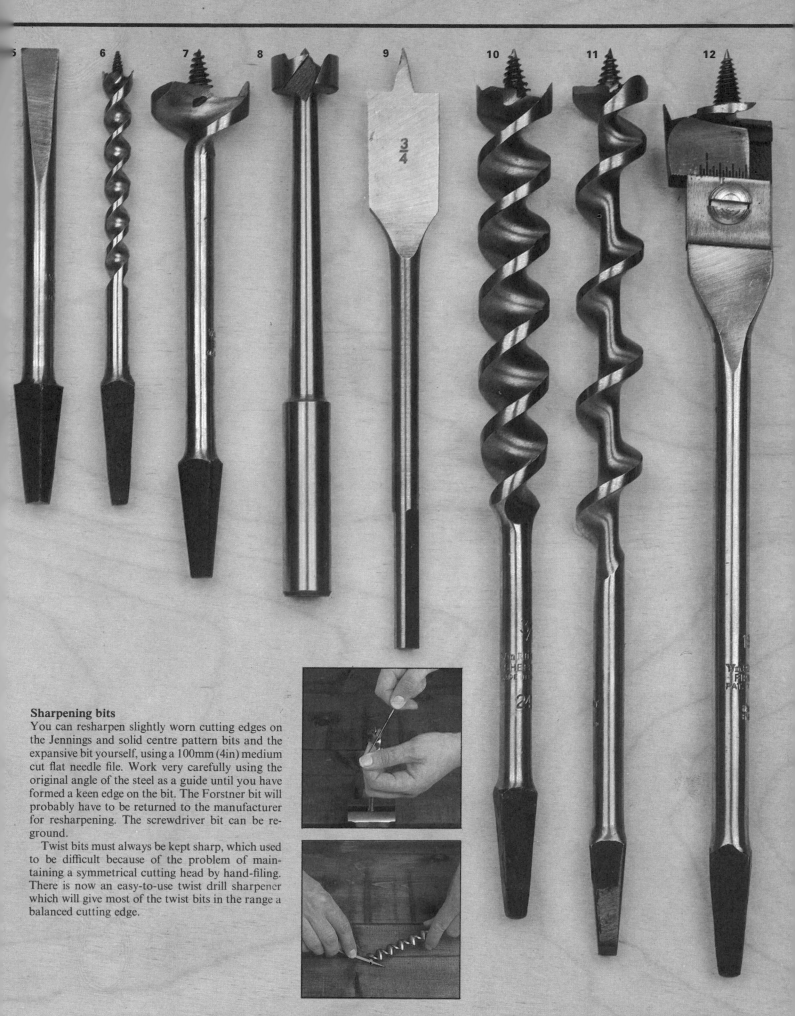

Sharpening bits

You can resharpen slightly worn cutting edges on the Jennings and solid centre pattern bits and the expansive bit yourself, using a 100mm (4in) medium cut flat needle file. Work very carefully using the original angle of the steel as a guide until you have formed a keen edge on the bit. The Forstner bit will probably have to be returned to the manufacturer for resharpening. The screwdriver bit can be reground.

Twist bits must always be kept sharp, which used to be difficult because of the problem of maintaining a symmetrical cutting head by hand-filing. There is now an easy-to-use twist drill sharpener which will give most of the twist bits in the range a balanced cutting edge.

Planes, chisels and gouges

Precision instruments such as planes are necessary if you want to be quite satisfied the end product results in a job well done. Chisels and gouges also help to give an expert touch to many woodworking tasks in the home.

When working with wood, it pays to use high quality tools for the best results. As with all your tools, when buying planes, chisels and gouges get the best you can afford and look after them.

Planes

The basic job of a plane is to smooth wood to exact dimensions. For this purpose three types – smoothing, jack and jointer planes – are available. Planes are also used for shaping wood: the block plane is for smoothing and shaping small work and there are various special planes for particular joints and shapes.

The blades of new planes have to be sharpened before use and regularly resharpened. If you do not want to go to the trouble of resharpening blades, you can buy a plane which takes throw-away replaceable blades. Other trimming tools are available, but are only suitable for jobs requiring less precision.

Most planes are now made of metal. Wood ones are very difficult to obtain and are rarely used by the home handyman.

Smoothing plane This comes in lengths of 200–250mm (8–10in) and is best used for smoothing small lengths of wood as it can create bumps and hollows on long lengths if not handled carefully.

Jack plane In 355 or 380mm (14 or 15in) lengths, this plane is long enough for most surfaces and less heavy than the jointer one.

Jointer plane Available in 560 and 610mm (22 and 24in) lengths, this plane is used for smoothing long pieces of wood. But it is heavy to use and quite expensive to buy.

Block plane A small plane which comes in lengths from 140–200mm (5½–8in), it can be used with one or two hands. The blade is set at a low angle with the bevel uppermost, making it ideal for cutting end grain. It is also used for shaping small work and is a convenient tool to use on chipboard and laminated plastic. However, the resin in these man-made materials quickly blunts the blade, which then needs frequent resharpening. Some planes have an adjustable mouth for coarse or fine work.

Special purpose planes The following planes are for specialized shaping jobs: a rebate plane cuts steps or grooves; an open-throat router makes grooves of uniform depth; a shoulder plane has a blade that cuts to the full width of the plane body so it can plane right into an angle. There is also a combination plane which can be fitted with various cutters.

Plane-type tools Aids to planing, such as the Stanley Surform and Aven Trimmatool, cannot be used with the same precision as conventional planes but are useful for levelling and shaping a variety of materials. They can also be used on painted wood and wood containing nails, which would normally ruin a conventional plane.

1 Combination plane with blades
2 Smoothing plane
3 Rebate plane
4 Jack plane
5 Jointer plane
6 Shoulder plane
7 Block plane
8 Open-throat router
9 Surform
10 Trimmatool

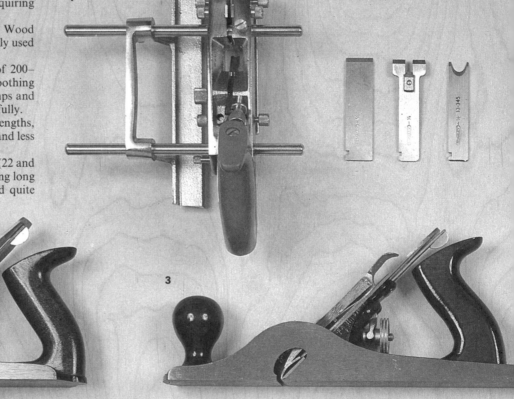

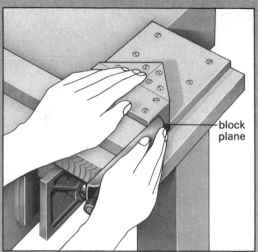

block
plane

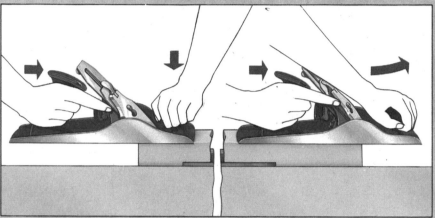

Using a plane

Before using a plane, make sure the blade is razor sharp and correctly adjusted to the required depth of cut. It takes experience to know just how far the blade should project for the desired cut, so it is worth practising planing on a piece of waste timber to find out how much the blade will remove when set in different positions. Turn the knurled knob to adjust the depth of the cut, then move the lever to straighten the blade along its width. Check the blade is parallel with the bottom of the plane; if the blade is not level, it will not cut evenly.

To level a long piece of timber, use a long plane since a small one will follow the undulations of the surface rather than straddle them. Always plane with the grain of the wood to get a really smooth finish. You will soon know if you are planing against the grain as you will tear the surface. This will be particularly noticeable on hardwood.

The right action Support the wood in a vice so you have both hands free to use the plane. Grip the knob at the front of the plane with one hand and place the other on the handle. At the beginning of each stroke press down on the front knob and gradually transfer the pressure so it is on the back of the plane when you finish the stroke. This action will keep the plane level with the surface of the timber and will prevent the ends being rounded off. You will find it easier if you put all your weight on your front foot (the left one if you are right-handed) at the beginning of the stroke and gradually transfer it to the back foot as you shift pressure on the plane.

When planing the edge of timber, concentrate on keeping the plane square to the timber. Check regularly with a try square after a few strokes.

When trimming end grain, check regularly with a try square that you are trimming square, or use a shooting board. Always work from each edge towards the centre. It is also important to keep the blade razor sharp and adjusted to only a very slight projection. If possible, use a block plane with an adjustable mouth and keep it tightly closed.

Warning When planing, check regularly to see the wood shavings are not trapped under the blade. If they are, release the blade and clear away the shavings. When you reassemble the plane, check the blade adjustment before continuing work.

6

Top left Hold bottom of plane squarely up to light to check blade is parallel to bottom
Top right Trim end grain on shooting board
Above When planing, work from right to left, gradually transferring pressure from front to back of plane

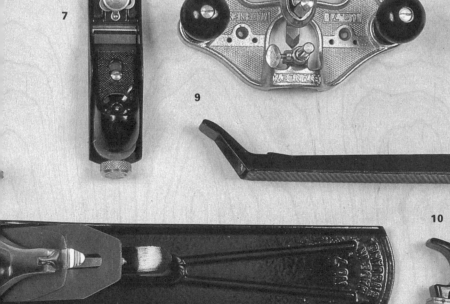

7

8

9

10

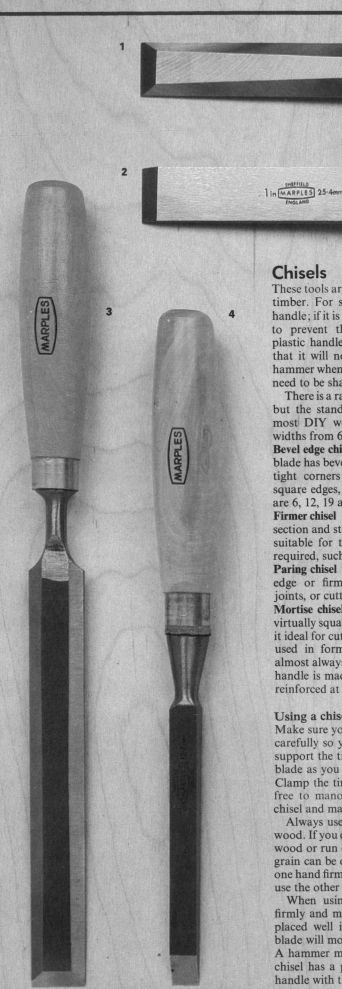

Chisels

These tools are for cutting out and paring pieces of timber. For some jobs you will have to tap the handle; if it is made of wood, you must use a mallet to prevent the wood splitting. A high-impact plastic handle is stronger and has the advantage that it will not be damaged if you tap it with a hammer when a mallet is not available. New chisels need to be sharpened before use.

There is a range of chisels to tackle different jobs, but the standard bevel edge type is suitable for most DIY work. Chisels are available in blade widths from 6–38mm ($\frac{1}{4}$–$1\frac{1}{2}$in).

Bevel edge chisel The most versatile type since the blade has bevelled edges which enable it to cut into tight corners where a firmer chisel, which has square edges, would jam. The most useful widths are 6, 12, 19 and 25mm ($\frac{1}{4}$, $\frac{1}{2}$, $\frac{3}{4}$ and 1in).

Firmer chisel Here the blade is rectangular in cross-section and stronger than that of a bevel edge. It is suitable for tougher jobs where less precision is required, such as in frame joinery.

Paring chisel This has a longer blade, either bevel edge or firmer type, useful for making larger joints, or cutting housings for wide shelves.

Mortise chisel The blade has square sides and is virtually square in cross-section. Its strength makes it ideal for cutting mortises (deep rectangular holes used in forming joints). As a mortise chisel is almost always used with a mallet, it is essential the handle is made of high-impact plastic or of wood reinforced at the top with a metal band.

Using a chisel

Make sure your chisel is razor sharp and handle it carefully so you do not damage the blade. Never support the timber with your hand in front of the blade as you could cut yourself if the chisel slips. Clamp the timber firmly so you have both hands free to manoeuvre the chisel or to work with a chisel and mallet.

Always use a chisel with or across the grain of wood. If you cut against the grain you may split the wood or run off the cutting line. Paring across the grain can be done using hand pressure only. Keep one hand firmly on the handle to exert pressure and use the other hand to guide the blade.

When using a mallet, grip the chisel handle firmly and make sure the flat side of the blade is placed well inside the marked cutting area; the blade will move towards the cutting line when hit. A hammer may be used instead of a mallet if the chisel has a plastic handle, but always strike the handle with the flat side of the hammer.

1 **Bevel edge chisel**
2 **Firmer chisel**
3 **Bevel edge paring chisel**
4 **Mortise chisel**
5 **Firmer gouge**
6 **Scribing gouge**

Note Cold chisels are used mainly for metal, brick and masonry work.

Right Pare across grain with chisel using hand pressure only; no mallet is needed

Gouges

A special kind of chisel, the gouge has a curved blade and comes in two types. The firmer gouge has a bevel edge on the back of the blade, the scribing gouge a bevel edge on the front. Sizes relate to the width of the blade, not its arc, and range from 6–25mm ($\frac{1}{4}$–1in).

Using a gouge

This is handled in the same way as a chisel but each type of blade has its own particular use. A firmer gouge is used to cut shallow depressions, such as finger grips on doors, and curved grooves. To do this, work alternately from each end of the cut towards the middle until the required depth is reached. A scribing gouge is used to trim curves to match a rounded surface, such as shaping a rail to join a round leg of a chair.

5   6

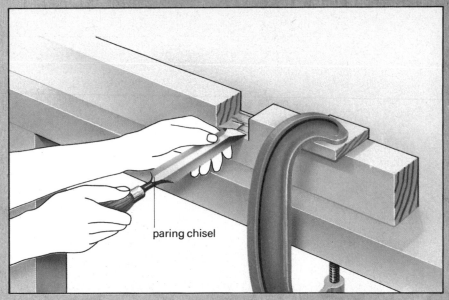

paring chisel

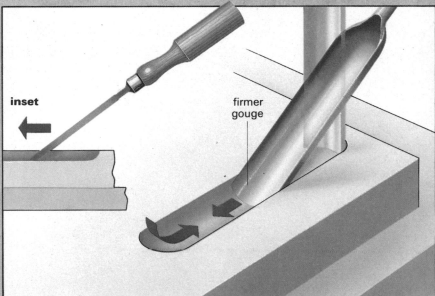

inset

firmer gouge

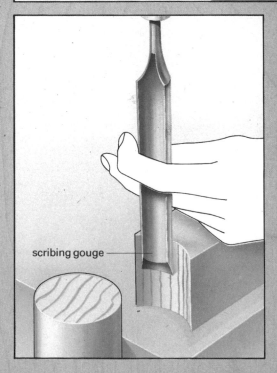

scribing gouge

Above Cut shallow groove, working alternately from each end with firmer gouge. When cutting along groove keep bevel edge of gouge parallel to bottom (**inset**)
Left Use scribing gouge to trim curve on rail to fit round chair leg

Marking and scribing

In any woodworking job it goes without saying that accurate marking out and scribing of timber is vital if you want to obtain the best results. As a general rule you can get by with the minimum of equipment, which includes a pencil, straight-edge, steel rule, or tape, and marking knife. More accurate tools are available, such as gauges, compasses and dividers, which are a worthwhile investment if you are doing a lot of joinery work.

If you fail to mark out timber correctly, you will end up with poor joints and probably an unstable construction; and if you have to start again, a lot of time and money will have been wasted. So marking and scribing are jobs you must take time and care over.

Of the two basic items, in principle a marking knife is used where precision is all important, such as in cabinet making; a pencil is used for more general carpentry work where such a high degree of accuracy may not be required. A pencil is also used to mark waste areas of timber which have to be removed and also to identify the face side and edge of timber.

Marking knife

This tool consists of an angled steel blade, which is ground and sharpened on one side only. When marking, the knife is held with the flat side of the blade against a metal straight-edge, which can be the blade of a try square or a steel rule. The cut the knife makes in the timber being worked will help prevent a saw or chisel splintering the work when cutting through.

The knife is suitable for marking the cutting lines on veneered surfaces. By sawing along scored lines you will be far less likely to tear the veneered surface; but because the scored lines are quite difficult to see, it is a good idea to go over them with a pencil so they show up quite clearly.

Multi-blade knife

Multi-blade knives for marking are also available; these are particularly useful since you can fit the relevant blade for the work involved. You can buy these knives with either fixed or retractable blade fittings. A range of blades is available for different types of work.

Normal duty A general purpose blade for marking out wood, trimming leather and suede and cutting paper, card and polystyrene tiles.

Heavy duty Used for scraping off paint or varnish and cutting plastic (not laminate), flooring tiles and roofing felt.

Hooked Ideal for cutting vinyl and textiles.

Angled Used for scoring long lines on timber and plastic and for cutting card. It can also be used for routing and cutting carpet, roofing felt and vinyl.

Concave Will cut carpet, roofing felt and vinyl. Also used for routing.

Convex Especially useful for cutting wallpaper; will also score most materials and cut carpet.

Laminate Designed especially to score laminate.

Warning Inaccurately scored lines cannot be removed. Until you are confident you can get it right first time, it is wise to set out the cutting lines on the timber to be worked with a pencil first.

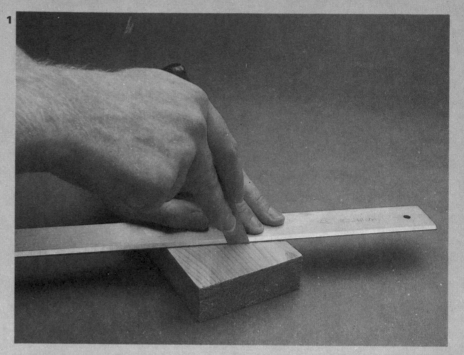

These can always be removed with a rubber or fine glasspaper. When you have checked for accuracy, you can score over the pencil marks.

Pencil

When marking timber, don't be tempted to pick up and use the first pencil stub which comes to hand. The pencil should be of a reasonable length so you can hold it comfortably for precise marking. It should be sharpened to a chisel point so you get clean, fine lines. For most work an HB grade pencil is suitable; this is hard enough to retain its point for some time, while soft enough not to damage the surface of the work.

Use an even softer grade pencil, such as a 2B, if

1 Using a marking knife held flat against a metal straight-edge to make an initial cutting line on a piece of timber
2 When marking the cutting lines on laminate, go over them with a pencil so they will show up more clearly as a guide for the saw
3 A cutting gauge, which has a blade instead of the point fixed to the normal marking gauge
4 A single point gauge

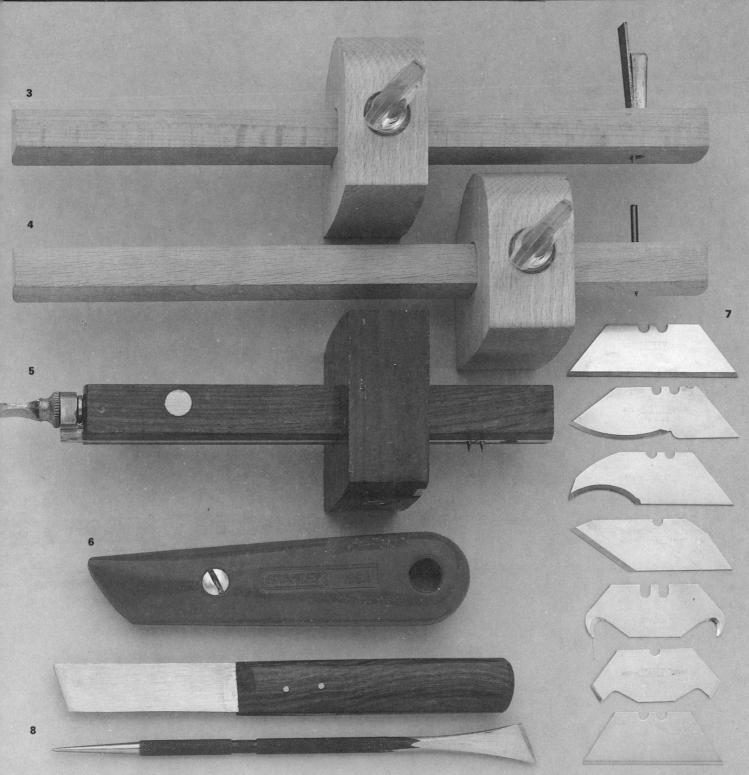

the timber is very soft or if you are just lightly marking the work for accuracy prior to using a marking knife. Use a harder grade pencil, such as an H or 2H, for fine marking where a marking knife is not available and where hard-surfaced timber is being worked.

For general marking of waste areas and with heavy work, it is best to use a carpenter's pencil, which has a wide rectangular lead available in soft, medium and hard grades. The medium grade is suitable for most work. The lead should be sharpened with a sharp knife and the end scraped to a chisel edge. If it wears down while working, you can rub it against medium glasspaper held on a flat work surface to renew the edge.

Gauges

Woodworkers' gauges are the most accurate tools to use when scribing or cutting lines in timber; their one limitation is that they can only be used to scribe or cut lines parallel to the edge or end of timber. To mark out curves and circles you will need a pair of compasses or – for larger areas – a timber lath, trammel heads or large blackboard-type compasses.

Single point The most widely used type is the single point marking gauge, the stem of which has a hardened steel point that protrudes about 3mm ($\frac{1}{8}$in) from it at one end. A stock slides along the stem and is held in place with a thumbscrew. To set the gauge, position the stock at the approximate

5 A mortise gauge: the two points – one of which is fixed and the other adjustable – mark out parallel lines

6 A multi-blade knife which holds a range of blades

7 Types of blade used with the multi-blade knife: (**from top**) heavy duty, convex, concave, angled, hooked, laminate and standard

8 Two types of marking knife which are fitted with a fixed, angled blade

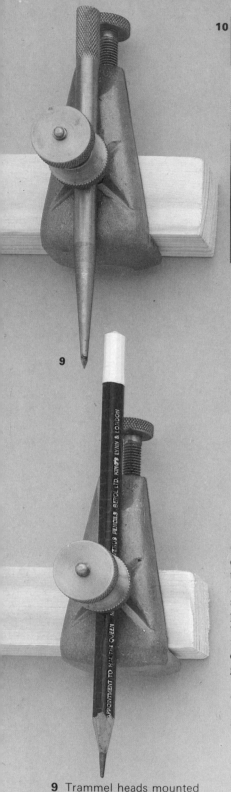

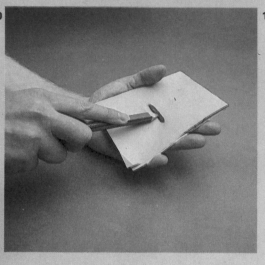

dimension required, then partially tighten the thumbscrew and tap the end of the stem gently on the bench until the point is the required distance from the stock, which can be checked with a rule. To mark the timber, grip the gauge with your thumb and first finger round the stock and your other fingers on the stem and run the gauge down the timber: keep the point at an angle to the work and the stock firmly against the edge of the work. Score lightly several times, allowing the point to mark a little deeper each time until the line can be seen clearly. If the gauge is not held firmly to the work, it can wander and follow the grain of the timber and you will not get an accurate parallel line. Always mark out with the stock on the face side of the work.

Keep the point sharp by using a small oilstone whenever necessary; when the gauge is not in use, slide the stock right up to the point in order to protect it.

Cutting This gauge is similar to the marking gauge, except that it has a blade instead of a point – and this is held in place by a wedge. Use it like the marking gauge when cutting through thin materials such as veneers, light plywood, card and thin plastic. Use the gauge on each side of the material until the cuts meet. A cutting gauge can also be used to mark out timber across the grain, since it cuts into the work and will therefore not tear the grain.

Mortise This has two points (one is fixed and the other slides) and a sliding stock. The gauge is used to set out the parallel lines when making mortise and tenon joints.

When a gauge is not available, a pencil and rule used carefully in conjunction with a try square can help you draw reasonably parallel lines. Hold the rule firmly in one hand with your thumb on the required measurement and your fingers steadying the rule underneath and touching the edge of the work. The end of the rule acts as a guide for your pencil. Check with a try square to make sure the line is parallel.

Compasses
Ordinary pencil compasses can be used to mark small radius curves and circles on timber. The legs are first set to the required distance apart and the point of the compasses is then placed at the centre of the circle; the leg holding the pencil is swung carefully round several times to mark out the curve or circle.

9 Trammel heads mounted on a timber beam are used for marking large accurate curves and circles
10 If your carpenter's pencil wears down when in use, sharpen it by rubbing on medium glasspaper
11 Using a single point gauge to mark timber
12 Wing dividers, which have points on both legs, are used for scribing equal distances on work

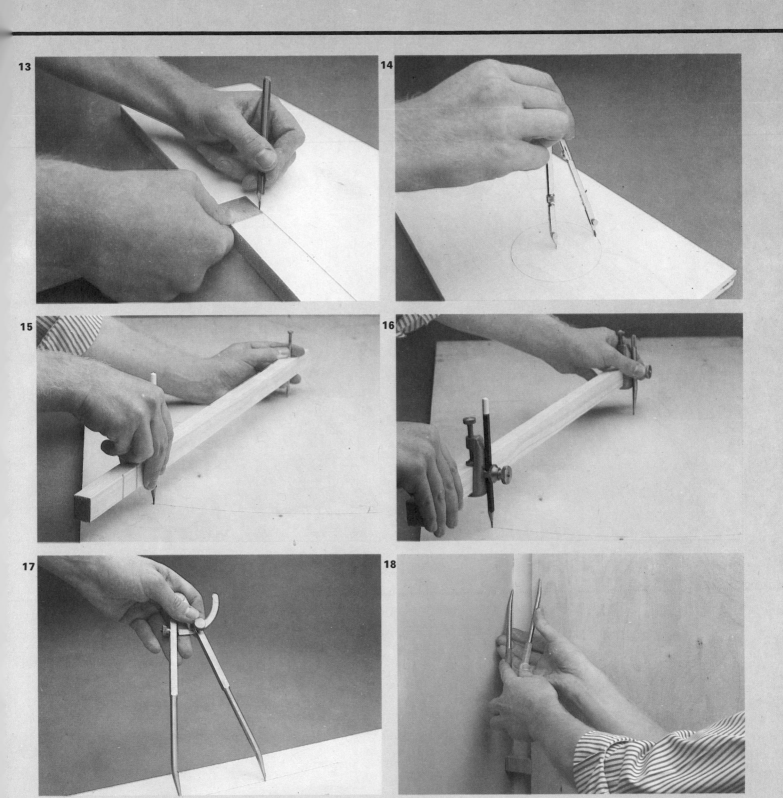

Wing compasses These are suitable for more accurate marking. One leg has a point and the other is flattened and sharpened so it scores the surface of the timber as it is moved. This helps to ensure a clean edge when cutting with a saw or chisel.

Timber lath This is useful for marking out larger circles. A nail or pin is driven in near one end of the lath to act as a pivot and a pencil is held in a notch or hole near the opposite end at the required distance from the nail for the radius to be marked on the work.

Trammel heads For really accurate marking of large curves or circles, trammel heads mounted on a timber beam should be used. Both heads are pointed for scribing and one usually has a socket so a pencil can be fitted. This apparatus is used in a similar way to compasses; place one point at the centre of the circle and move the other point (or pencil) to mark the required radius.

Wing dividers With points on both legs, these are used for stepping out equal distances along a length of timber. They can also be used to scribe a line along a length of timber when it is necessary to fit this to an irregular surface; the outline is transferred from the irregular surface onto the timber to be fitted.

13 Marking a parallel line with a rule and pencil; check with a try square
14 Using compasses to mark small curves
15 Using a timber lath to mark large curves
16 Using trammel heads on a beam to mark large curves
17 Using wing dividers to step out equal distances on a piece of timber
18 Using wing dividers to scribe irregular outlines onto work to be fitted

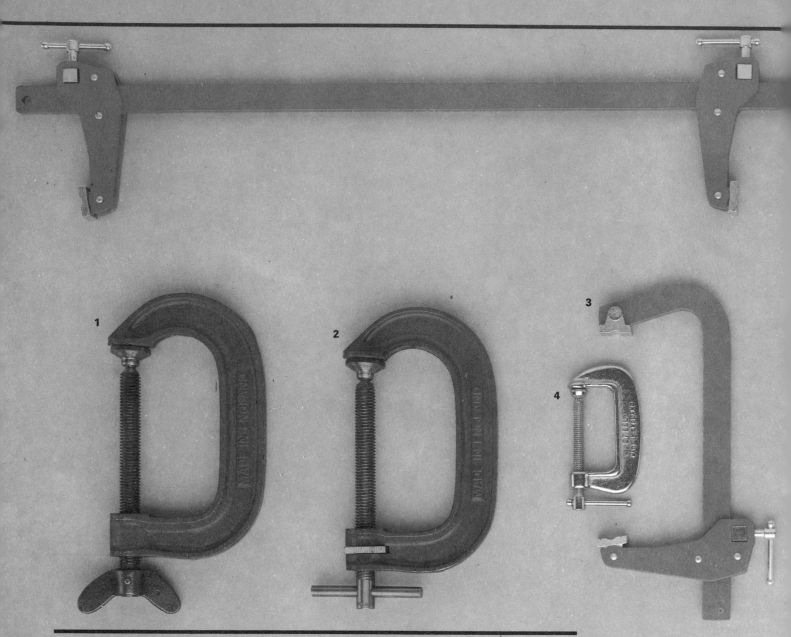

Clamps and grips

Besides woodworking vices and bench holdfasts there are other clamping (or cramping) tools you can buy. Some of these are expensive, but they do enable you to carry out a whole range of jobs which are often beyond the scope of the simpler devices.

G-clamps

You will find these tools nearly as useful as the woodworking vice. They can be used to clamp together two items which are being glued or they can be used to hold timber down on a bench while it is worked.

G-clamps are available in many sizes, the most common being about 50–300mm (or 2–12in). The size indicates the width of the jaw opening. Special long reach or deep-throat clamps with extra deep openings are also available in sizes from about 50mm (or 2in) to 100mm (or 4in). The screw jaw is fitted with a swivel shoe which adapts to uneven surfaces. The strongest clamps have ribbed frames of malleable iron or steel with steel screws, while

those for lighter work, such as fretwork clamps, have spring-tempered all-steel frames.

When using a G-clamp place scraps of wood between it and the timber being worked to protect the timber from marking. If the timber is being glued, put greaseproof paper between the work and the protective scraps to prevent them sticking together. You should never overtighten a G-clamp since this will dent the work and may bend the frame of the clamp.

Edging clamp A special version of the G-clamp, this is used to hold edging strips and lippings to a straight or curved workpiece. The width of the jaw opening is usually about 60mm (or 2⅜in) and the throat depth up to 32mm (or 1¼in). Attach the clamp to the workpiece and tighten the secondary screw onto the edging.

Quick-acting cramps

There are many models of quick-acting cramps manufactured, but most work on the principle of a

1 Light duty G-clamp (Record Ridgway 120)
2 G-clamp with spin release action (Record Ridgway Spingrip 127)
3 Quick-acting G-clamp (Mole Rak)
4 Mini G-clamp (Record Ridgway Junior 119)
5 Edging clamp (Record Ridgway 129)
6 Fretwork clamp (Finnie)
7 Quick-acting multi-directional sash cramp (Mole Rak)
8 A multi-directional cramp will hold pieces of work together or apart; two or more sets of jaws can be used on one bar
9 Several sash cramps can be used to hold a frame together. Place them at the edges of the frame, two on top in one direction and two underneath the other way

7

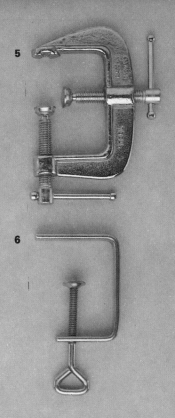

5

6

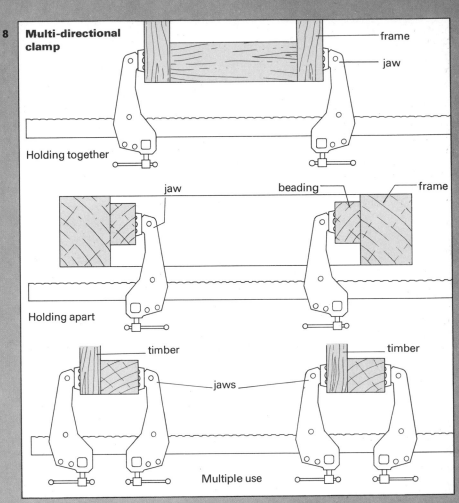

8 **Multi-directional clamp**

frame

jaw

Holding together

jaw

beading

frame

Holding apart

timber

timber

jaws

Multiple use

9 **Sash cramps**

sliding cramp arm which can be moved and locked in any position on a steel bar. A particularly useful type is multi-directional, with two or more arms which can face either way on the steel bar to handle the most complicated cramping jobs. It can be used to cramp pieces of timber together – and to force them apart – and is supplied on a standard 305mm (or 12in) bar, though bars up to 1220mm (or 48in) are available. Maximum throat depth for this type of cramp is 92mm (or $3\frac{5}{8}$in).

Sash cramps

These relatively expensive cramps are used for holding large frames or panels while they are glued. Most have a rectangular cross-section steel bar on which the shoes slide. You place one shoe in position according to the width of the work and fix it with a pin through the bar and then adjust the tension by screwing up the other shoe.

Depending on the thickness of the bar, the capacity of a sash cramp can be about 457–1676mm (or 18in–5ft 6in). Lengthening bars can increase the capacity of some sizes by a further 1220mm (or 4ft). Alternatively, you can make two sash cramps into one large one by removing the pegged shoes and linking the two cramps with nuts and bolts passed through the adjusting holes so the screw heads are at either end.

Rectangular section sash bar cramps tend to bend in use and to combat this, use three cramps on the workpiece – one on one side and two on the other. Alternatively you can use a stronger, more expensive T-bar sash cramp. The heavy weight of sash cramps, particularly in the larger sizes, can pull a frame out of true; to overcome this, make sure the

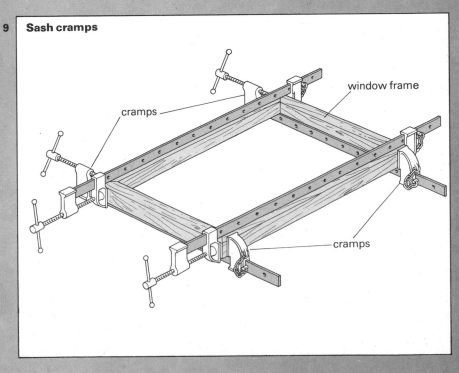

window frame

cramps

cramps

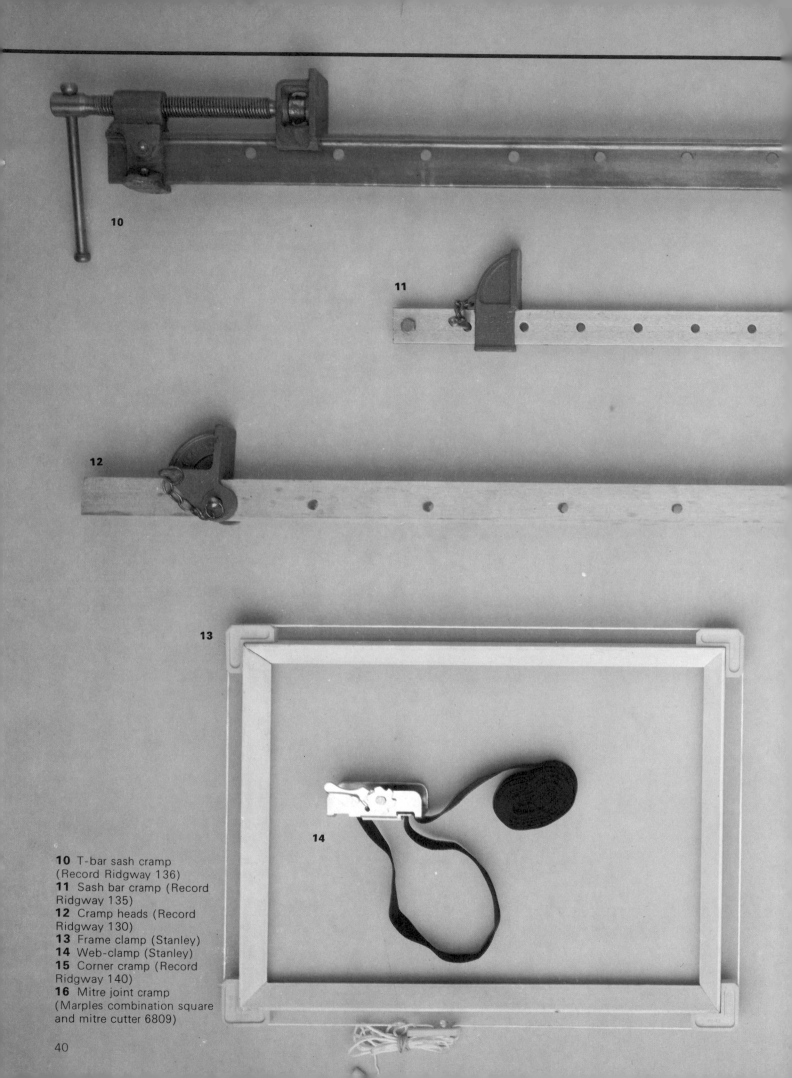

10 T-bar sash cramp
(Record Ridgway 136)
11 Sash bar cramp (Record
Ridgway 135)
12 Cramp heads (Record
Ridgway 130)
13 Frame clamp (Stanley)
14 Web-clamp (Stanley)
15 Corner cramp (Record
Ridgway 140)
16 Mitre joint cramp
(Marples combination square
and mitre cutter 6809)

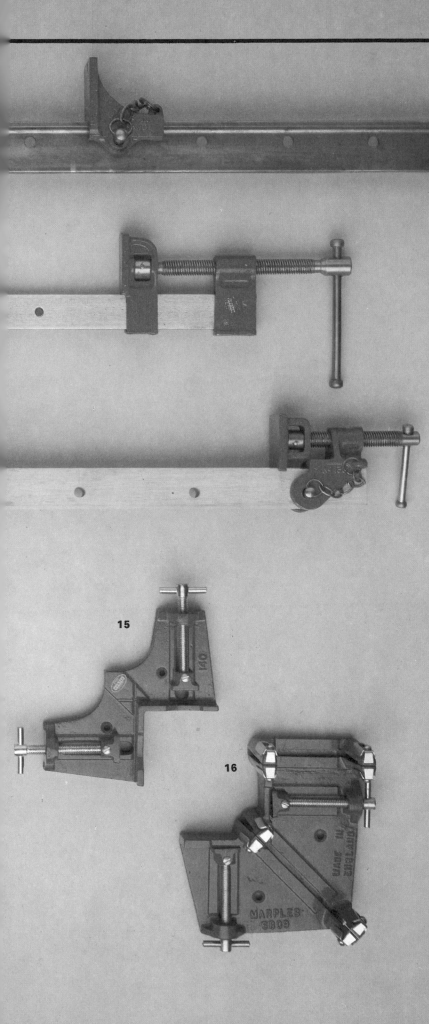

framework is well supported. Similarly, the weight of the cramps can make a frame seem flat when they are in place, but when they are removed the frame may revert to its original shape.

Cramp heads
These are much cheaper than all-metal sash cramps, since you buy only the cramp heads themselves and use them in conjunction with a length of 25mm (or 1in) thick hardwood, which is of sufficient width to take the strain of cramping without bending. You need to drill holes for the locking pins at approximately 100mm (or 4in) intervals along the length of the beam.

Web-clamps
As a cheap means of holding large frames and panels for gluing, you can use a web-clamp – basically a more sophisticated version of the Spanish windlass. A length of nylon webbing tape around the work is tightened by passing the free end through a steel clamp, which has a ratchet handle and a mechanism to tighten the tape. You can use web-clamps on almost any shape of framework with an all-round measurement up to slightly less than the length of the webbing supplied, which is usually about 3.5m (or 12ft).

Frame clamps
These are another alternative to the Spanish windlass, but this time used for holding light work such as a picture frame. The frame clamp has four right-angle jaws of polypropylene plastic, which protect the corners of the frame, and 3.5m (or 12ft) of terylene cord, which you pass through a plastic cleat to draw the corner pieces together.

Corner cramp
This is another cramp for holding a framework at the corners. Also known as a mitre cramp, it is particularly useful for holding mitre joints at a right-angle while they are pinned and glued. The cramp point is designed so only a minimal mark is made on the moulding. The cramps can also hold awkward shapes and they usually have a capacity of 50–108mm (or 2–$4\frac{1}{4}$in).

You can make corner cramps yourself by cutting springs from an old upholstered spring chair or bed into the shape of a C.

Mitre joint cramps
Cramps of this type are particularly suitable for holding picture frame joints under light pressure. They are made of spring steel and you apply them to the corners of the frame by expanding and relaxing them with special mounting pliers.

This type of cramp incorporates a saw guide at 45 and 90 degree angles so you can use the cramp to make accurate corner joints. They are available in six sizes with the smallest taking mouldings of 10–15mm (or $\frac{3}{8}$–$\frac{5}{8}$in) wide and the largest taking mouldings of 65–90mm (or $2\frac{1}{2}$–$3\frac{1}{2}$in) wide.

Left Aids to woodworking; before you use any of the vices shown, remember to fit plywood facings inside the jaws to protect your work
1 Woodworking vice with quick-release mechanism (Paramo 150)
2 Clamp-on woodworking vice (Record Ridgway Junior woodwork vice)
3 Plain screw woodworking vice (Paramo 61)
4 Clamp-on vice with L-shaped jaws (Stanley)
5 Portable workbench with built-in vice (Black & Decker Workmate WM 625)
6 Bench holdfast (Record Ridgway)
7 Home-made bench hook
8 Holding a frame together with Spanish windlasses; make sure you place scrap wood between the string and the frame to prevent marking the timber
9 On a framework with mitred joints, wrap the Spanish windlass round the frame, using protective corner blocks (notched to guide the string)
10 Use an ordinary bench vice with pieces of scrap wood to clamp small frames

Woodworking vices

Clamps and cramps are indispensable woodworking aids in certain circumstances, while your range of devices can be improved by several simple improvised pieces of home-made equipment. However, there is no real substitute for that most versatile clamping device, the traditional woodworking vice. Used properly, with plywood facings inside the jaws to protect the work from damage, a woodworking vice will prove to be the most useful piece of clamping equipment you can buy. Some vices are permanently mounted below the bench top, while various other models clamp on and can be removed as necessary. The jaws should have the largest possible surface area to minimize damage to the work, while at the same time giving a strong grip; they should also open wide enough to accommodate large cross-sections of timber. For best results, use a vice where the jaws have been drilled to allow replaceable protective plywood facings to be fixed easily in place. It is also useful to work with a vice which has a quick-release mechanism so you can open and close the jaws in seconds.

Some aluminium body vices have L-shaped jaws, which hold the work horizontally or vertically, and an offset clamp, which allows the vice to be fixed to the front and side of a bench and which can also be used as a G-clamp. A more versatile device is an all-purpose portable workbench. This has as its top a vice, which can be as wide as 740mm (or 29in) with a 100mm (or 4in) wide jaw opening, although there are smaller models available. On the largest model, swivelling vice pegs which press into the top of the bench allow items up to about 250mm (or 10in) wide to be gripped, while extender arms will accept sheets of wood up to about 1800 × 900mm (or 6 × 3ft) and picture, door and window frames. The vice jaws can be operated either in parallel or with a taper action.

Bench holdfast

This is used to hold wood down firmly on a bench top during work. The notched step of the cramp is passed through a hole in the bench top and levered over sideways by an arm. The arm exerts considerable pressure on the workpiece as the adjusting screw, which bears down on the top of the stem, is tightened. A holdfast can hold long timbers or large panels either on, or over, the edges of a bench. It is important you protect the surface of the workpiece by placing a piece of scrap wood under the pressure point.

When fitting a holdfast, make sure the bench top is thick enough to take the iron collar, which comes with the tool, without bending. If necessary, reinforce the area where the collar will be fitted by gluing and screwing a 25mm (or 1in) thick hardwood block under the bench. Also make sure the collar is fixed away from under-bench drawers and cupboards. It is usually fitted at the end of the bench opposite the vice and you should keep it on the centre line of the bench top, about 450mm (or 18in) in from the end. The collar is countersunk in the bench top and screwed in place so it is level with the surface. There are two sizes commonly used: one with a maximum opening of 175mm (or $6\frac{7}{8}$in) and the other with a maximum opening of 194mm (or $7\frac{5}{8}$in). Extra collars are available to enable a holdfast to be used in several positions. When not in use the holdfast can be removed from the workbench and stored out of the way.

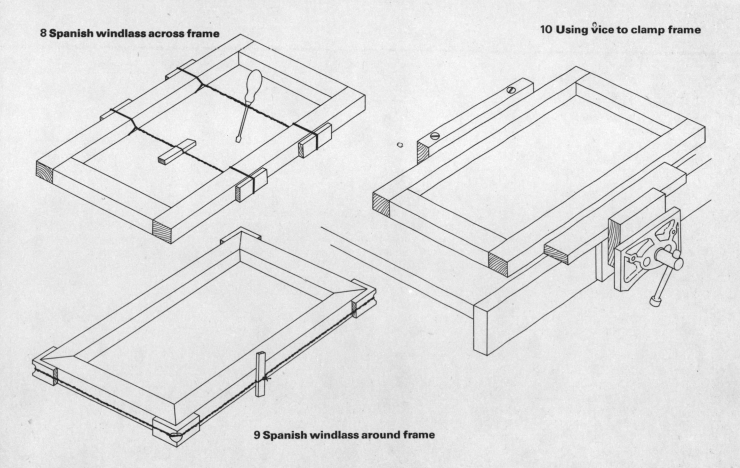

8 Spanish windlass across frame

9 Spanish windlass around frame

10 Using vice to clamp frame

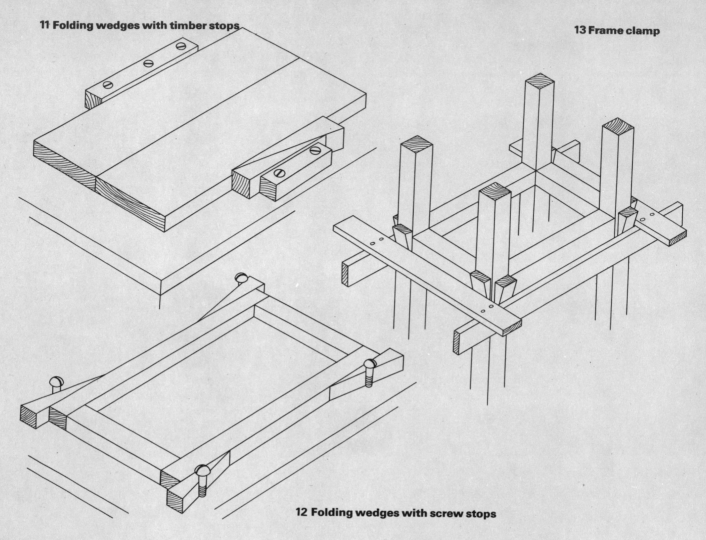

11 Folding wedges with timber stops

13 Frame clamp

12 Folding wedges with screw stops

Bench hook

Although not strictly a clamping or gripping tool, the bench hook is useful for holding small pieces of timber while they are cut across the grain with a tenon saw. It is made of hardwood with a batten on the underside which rests against the top edge of the bench, and another on the top surface, where the wood rests and where you grip it by hand when cutting. You can make a bench hook from 18mm (or ¾in) thick hardwood. A useful platform size is 250 × 230mm (or 10 × 9in).

Home-made clamps

Purpose made clamps can be quite expensive, especially the larger size ones which you probably will not use very often. To save unnecessary expense, and with a minimum of time and effort, you can make highly effective clamps yourself.

Spanish windlass This can be used in many situations where clamping is required. It is a loop of cord or strong string which is placed around the framework to be held together; you twist a lever, such as a screwdriver or scrap of wood, round in it to increase the pressure. To prevent the string from damaging the wood you should protect the edges with scraps of timber or man-made boards. For large frames, use two loops across the frame or place the loop right round the frame to pull the corners together. The latter arrangement is particularly suitable when you are gluing mitred edges together; in this case it is important you also have

four notched corner blocks to guide the string and act as buffers.

Workbench vice To clamp frames small enough to rest on your workbench, you can use an ordinary workbench vice. Screw a length of timber to the bench to act as a temporary stop and rest one side of the framework against this with the other side close to the vice. Fix a piece of stout timber to the face of the vice with the top edge above the level of the bench top. When you tighten the vice against the length of fixed timber the frame is securely clamped.

Folding wedges Two wedges placed face-to-face make a versatile clamping device. You can cut the wedges from any type of scrap timber; but it is better to make them from hardwood if you are going to use them frequently, since this type of wood is more durable than softwood.

Place the framework or timber to be clamped on a flat surface. Rest one side of the work against a timber stop and fix another stop close to the opposite side of the frame, leaving room for the folding wedges. Place the wedges together and use a wood mallet to tap their ends inwards to increase pressure on the workpiece. Alternatively, you can use stout screws as the stops and drive the wedges between the screws and the workpiece.

Timber frame When the workpiece to be clamped cannot be held flat on a bench, you can make a timber frame to fit around the work. Place folding wedges between the temporary frame and the workpiece to clamp the joints tightly.

11 A simple clamping method using folding wedges. The workpiece is placed between two timber stops and the wedges driven in to secure the work

12 Alternatively use screws as stops and drive the wedges between these and the work

13 When it is difficult to hold the work flat on a bench, construct a rough timber frame and place this around the work, with wedges in between to hold the joints tight

Ladders

1 A step stool is adequate for many jobs around the house and provides an extra kitchen seat
2 A stable base for tools and materials is a useful feature of the platform step ladder
3 The versatile combination ladder opens out to form steps
4 For work on a staircase, the combination ladder is ideal

Whether you are changing a light bulb in a high-ceilinged room, decorating or doing general maintenance work, you will need steps of some kind sooner or later. Look at the range available and decide what kind you need before hiring or buying. For occasional work it will be cheaper to hire what you want, although in the long run it is probably worth your while buying some multi-purpose steps.

Ladders

If you live in a flat with limited storage facilities and low ceilings, a sturdy step stool will cope with most jobs. If you have high ceilings or do a lot of decorating, you should invest in a step ladder or combination ladder. For external maintenance or decorating an extension ladder is essential.

Platform step ladder This type opens up to a free-standing position and has a small platform on top on which to stand a bucket, paint can or tools, thus leaving your hands free. It is very stable and extra safe if fitted with a handrail above the platform. When choosing a platform ladder, make sure the treads are wide enough to allow you to stand comfortably for long periods.

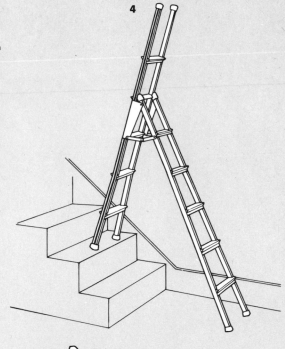

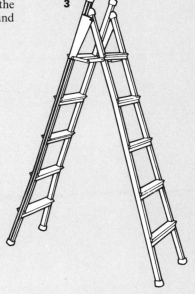

Combination ladder/steps If you need to reach different heights or work on a staircase, a combination of ladder and steps is ideal. Adjustable for three different jobs, the combination is still compact and easy to store. It consists of a pair of ladders which can be opened to form a step ladder without a platform or extended to a small double extension ladder long enough for most jobs on the outside of a bungalow. The two sections can also be adjusted to straddle different levels of a staircase.

Extension ladder This consists of two or three parts extending to the required length. A double (two part) extension is suitable for most two-storey properties. Long ladders are extended by means of a rope secured on a cleat. Smaller ladders extend by hand and are secured with stay locks which clip onto the selected rung.

It will probably be more economical to hire rather than buy an extension ladder, especially if upper storey work is planned to be completed in a short time. If you use an extension ladder frequently, it will be less expensive to buy one.

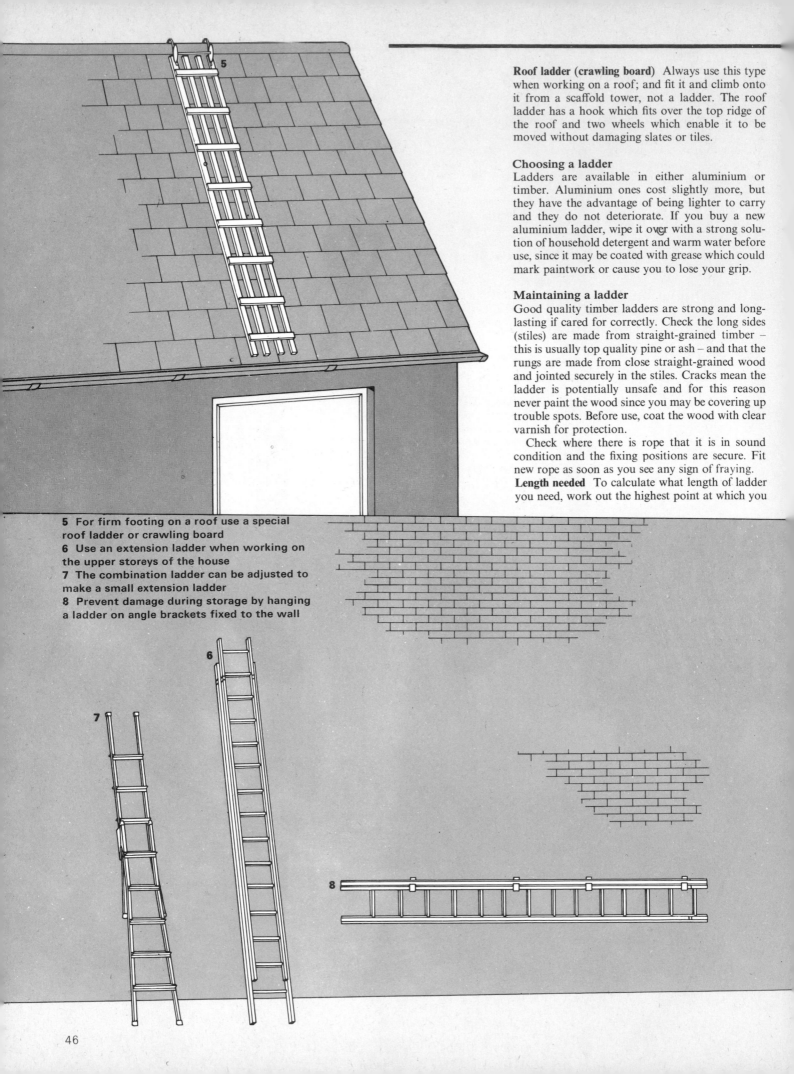

Roof ladder (crawling board) Always use this type when working on a roof; and fit it and climb onto it from a scaffold tower, not a ladder. The roof ladder has a hook which fits over the top ridge of the roof and two wheels which enable it to be moved without damaging slates or tiles.

Choosing a ladder

Ladders are available in either aluminium or timber. Aluminium ones cost slightly more, but they have the advantage of being lighter to carry and they do not deteriorate. If you buy a new aluminium ladder, wipe it over with a strong solution of household detergent and warm water before use, since it may be coated with grease which could mark paintwork or cause you to lose your grip.

Maintaining a ladder

Good quality timber ladders are strong and long-lasting if cared for correctly. Check the long sides (stiles) are made from straight-grained timber – this is usually top quality pine or ash – and that the rungs are made from close straight-grained wood and jointed securely in the stiles. Cracks mean the ladder is potentially unsafe and for this reason never paint the wood since you may be covering up trouble spots. Before use, coat the wood with clear varnish for protection.

Check where there is rope that it is in sound condition and the fixing positions are secure. Fit new rope as soon as you see any sign of fraying.

Length needed To calculate what length of ladder you need, work out the highest point at which you

5 For firm footing on a roof use a special roof ladder or crawling board
6 Use an extension ladder when working on the upper storeys of the house
7 The combination ladder can be adjusted to make a small extension ladder
8 Prevent damage during storage by hanging a ladder on angle brackets fixed to the wall

will want to stand when working and allow for the ladder to extend at least three clear rungs above this point.

Storage An ideal place to store a ladder is the garage, where it can be kept dry and under lock and key. Preferably hang the ladder along the wall on strong hooks or angle brackets and make sure it is well supported in the middle. This is particularly important with wood ladders, which may sag under their own weight if supported only at the ends.

Putting up a ladder

Place the ladder flat on the ground at right-angles to the wall with the foot of the ladder against the wall. Pick up the ladder by the top rung and walk towards the wall, gradually raising the ladder above your head by passing your hands over each rung. If the ladder is heavy get someone to hold the foot of it steady. When it is flat against the wall, pull the foot of it away from the wall so the distance between the foot of the ladder and the wall is one quarter the length of the ladder.

Extending a ladder

Always put up a ladder before extending it. Raise it to the required height, using the wall as support for the top. Get someone to hold the foot of the ladder steady. Make sure at least a quarter of the top ladder is supported by the one below and that the stay clips are engaged or the rope secured firmly. Check the distance between the foot of the ladder and the wall is one quarter the length of the extended ladder.

Additional safety

Always check the ladder is not damaged before using it and always stand it on a firm, level surface for working. If the ground is uneven, put the ladder on a paving stone or wood platform and place a sturdy piece of wood or sandbags in front of it to prevent it slipping. For additional security, drive one or more pegs into the ground and tie the bottom of the ladder to them. Aluminium ladders should have rubber feet to give a non-slip base and similar rubber cups are usually fitted to the top, also to prevent slipping.

Avoid using an extension ladder in windy conditions, especially if you are inexperienced. Avoid resting a ladder against any gutter unless of stout metal and securely fixed; never rest a ladder against a plastic gutter.

When working around roof eaves, make sure three rungs project above the line of the eaves. Where possible secure the ladder by tying one rung to a ring bolt screwed into the fascia. This will prevent the ladder sliding sideways. If you have plastic guttering, use a ladder stay. Never lean out from a ladder; work only as far as you can comfortably reach. Follow this rule strictly, even when the ladder is tied top and bottom.

Don't move a ladder or pair of steps if something is still hanging from it or on the platform. Wear strong shoes when working on a ladder for long periods, since with thin-soled shoes your feet will soon ache and fatigue can cause you to slip, especially on round rungs. Don't wear boots, since they make it difficult to locate the rungs.

9 To raise a ladder, place the foot of the ladder against the wall. Hold the ladder by the top rung and walk towards the wall, passing your hands down the rungs
10 When the ladder is flat against the wall, move the foot of it away from the wall
11 When extending a ladder make sure the overlap is at least a quarter the length of a single ladder

Working from a ladder

If you are right-handed, work from right to left so you are always moving the ladder away from your work and do not need to rest it against fresh paintwork. Left-handed people should, of course, work from left to right.

When you move a ladder to a new work position, lift it clear of the wall before repositioning it. Do not slide the top of the ladder along the wall as this may damage pebble-dashing or paintwork.

If the top of the ladder has to be placed in front of a window, tie or bolt a strong, flat batten, 100 × 25mm (4 × 1in), to the top end of the ladder so each end of the batten rests against the wall either side of the window. This will provide firm support for the ladder.

Useful accessories

Various ladder accessories can be bought or hired. Some of them are worth using as they make working at a height more comfortable and convenient.
Ladder platform Clips onto a rung to provide a more comfortable area to work on.

Ladder stay Enables you to paint the underside of an overhanging roof without having to lean back. One end locks onto the top two rungs of the ladder and the other end rests against the house wall so the ladder is held securely a short distance from the wall. The ladder can still be tied to a ring bolt.
Tool rack This attachment holds bucket and tools in a high position. A stout 'S' hook may also be used to suspend a bucket or paint can, but is less versatile.

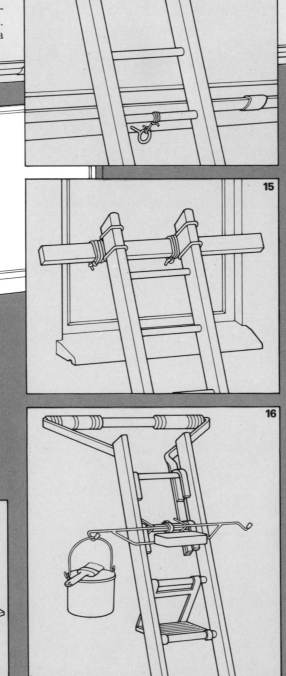

12 When working on a ladder, take care not to lean out

13 On uneven ground stand the ladder on a flat board and place a heavy block of wood against it to prevent it slipping. Tie the bottom of the ladder to pegs for additional safety

14 When working around the eaves, have the ladder projecting above the eaves by three rungs and secure it to the fascia by tying it to a ring bolt

15 To hold the top of a ladder away from a window, tie a bar of wood to the ladder so each end rests against the wall

16 Ladder accessories make working at height more comfortable: fit a ladder stay to the top rungs to hold it away from the wall so you can paint the underside of the roof easily; a ladder platform gives a stable base to work from and a tool rack holds paint cans, buckets and tools

Scaffold towers

If you feel unsafe on a ladder, you may prefer to work from a scaffold tower, which provides greater stability and gives access to a larger work area. It is more expensive to hire than a ladder, so it may be worth buying one in partnership with other house owners. One big advantage is a tower can be used inside or outside.

If you want to paint the outside of your house, for example, there is no need to hire scaffolders as versatile scaffold towers can be erected by the DIY enthusiast in a very short time – you simply interlock tubular frames and build them up to the height you need. The frames are available in widths of 600 and 1200mm (24 and 48in) and can be used in any combination.

Several manufacturers make easy-to-assemble tower kits for the home handyman. There are no nuts and bolts to fix since the tower consists of tubular frames which interlock and build up to the required height. The frames are available in widths of 600 and 1200mm (24 and 48in) and can be used in any combination.

The basic kit consists of the frames, diagonal braces which reinforce the frames, handrail posts and handrails. There are various feet for fitting onto the bottom rails. The standard base plate can be used on a level surface and adjustable feet are available for uneven ground or stairs. These jack up the appropriate part of the frame to the required level. Castors can be fitted to make the tower mobile and can be locked when the tower is in the required position. But only use them on a firm, level surface. Rubber feet are available for use indoors. Platform boards slot onto the frames to give a base to work from and toe boards may be fitted to prevent tools being kicked off the platform.

Some kits include a ladder which is fitted inside the frame. Outriggers – angled supports attached to the outer part of the frame – increase the base area, giving greater stability and allowing height to be increased. This, however, should not exceed three times the minimum base dimensions.

The design of the kit varies slightly between manufacturers, but all kits are assembled in a similar way.

Assembling a tower
Select the appropriate feet and fit them onto the bottom of the first pair of frames. If using castors, lock them. Place the two frames opposite each other with the spigot (the narrow end of the frame) uppermost. Slot a diagonal brace onto two diagonally opposite uprights then interlock two more frames at 90 degrees to the first pair, placing the wide ends over the spigots of the first set of uprights. Continue until you reach the desired height and, as you get higher, use a platform board to stand on while assembling the tower. On the last but one frame place another diagonal brace in the opposite direction to the one below. Place the platform boards at working level and fit the handrail posts and handrails.

Cantilever structures can be built onto the tower to reach flat garage roofs and other split-level work areas such as large stairwells and landings.

Safety precautions
Follow the manufacturer's instructions carefully when assembling the tower. Make sure you start from a firm base and use the various parts of the kit in the correct way. Fit a safety toe board around the sides of the platform to prevent tools being kicked over the edge of the tower.

Wherever possible, tie the top of the tower to a fixing on the building for extra safety. This is particularly advisable for heights over 3m (or 10ft). A ring bolt screwed securely into the building makes an ideal fixing.

Never try to move a tower or adjust the legs when someone is on the platform or when tools or equipment are on it.

After moving the tower, check the adjustment of base legs on uneven ground and relock the castors. If the tower is higher than 3m (or 10ft) and is not fitted with castors, dismantle it before moving it to a new position.

Assembling a scaffold tower:
1 Join two parallel base rails with a diagonal bar
2 Place the next pair of rails at right-angles to the first pair. Repeat the whole procedure, alternating the direction of the diagonal bar until the required height is reached
3 Place planks at the top of the tower to form a platform and fit a handrail

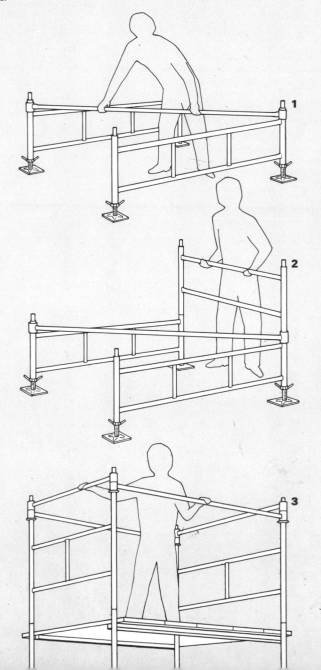

Spanners and wrenches

Never use anything but a good quality spanner of the correct size to turn a nut or bolt; if you use a gripping tool, the damage caused could render the work useless. If you want to grip work, there are two main points to bear in mind when selecting the tool for the job: it must grip the work securely and not slip and it must not damage the work – although there may be occasions when, due to the nature of the work, it will not matter if your gripping tool marks the work surface.

Spanner sizes
Spanners are available in a range of sizes, depending on the system of the work in hand and are made with either standard or short-length shanks.

Whitworth and BSF The size of the hexagons on British Standard Whitworth and British Standard Fine bolts differs for any given diameter of bolt. In practical terms this does not matter, since the same set of spanners will fit both series of bolt and nut hexagons. This means a spanner designed to fit the hexagon head of a $\frac{1}{4}$in BSF bolt will also fit the hexagon head of a $\frac{3}{16}$in BSW bolt; a similar relationship exists throughout the range.

The normal set of spanners will range up to 2in BSF, but there is little need for the largest sizes. A suitable range of BS spanners for use in the home workshop would be: $\frac{1}{4} \times \frac{5}{16}$, $\frac{3}{8} \times \frac{7}{16}$, $\frac{1}{2} \times \frac{9}{16}$, $\frac{5}{8} \times \frac{11}{16}$, and $\frac{3}{4} \times \frac{7}{8}$. The Imperial sizes indicated are those found marked on the jaws of the spanner and indicate the bolt diameter. Most spanner sets are arranged in such a way that the larger size on one spanner is the same as the smaller one on the next spanner up. Thus a $\frac{7}{16} \times \frac{1}{2}$in follows on from a $\frac{3}{8} \times \frac{7}{16}$in, which means you can use one of the $\frac{7}{16}$in ends on the bolt and the other $\frac{7}{16}$in end on the nut.

American and Unified series Spanners made to fit these series of nuts and bolts are identified by the distance measured across the flats of the hexagon – and not by the bolt diameter. For example, a spanner marked $\frac{7}{16}$ A/F (across flats) measures $\frac{7}{16}$in across its jaws and is designed to be used on a bolt with a diameter of $\frac{1}{4}$in. The most useful set of spanners in these series for home use would be: $\frac{5}{16}$ A/F $\times \frac{3}{8}$ A/F, $\frac{7}{16}$ A/F $\times \frac{1}{2}$ A/F, $\frac{9}{16}$ A/F $\times \frac{5}{8}$ A/F, $\frac{11}{16}$ A/F $\times \frac{3}{4}$ A/F and $\frac{13}{16}$ A/F $\times \frac{7}{8}$ A/F.

Metric series These spanners are also identified by the measurement across the flats of the bolt head. The most useful set would be of 9–22mm spanners. Unfortunately the ends of these spanners may not coincide with the next spanner in the set and therefore to hold both the nut and the bolt at the same time you need two similar spanners. The metric series is becoming more widely used than the other series, particularly on such things as cars and appliances. Bear in mind metric spanners are not interchangeable with those of other series.

Open-ended spanner
The most common type of spanner is the open-ended version – and it is often the most abused, bearing in mind how versatile it is. A good quality open-ended spanner will operate very efficiently, with the advantages of being easy to slide onto a nut or bolt where access is limited, of needing access to only two flats of the nut or bolt in order to turn it

and of being able to operate even when the spanner shaft is not quite at right-angles to the bolt axis.

The head of the spanner is set at an angle to the shaft; this angle, of 15 degrees, is exactly a quarter the angle through which an ordinary hexagonal nut turns when it moves one flat. In a restricted area, therefore, the spanner needs to be turned only 30 degrees, removed from the hexagon, turned over and back through 30 degrees to hold the next flat. The next time it is turned over and moved back 30 degrees, the jaws take another hold on the same flats. This is repeated as often as necessary, with only a 30 degree turn required each time.

Ring spanner
While the open-ended spanner offers accessibility, the ring spanner has the advantage of power and safety, since it holds all six points of the hexagon and will not slip if used properly. This type of spanner is sometimes called the 12-point spanner because the inside of the ring has 12 points, six of which fit around the points of the nut in one position and the other six of which come into operation when the spanner is repositioned on the nut. In this way the ring spanner can also be used to turn a nut or bolt with only a 30 degree movement.

Ring spanners come in two designs: plain, where the spanner head is in the same plane as the shaft,

1 Offset ring spanners
2 An open-ended spanner offers accessibility since it can be used even when its shaft is not at right-angles to the axis of the bolt
You can use an open-ended spanner to turn a nut in a restricted space:
3a Slide the spanner onto the nut
3b Turn it through 30 degrees
3c Remove the spanner and turn it over to hold the next flat
3d Turn the spanner back through 30 degrees. Repeat this procedure as necessary
4 A range of open-ended spanners
5 Combination spanner

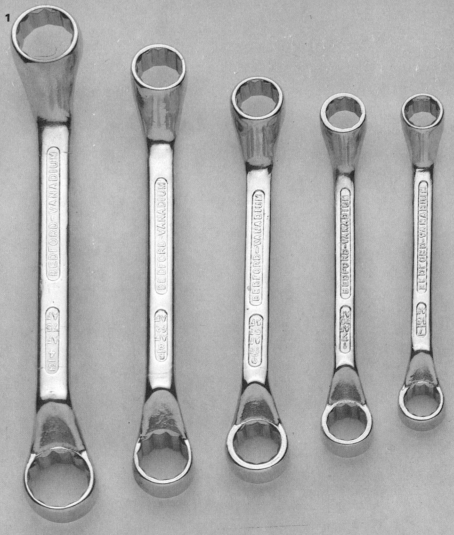

1

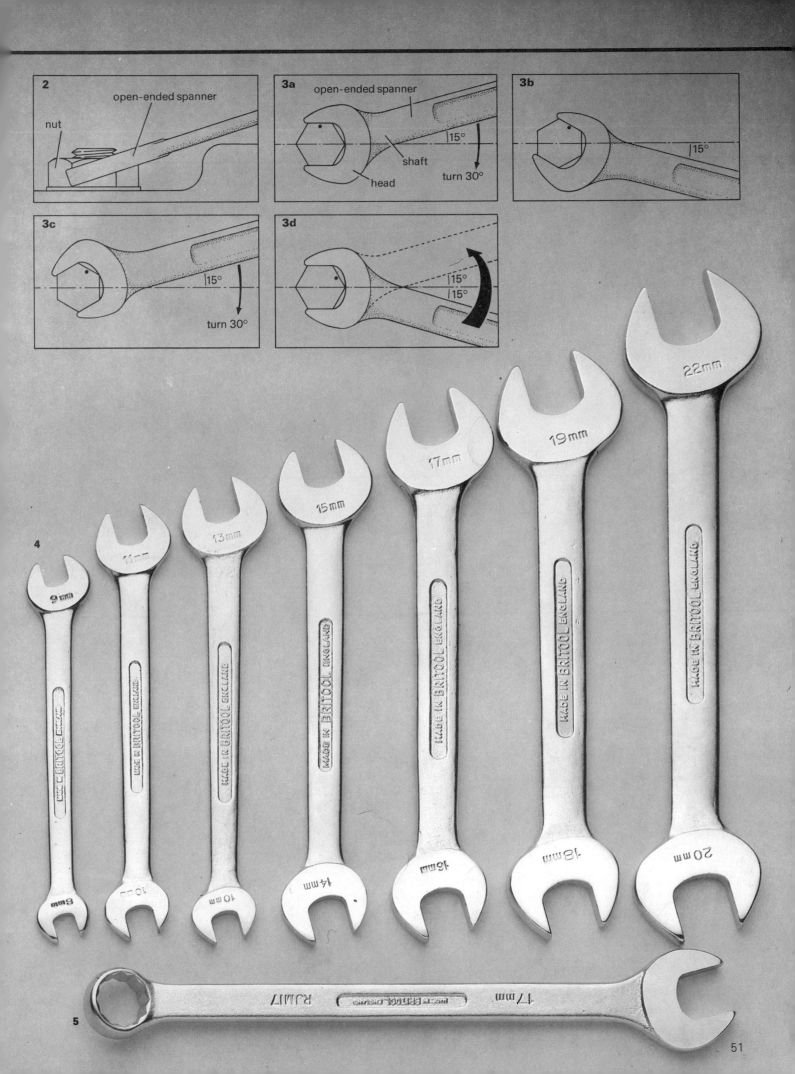

2

nut

open-ended spanner

3a

open-ended spanner

shaft

head

15°

turn 30°

3b

15°

3c

15°

turn 30°

3d

15°
15°

4

9mm
11mm
13mm
15mm
17mm
19mm
22mm

MADE IN BRITOOL ENGLAND

8mm
10mm
12mm
14mm
16mm
18mm
20mm

5

17mm

RJM17

MADE IN BRITOOL ENGLAND

and offset, where the head is set to one side of the shaft to give greater accessibility.

Combination spanner

Although it is useful to have a set of both open-ended and ring spanners, the advantage of both types can be gained with a combination spanner. One end of the spanner is open and the other has a 12-point ring, as described earlier. The only disadvantage with this type of spanner is that more are needed to cover any given range of sizes since each spanner fits only one size of nut or bolt.

Obstruction spanner

This type of open-ended spanner is specially designed for use in restricted working conditions. It is shaped in such a way that it requires only a 17 degree movement to turn the nut or bolt. It is not normally bought in set form, but rather as a one-off purchase when needed to tackle a particular fastening problem.

Box spanner

For nuts which are really deeply recessed, a box spanner is a most useful type to have; the inside of the head has only six sides and the whole of the working part fits around the hexagon. It does not have a fitted handle, but there are normally two holes in the tube at right-angles to each other which offer a choice of levering positions when you insert a lever (known as a tommy bar); this turns the spanner.

While this type of spanner is comparatively inexpensive, it is not satisfactory for tough jobs.

Socket spanner

The socket spanner is undoubtedly the most versatile type, since it combines the strength and accessibility of the ring spanner and has a vast range of interchangeable components which can be fitted to it. The socket sizes come in metric, Imperial, Unified or American systems and the socket has a square hole in the opposite end to take the driving

6 Box spanner with tommy bar
7 Various size sockets
8 Speed brace
9 Universal joint attachment
10 Explaining torque
11 Sliding bar lever
12 Ratchet driver
13 Extension bar
14 Driver with universal joint
15 Torque wrench

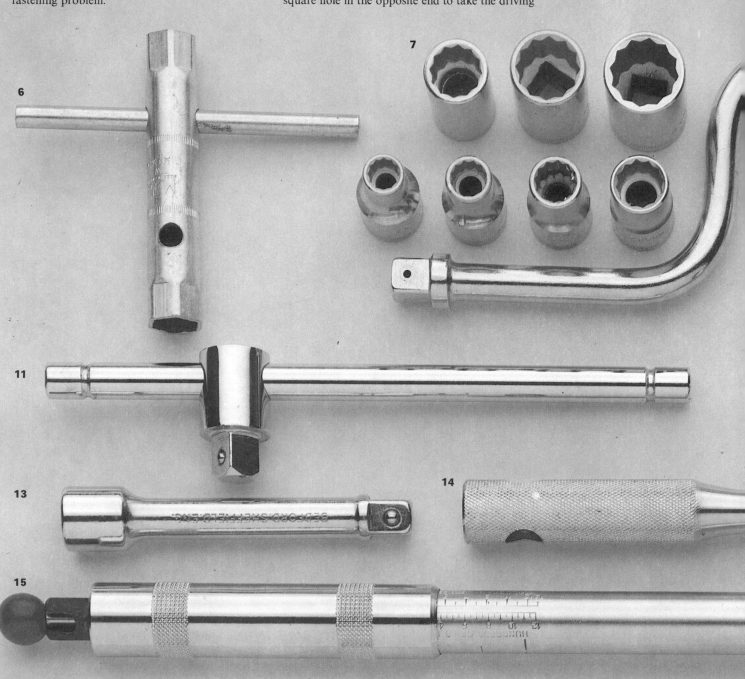

handle. The drive size most commonly used is $\frac{1}{2}$in across the flats of the square, although $\frac{1}{4}$, $\frac{3}{8}$ and $\frac{3}{4}$in sizes are also available. The size depends on the size of the hexagon being turned – and the $\frac{1}{2}$in accommodates most jobs likely to be tackled at home.

Types of driver The most useful driver is the ratchet type with reversible setting; the number of ratchet stops is usually about 30, which means only about a 13 degree movement is needed to turn the hexagon of a nut or bolt.

Another driver is the sliding bar lever, which comprises a simple square that slides along a plain bar. Other drivers incorporate universal joints so the socket can be driven from almost any angle.

There is a universal joint attachment which fits behind the socket; this type is particularly useful when an extension bar is being used. Various lengths of extension bar are available, which can also be fitted end to end to suit the job in hand; each comprises a square at one end of a steel bar with a matching socket at the other end.

Torque wrench

The torque wrench is designed to accept sockets from a socket spanner set. It is fitted with a ratchet mechanism so the socket can be turned in either direction as necessary. The most important aspect of this type of wrench is that it incorporates a device which can be adjusted to control the torque or turning effort which is applied to the nut or bolt.

Torque This is measured by multiplying the force applied to the spanner by the perpendicular distance between the point of application of the load and the centre of the nut or bolt. It is expressed in kilogram force centimetres or metres (kgf cm/m), pound force inches or feet (lbf in/ft) or Newton metres (Nm). On vehicles, for example, almost all important bolted joints have to be tightened to a particular torque loading to avoid overstressing.

Wrench (Allan) key

The wrench (or Allan) key is used solely to tighten or undo hexagon socket screws which have a round

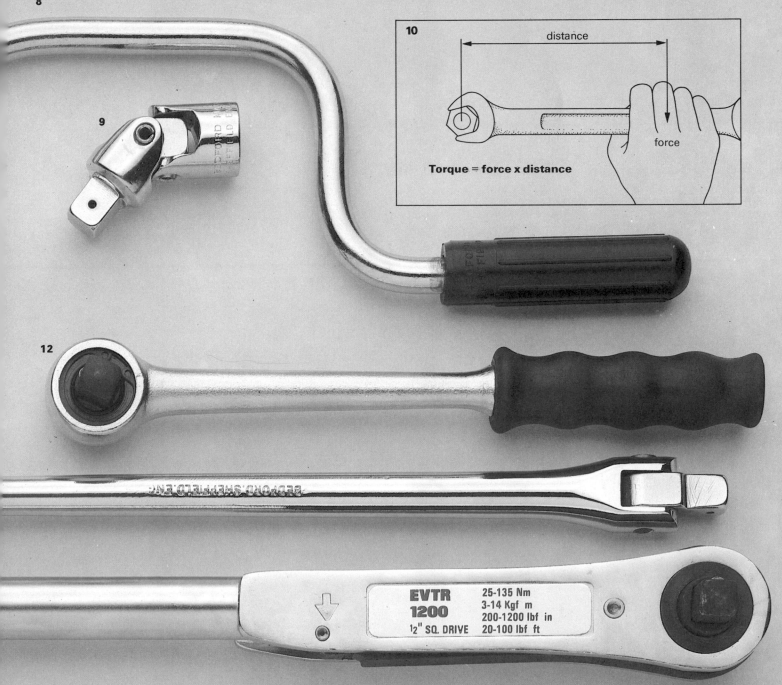

10 distance

force

Torque = force x distance

EVTR
1200

$\frac{1}{2}$" SQ. DRIVE

25-135 Nm
3-14 Kgf m
200-1200 lbf in
20-100 lbf ft

head with a hexagonal hole in the centre; the mating hexagonal key fits into this hole. Hexagon socket screws are expensive, but they are often used on good quality machines because the head requires very little space and can often be sunk into a bored hole to prevent a protruding screw head. They can also be used to secure a neat joint in furniture which needs to be dismantled and reassembled easily. Hexagon socket grub screws, which have a pointed tip, are often used for fixing pulleys and collars on rotating shafts, such as in washing machines. A set of hexagonal keys is not expensive – and the keys are the only means of removing a hexagon socket screw without damaging the screw or the parts held together by the screw.

Adjustable spanner

The purist will only turn to the adjustable spanner when absolutely stuck for the correct tool. This type has adjustable jaws to fit any size of hexagon on a nut or bolt. Although well engineered, this spanner is still subject to wear and can slip if not used carefully, particularly when working on a tough job.

Girder spanner Although regarded as a last resort, there is one particularly useful small adjustable spanner – the girder spanner. Because of its size, it is used only on work which does not require much force to be moved, such as nuts on electrical terminals.

Self-grip wrench

The self-grip wrench, which has a locking action, is one of the most useful hand-gripping tools. Once placed on the work, it can be locked in position and will stay there unsupported, allowing you the freedom to use both hands to manipulate the other parts of the job. This type of wrench is available with either flat or rounded jaws (for gripping circular objects) with a variety of locking and release mechanisms, depending on individual manufacturers.

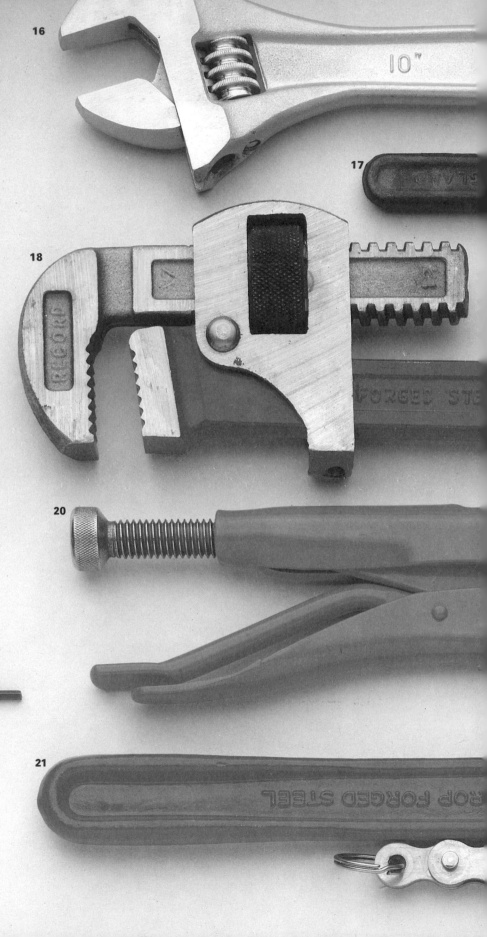

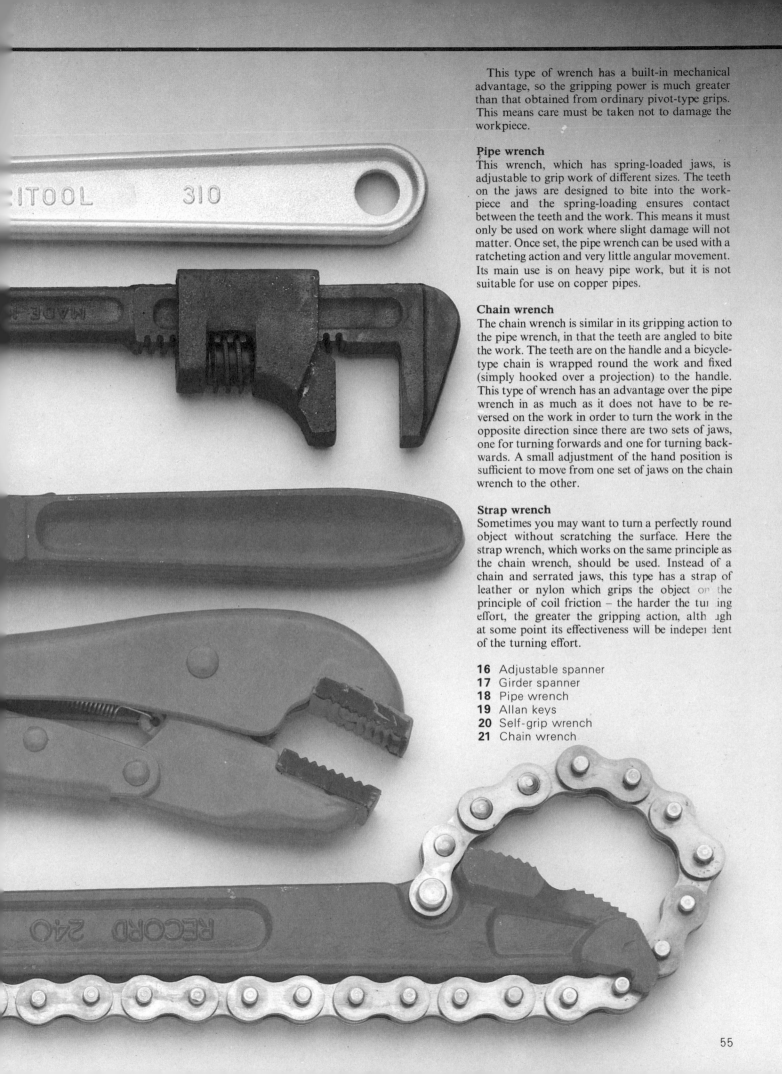

This type of wrench has a built-in mechanical advantage, so the gripping power is much greater than that obtained from ordinary pivot-type grips. This means care must be taken not to damage the workpiece.

Pipe wrench
This wrench, which has spring-loaded jaws, is adjustable to grip work of different sizes. The teeth on the jaws are designed to bite into the work-piece and the spring-loading ensures contact between the teeth and the work. This means it must only be used on work where slight damage will not matter. Once set, the pipe wrench can be used with a ratcheting action and very little angular movement. Its main use is on heavy pipe work, but it is not suitable for use on copper pipes.

Chain wrench
The chain wrench is similar in its gripping action to the pipe wrench, in that the teeth are angled to bite the work. The teeth are on the handle and a bicycle-type chain is wrapped round the work and fixed (simply hooked over a projection) to the handle. This type of wrench has an advantage over the pipe wrench in as much as it does not have to be re-versed on the work in order to turn the work in the opposite direction since there are two sets of jaws, one for turning forwards and one for turning back-wards. A small adjustment of the hand position is sufficient to move from one set of jaws on the chain wrench to the other.

Strap wrench
Sometimes you may want to turn a perfectly round object without scratching the surface. Here the strap wrench, which works on the same principle as the chain wrench, should be used. Instead of a chain and serrated jaws, this type has a strap of leather or nylon which grips the object on the principle of coil friction – the harder the turning effort, the greater the gripping action, although at some point its effectiveness will be independent of the turning effort.

16 Adjustable spanner
17 Girder spanner
18 Pipe wrench
19 Allan keys
20 Self-grip wrench
21 Chain wrench

Files

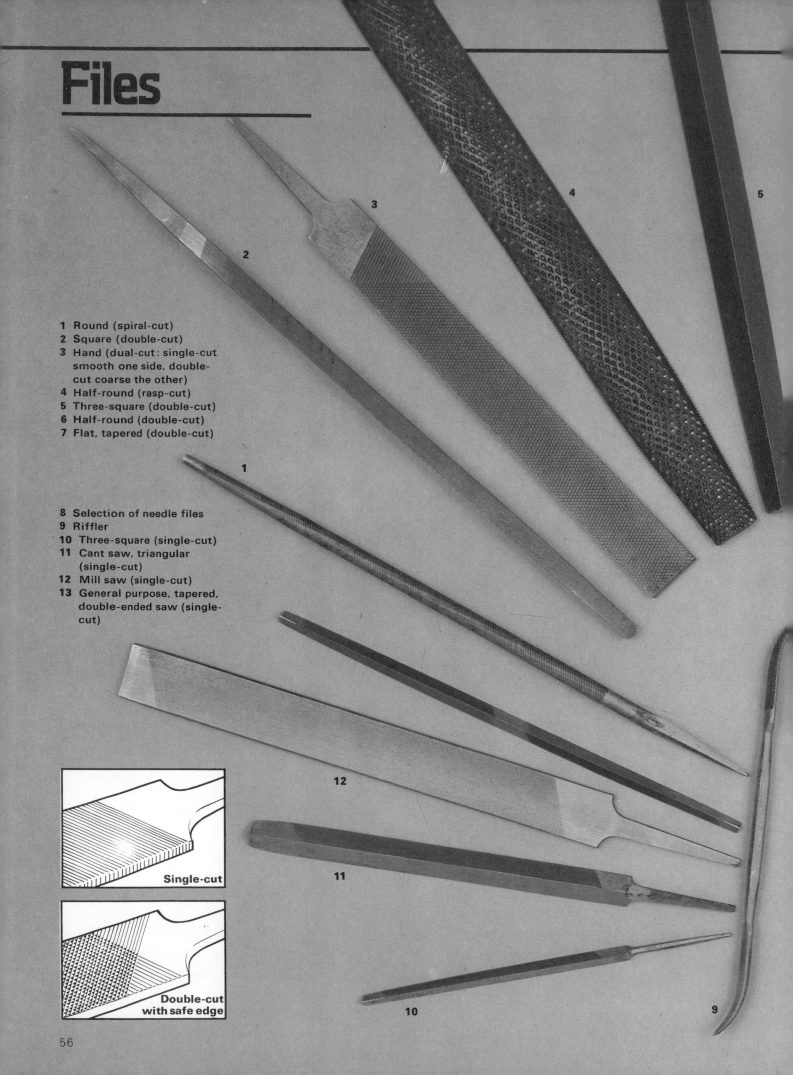

1 Round (spiral-cut)
2 Square (double-cut)
3 Hand (dual-cut: single-cut
  smooth one side, double-
  cut coarse the other)
4 Half-round (rasp-cut)
5 Three-square (double-cut)
6 Half-round (double-cut)
7 Flat, tapered (double-cut)

8 Selection of needle files
9 Riffler
10 Three-square (single-cut)
11 Cant saw, triangular
   (single-cut)
12 Mill saw (single-cut)
13 General purpose, tapered,
   double-ended saw (single-
   cut)

Single-cut

**Double-cut
with safe edge**

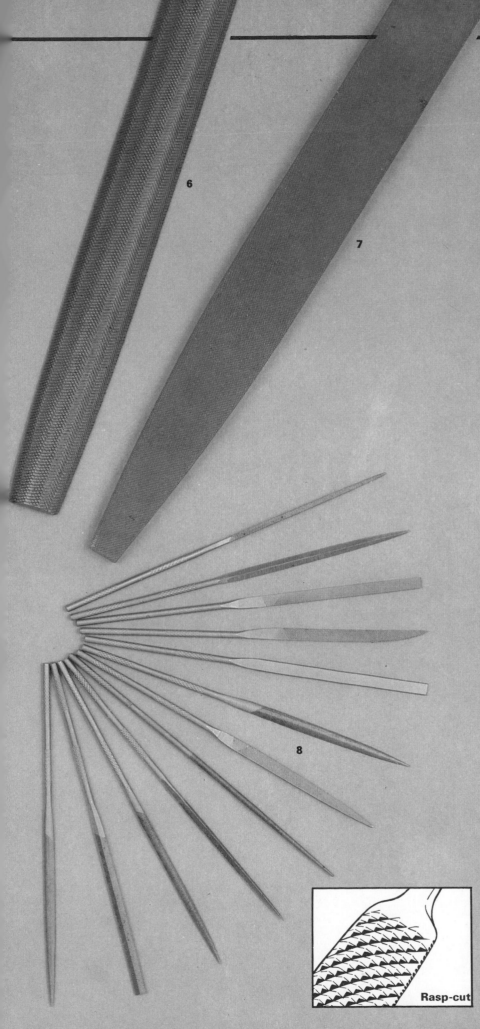

Files come in many shapes (flat, tapered, round, half-round, square, three-square or triangular) and sizes, with various grades of teeth and cut. Shape and type of cut vary according to the work involved, the amount of material to be removed and the finish required. Usually, the bigger the job the larger the file you should use. Although the file is basically designed to be used for metalwork, you can do some fining down on wood or laminate edges with a file.

There are two basic styles of cutting edge on files: single-cut and double-cut (**see details opposite**) and each has a different tooth formation for different filing effects.

Single-cut Here the teeth are arranged in one direction only, to give a smooth cut and to remove a fair amount of material with each stroke.

Double-cut With two sets of diagonal teeth crossing over to make the double cut.

There are three main degrees of coarseness (applying to both single and double-cut files) known as bastard, second-cut and smooth.

Bastard With a very coarse face, this type is used for removing material rapidly at the start of a job.

Second-cut Finer than bastard files and suited to in-between work.

Smooth Finer still, this cut is used for finishing off the surface.

There is no point in removing a lot of material with a fine file – all you will achieve is aching muscles and a worn-out tool.

Many files are made with a 'safe' edge – that is, one edge without teeth. If by accident you rub the file against the face adjacent to the one you are working on, you will not remove any material. Always use a file with a safe edge when working in restricted space or when you want to produce an accurate cut-out or right-angle.

Multi-purpose files

Several manufacturers have produced multi-purpose files for general use. These are dual-cut with very coarse teeth on one side and finer teeth on the other.

Specialist files

There are special files available for use on awkward corners or angles where conventional ones would be too big; you can also buy a range of small saw files which are designed for sharpening the teeth of specific saws.

Needle files Very thin, fine files which come in a variety of shapes. They are ideal for delicate work such as clockmaking.

Rifflers With curves or hooks at each end, or curved at one end and tapered and pointed the other, these come in many shapes. They can cope with intricate jobs and are mainly used by toolmakers and silversmiths.

Mill saw files Extremely useful for sharpening the teeth of a circular saw, these are single-cut with rounded edges that fit the gullet of the saw blade; you maintain the depth of the teeth as well as filing the top edge.

Cant saw files Triangular, single-cut for sharpening saws with long, slender teeth, such as pruning saws.

Round files These have a special spiral cut for filing the gullets of chain saws.

Rasp-cut files With individually formed teeth in varying degrees of fineness (**see detail at left**), they can be used on most types of material, including wood, plastics and soft metals.

Rasp-cut

Using files

Clamp the work in a vice to leave both hands free. Make sure the vice is at such a height that, when you hold the file with its far end resting on the work, the file is horizontal and the file tip, your hand and arm are all in a straight line.

The jaws of a vice are usually serrated to grip firmly, but these edges will badly mark fine work. To overcome this problem, buy a pair of smooth face jaws (or grind off the existing ones) or use a pair of vice linings – shaped pieces of lead, plastic or other soft material which fit around the jaws to protect the work.

The stance you adopt for filing is important. Stand with your legs slightly apart, with the left foot forward and the right foot pointing sideways (if you are left-handed, reverse the position).

Accuracy depends on the correct grip: hold the handle of the file in your right hand, place the palm of your left hand over the end of the file and wrap your fingers underneath to grip it tightly (again reverse the position if left-handed). This will enable you to apply considerable pressure. For lighter work, particularly when sharpening small saws with a triangular file, change your hand grip to a finger-tip hold. Place the file on the work and push it across the surface, using firm strokes the full length of the blade and lifting the file on the backward stroke.

You will find the angle of the teeth allows you to vary the cutting action simply by changing the direction of the stroke. To ensure accuracy on long lengths, use the file in a sideways action, making sure the teeth are at right angles to the direction of the cut – if they go the other way you will score the surface.

Draw filing This gives a much finer finish than straight filing. You hold the file across your body, with one hand gripping each end. Stand at right angles to the work and draw the file across it, towards the body, giving a slicing action to the file teeth.

Care of files

The teeth of a file are accurately cut on the face of extremely hard steel and, as with most very hard materials, this is rather brittle. Always keep your files on a rack; if they are jumbled together in a drawer, their teeth will blunt and chip and they will never again cut with the same efficiency.

Certain soft materials, particularly aluminium, tend to clog the file teeth, reducing their efficiency. When filing such materials keep a wire brush handy and use it along the line of the teeth to keep them clean.

A better tool for cleaning the teeth is a file card. This is a piece of very thick, strong, woven material into which are embedded hundreds of tiny wire strands making, in effect, a very wide wire brush with fine bristles about 6mm ($\frac{1}{4}$in) long. You can either use the card in this flexible state or stick it to a piece of wood to make a flat, rigid structure.

One way to cut down, if not eliminate, the problem of clogging is to keep some French chalk handy and liberally dust this on the file when cutting soft metals. The chalk acts as a lubricant and prevents the metal from sticking to the file.

Warning Always fit your files with proper handles. These may cost a few pence each, but they can prevent personal injury since a slight slip, a file catching on a sharp edge or a careless moment may result in a nasty hand wound.

Top Always clamp the work you are filing in a vice and use the file with your hand and arm in a straight line
Above Draw filing involves holding the file at both ends, standing at 90 degrees to the work
Right You can clean the teeth of a file with a special file card

Pliers and pincers

Usually bought as general purpose tools, pliers are part of a large family – including pincers and nippers – each suited to a particular job.

Engineer's (Combination) pliers
The best general purpose pliers since they have both a round and flat gripping area and two sets of cutters. Lengths are 125–250mm (5–10in), with or without insulated handles.

Electrician's pliers
Special version of the engineer's pliers with insulated handles to withstand up to 10,000 volts. Lengths are 150–200mm (6–8in).

Long nose pliers
These tools perform the holding and cutting functions of engineer's pliers, but are less bulky. Their long jaws make them particularly useful for work in tight places, such as motor engines, and for electrical work. Lengths are 140–200mm (5½–8in), with or without insulated handles.

Bent long nose pliers
Nose is bent to a 45 degree angle, making these pliers invaluable for working behind obstructions. 200mm (8in) long.

Water pump pliers
Combination of pliers and spanner, these are used instead of a spanner or wrench where a light, adjustable, long-handled tool is needed. They have four adjustment positions. 240 or 250mm (9½ or 10in) long.

Glass pliers
Pliers with wide, flat, serrated jaws used to snap glass. Lengths are 200–250mm (8–10in).

Nippers (cutters)
For cutting wire of all types, the most popular are the diagonal cutting ones. Lengths are 100–190mm (4–7½in).

Wire strippers
As the name suggests, used for easy stripping of insulation from wire. They can be adjusted to cope with various thicknesses of wire 150mm (6in) long.

Pincers
These are gripping, not cutting, tools designed for prising and pulling out nails and tacks. Lengths are 150–250mm (6–10in).

1 Nippers. **2** Glass pliers. **3** Electrician's pliers. **4** Long nose pliers. **5** Engineer's pliers. **6** Pincers. **7** Wire strippers. **8** Bent long nose pliers. **9** Water pump pliers

Tools for bricklaying

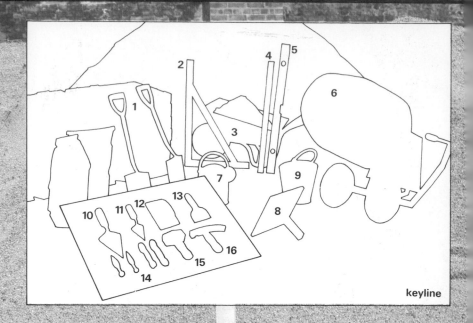

keyline

1 Shovels You need two – one for mixing the mortar and the other exclusively for shifting dry cement from the sack to the mix

2 Builder's square To check the first few courses of your wall are at right-angles to the concrete foundations

3 Wheelbarrow A sturdy model is essential for carrying bricks and mortar

4 Gauge rod Used to check the mortar joints are being kept to a uniform thickness. A 75 × 25mm (3 × 1in) softwood batten (about two metres or six feet long) will do. Mark the batten in 75mm (3in) graduations (the depth of a brick and its mortar). When checking with the gauge rod, each graduation should align with the top edge of a brick course

5 Spirit level A 1m (or 3ft) level is needed to check the bricks are being laid accurately – horizontally and vertically. A 150mm (6in) level is useful for the beginner for levelling each brick as it is laid against the previous one in the course

6 Cement mixer Many consider hiring one essential, especially for larger jobs. It all depends on your muscles and your money

7 Watering can Must be fitted with a fine rose for adding water to the mix

8 Mortar board or hawk For holding small quantities of mortar while working. Make it yourself from a 13mm ($\frac{1}{2}$in) thick piece of board with a 100mm (4in) length of broom handle screwed to it

9 Bucket You need two; keep one for cement only. If the buckets are the same size, it makes it easy to add the various ingredients to the mix in the correct proportions

10 Laying trowel For spreading mortar on the bricks

11 Pointing trowel For cleaning and shaping the mortar joints between the bricks. The joints can be flush with bricks or sloped to allow water to drain

12 Steel float If you want a really smooth finish on your concrete foundation, you can use a steel float

13 & 15 Bolster chisel and club hammer Use these together when you need to cut a brick in half. Lay the brick on a firm, level surface and make grooves on both sides of the 112.5mm ($4\frac{1}{2}$in) face. Place the bolster chisel at right-angles on the grooved line and tap gently with the hammer. Two more sharp blows with the hammer should leave you with a clean brick. Remember to practise first with some unwanted bricks. You can also use these tools to remove old mortar from second-hand bricks

14 Bricklayer's pins and string Use the line as a running guide in conjunction with a spirit level to ensure each course of bricks is laid horizontally. Knock the pins into the mortar course at each end of the wall and stretch the line taut between them. As you complete each course, reposition the line for the course above

16 Bricklayer's hammer Used for cutting bricks when only a small amount has to be trimmed.

Tools for laying concrete

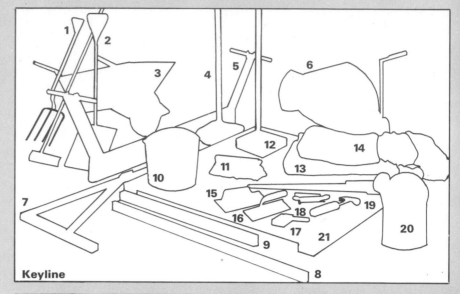

Keyline

You need a surprising number of tools for mixing and laying concrete; many of them you will probably have already, some you can make yourself and some you can hire. All equipment which comes into contact with concrete should be thoroughly scrubbed at the end of each work session to prevent the concrete setting.

1 Fork For digging out foundations. You will also need a spade to clear the site

2 Shovel & rake For shovelling the concrete into the formwork and spreading it slightly proud of the formwork timbers

3 Wheelbarrow A sturdy model is essential if the ballast and cement has to be carried from the storage area to the mixing site or if the mixing site is any distance away from the formwork. If the barrow has to be pushed over soft ground, lay down a line of strong planks

4 Ramming tool For compacting the subsoil or hardcore used in foundations, if a roller is not available. Fill a timber mould (about 200 × 150 × 100mm/8 × 6 × 4in) with concrete, insert a piece of iron pipe or a broom handle in the mould and keep it supported until the concrete has set. A punner (**12**) may also be used

5 Tamping beam For levelling drives and wider sections of concrete. Make it from 150 × 50mm (6 × 2in) timber. Strong handles help you move the tamper more easily

6 Hand-operated concrete mixer This comprises a mixing drum on a trolley. The cement, ballast and water are poured into the drum and the machine pushed along a hard, level surface to rotate the drum and mix the concrete. Electric, petrol and diesel-powered mixers are also available (all can be hired). Tipping stand facilitates pouring of concrete into barrow; while one load is being spread, another can be mixed

7 Builder's square To check the corners of the form for squareness. Make one by joining three lengths of wood with sides in the proportion of 3:4:5. A good size is 450 × 600 × 750mm (or 18 × 24 × 30in). Use an L-shaped bracket and screws to make rigid joints. If the proportions are accurate, the angle between the shortest sides will be 90 degrees

8 Spirit level For checking formwork and crossfall

9 Timber straight-edge For setting out fall of concrete if drainage is required. You can also use it for levelling narrow sections such as paths; a 100 × 50mm (4 × 2in) straight-edge is sufficient

10 Bucket You will need two of these (both the same size) for measuring and two shovels (again of equal size) for mixing. Keep one bucket and shovel for measuring out and adding cement to the mix. The second bucket and shovel can be used for adding ballast and water and for mixing. Using equal sized buckets gives an easy guide to quantities; for example, a 1:5 mix needs one bucket of cement and five buckets of ballast

11 Coarse brush You can give a textured finish to concrete by sweeping the surface with a coarse brush fitted to a long handle

12 Punner This is used for compacting concrete in a trench. It may also be used for compacting the foundation. To make a punner, nail together several layers of timber and fix a broom handle vertically

13 Polythene sheeting Used to protect concrete from the elements while it is curing

14 Straw & sacking Either can be used to protect new concrete from frost

15 Wood float For giving a textured finish to concrete

16 Steel float Also for finishing concrete

17 Measuring tape For measuring out a large site or path

18 Pegs & string Use with the measuring tape to mark out the site

19 General purpose saw & claw hammer For making formwork

20 Watering can This is useful to control the rate at which water is added to the mix

21 Mixing platform Use where there is no suitable solid area for mixing concrete. Nail boards together for the base and add side pieces to keep the concrete on the platform. Or fix side pieces to a large sheet of 18 or 25mm (¾ or 1in) plywood

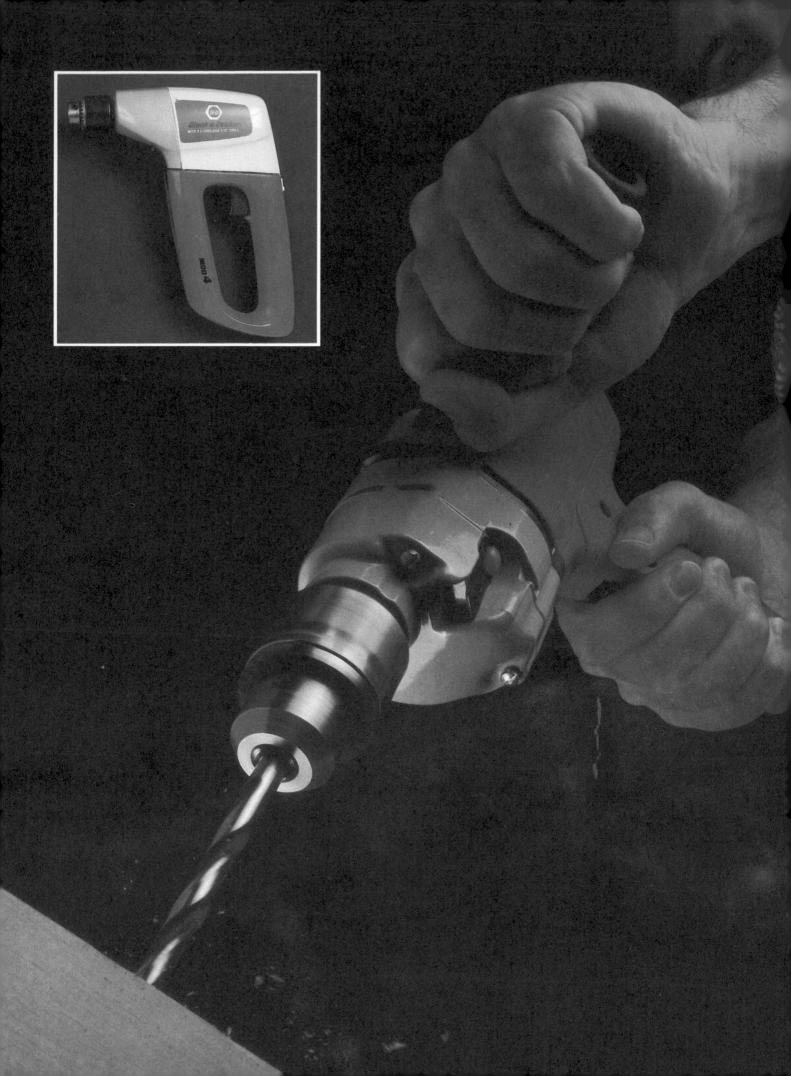

Power tools

The electric drill is no longer an expensive luxury for the home handyman, but an essential part of the DIY tool kit. Apart from just drilling holes, it provides the basic power unit for a wide range of attachments – from saws to polishers – which can be bought separately as required. Electric tools also tire less easily than human muscles and allow you to tackle jobs too physically demanding to be enjoyable.

Attachments are inexpensive and are undoubtedly useful for many sanding, sawing and polishing jobs, but for heavy and regular use, the purpose-built equivalents with their own power unit are worth considering. The integral circular saw unit, for example, runs at a greater speed than the standard electric drill, giving more efficient cutting. A jigsaw attachment can be used to full advantage to cut through a variety of materials only with a two-speed drill. Anyone with a single-speed drill would, in the long term, be saving money by buying a purpose-built jigsaw.

Both these tools are described in detail on the following pages, with tips for safe and efficient use. It is with both safety and efficiency in mind that we recommend considera-tion of a power saw bench, to which a power saw can be attached, leaving both hands free to manipulate the material being cut. Although a hand-operated circular saw is safe in careful hands, there are obvious safety advantages in fixing the saw, where the current-carrying lead is in no danger of contact with the cutting edge.

Those who decide to use their electric drill to its full potential by adding a collection of attachments will no doubt need to change attachments frequently. Even for simple drilling jobs such as fixing a shelf to a wall, the need for both wood and masonry bits, plus perhaps a countersink bit, will mean regular use of the drill's chuck key. It is both easy and frustrating to lose the key unless it is permanently attached to the drill lead. This should be the first and most practical 'attachment' in anyone's power tool kit.

In time, hard use will cause wearing of the drill's brushes and bearings. Before you buy a power tool, check that the manufacturer can supply DIY repair kits for simple main-tenance jobs, and that proper servicing facilities are available for more important repairs.

Electric drills

One drill tends to look much the same as another, but there is quite a difference in price, performance and versatility between models. It will be worth your while to shop around to compare the considerable discounts that some shops offer.

Nearly all drills are mains-operated, although rechargeable battery-powered ones are available. Battery-only types are useful if you are working a long way from a power outlet or if you simply want a lightweight tool. Otherwise choose one that operates off the mains.

Make sure the drill you buy offers a full range of attachments to fit it and check on the after-sales service before deciding on the best one for your needs.

The power of the drill is rated in watts, generally between 350 and 500 – the higher the wattage, the more powerful the drill. Higher-wattage drills are the most expensive, but they are also the strongest.

Chuck capacity Drills offer a range of chuck capacities. This capacity refers to the maximum size drill bit shank that can be fitted and the maximum size hole that can be drilled in steel. Special drill bits enable you to make holes twice as large in wood and up to one and a half times larger in masonry.

Usually the larger the hole to be drilled and the harder the material, the slower the drill speed you need. If you are likely to want to drill a variety of materials, using various attachments, you should buy a variable-speed drill.

Variable-speed drill If the drill is fitted with an electronic switch, its speed can be varied between nil and maximum revs according to the pressure on the trigger switch. When the speed is reduced electrically, torque is also reduced unless the drill is fitted with an electronic feedback controller. There are other variations which you should ask your supplier to explain before you buy a drill.

Most drilling and other work with attachments, such as sanding and sawing, will be done at the top speed of around 2,000–2,400rpm. Drilling brickwork, concrete and holes of more than 6mm (¼in) diameter in steel calls for a lower speed of around 900rpm. The very low speeds you can get with a variable-speed drill are also useful for making an accurate start to drilling (where otherwise the bit might bounce off the surface) and for drilling hard materials such as glass and ceramic tiles which might break or crack easily.

Two-speed drill Normally has a gearbox that mechanically reduces the working speed and simultaneously increases the torque or turning force.

Single-speed drill Operates at about 2,800rpm. You can use it to make holes in masonry, but the drill bit must be removed frequently from the hole to clear the waste dust and allow the tip to cool. You can get a plug-in electronic speed controller to fit in the supply cable, but it is better to buy a variable-speed drill to start with if you intend doing work that requires a slower speed.

Warning If you apply excessive pressure to the drill or try to make it work under strain, perhaps by using a blunt drill bit, the motor windings may overheat and burn out. To avoid this, remove the drill from the work at regular intervals and let it run freely to allow the fan to cool the windings. This is very important when using an electronic control drill at low speed because the fan only works efficiently at maximum speed. Some drills have an automatic overload cut-out to protect the windings from overheating.

Hammer (impact) action Generally a built-in feature that can be selected when drilling tough materials like concrete, stone or hard bricks. Hammer action is created by a ratchet-like rotary mechanism that delivers up to 40,000 percussions a minute as the chuck revolves. A specially strengthened masonry drill bit, called a percussion drill bit, should be used for this type of work.

Drill safety
Used sensibly, the electric drill is a very safe tool; but because it works fast, never take your mind off what you are doing.

● Keep children and pets away from the working area and always unplug the drill before making adjustments or changing the drill bit.

● Always use the chuck key to tighten the bit in the chuck and never try to tighten it by holding the chuck while the drill is still running or you could be seriously injured.

● Make sure the flex is well clear of the work area, don't wear a tie or scarf and if your hair is long tie it back; this will prevent anything getting tangled up in the drill, possibly throwing it out of control or again causing injury.

● Wear protective spectacles to guard your eyes against flying particles.

● Always check the extension lead is in good condition and suitable for the drill being used.

● Never use drills in the rain or under damp conditions.

● Make sure your drill is properly earthed (unless it is double-insulated and supplied with a two core flex) and the plug is fitted with a 13 amp fuse.

Below A Wolf two-speed electric drill

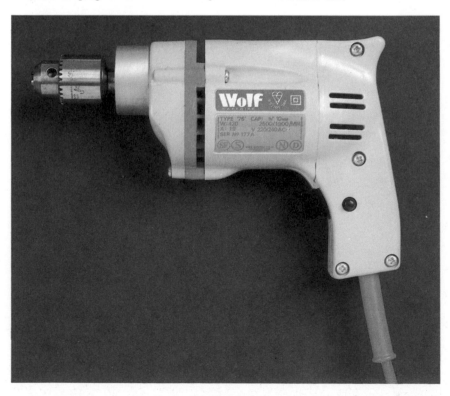

Circular saws

If you have a lot of accurate saw cutting to do, you may find the purpose-built unit, rather than an attachment to your electric drill, is worth buying. The attachment does provide a faster and more accurate cut than a conventional hand saw; and used with the correct blade you can cut all types of timber, as well as ferrous metals, aluminium, lead, asbestos and ceramic tiles, laminated chipboard and other laminates. But the attachment runs at lower speeds than the purpose-built unit and is therefore less efficient.

The saw blade is most efficient when used at high speeds: and the larger the blade diameter, the more power needed for maximum efficiency. Blades are commonly available in diameters of 125–229mm (5–9in). Larger blades are available for bigger saw units. When buying extra blades make sure they will fit your unit because just as blade sizes vary, so do methods of fitting them. And before you buy an attachment you should check with the manufacturer or supplier whether your power drill is suitable to take the attachment you want. The power of the average drill offers a maximum speed of around 2400rpm, while an integral unit gives a speed of 3000rpm.

Saw blades

A general purpose blade – normally supplied with the attachment or integral unit – is a combination of a rip and cross-cut blade, suitable for cutting across and along the grain. Usually a 24 point blade, it can also be used for light boards. Several blades and cutting discs are available for use with either type of saw, as well as some more specialist blades.

Cross-cut blade Used for cutting timber to length.

Rip blade For sawing timber along its length and parallel to the grain.

Planer blade Hollow ground to give a smooth finish to a saw cut.

Tungsten carbide blade The hardened steel teeth cut more quickly, therefore making it suitable for cutting materials with a high resin content, such as plastic laminate and chipboard, which generally blunt normal steel teeth.

Metal cutting blade Has fine teeth and will cut most soft metals.

Flooring blade Suitable for cutting floorboards. It will also cut through nails.

Metal cutting wheel Used for cutting metals and plastics.

Masonry cutting disc This will cut brick, ceramic tiles, slate, marble, soft stone and non-ferrous metals.

Laminate blade Available in a tungsten carbide-tipped version. Because plastic is a difficult material to cut we recommend you sandwich it between two pieces of scrap wood and saw through all three layers to achieve a clean cut and prevent damaging the decorative surface.

Reinforced abrasive blade This will cut marble.

Friction blade For high-speed cutting of corrugated and flat steel sheets.

A range of circular saw blades used for (**top to bottom**) aluminium, stone, laminates, corrugated and flat sheet metal, metal, man-made boards, ripping, flooring, general purpose, smoothing wood cuts, cross-cutting

Warning Before fitting a blade make sure the saw is not connected to the power supply. You must always treat the electric saw with respect and care: it is one of the most useful tools in the home, but it can be one of the most dangerous if not handled properly. Never leave it on a bench where children may have access; when you have finished using it, always lock it away.

Fitting the blade
It is vitally important you fit the blade correctly. The direction of the blade is usually marked on the outer side by the manufacturer so there can be no mistake in fitting it. Check your blades regularly to make sure they are sharp: working with a blunt blade will cause it to overheat and be damaged; it will also spoil your work.

Changing the blade
This is a simple operation if you follow a set procedure. Hold the blade in a fixed position by inserting a screwdriver or special key into a hole drilled through the saw blade (making sure the power is switched off). Loosen the blade retaining bolt with a spanner, remove the old blade, and fit the replacement blade, retightening the retaining bolt. On most models the blade guard will have to be pulled back to do this.

Depth of cut This is adjusted by releasing a locking nut and raising the sole plate so the required depth of blade protrudes through the sole plate opening and relocking the nut to the hold position.

Using the saw
With a circular power saw the cut is usually made by one run of the saw blade, when the blade should be set slightly deeper than the thickness of the material being cut. When sawing thick timber or hard materials, however, you should cut in two stages. On the first run, set the blade depth to about half the thickness of the material you are cutting and follow up with a second run, setting the depth of cut to complete the sawing. This will prevent unnecessary stress and wear on the blade.

Rip fence guide This passes through a slot in the sole plate and is locked into position when the 'T' section of the fence is set at the required distance

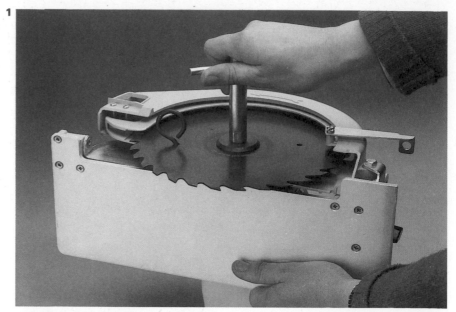

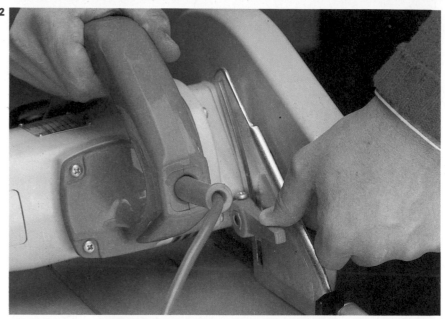

from the blade. Because it is adjustable it enables an accurate parallel cut to be made to a true straight edge of a piece of timber. This is particularly useful when ripping along a length of timber where a uniform width of cut is required. It can also be used across the grain if sufficiently close to the end. Remove the fence guide when using the saw to cross-cut timber beyond the reach of the fence.

When ripping through a long length of timber, the cut might be inclined to close behind the saw blade, causing it to overheat. You can prevent this by inserting a thick wedge of timber at the start of the cut before proceeding past the halfway mark on the timber being cut.

Large boards can be cut through the centre along an accurate line by clamping or pinning straight edge timber to the surface. This will act as a guide to the edge of the sole plate and the blade can be set at an accurate distance from the edge of the guide timber.

Warning Make sure the board is well supported along all edges and that sufficient clearance is provided under the cutting line.

Angle sawing This can be done by a simple adjustment to the sole plate, allowing the saw to cut accurately at a constant angle of 5–45 degrees. A protractor scale is a standard fitting to most units and attachments so the required angle can be set against the scale for accuracy. Once the angle has been set and locked, the blade can be set for the depth of cut as previously described. The teeth should project through the base of the material as for vertical cutting.

1 Changing blade with special key holding it in place
2 Adjusting depth of cut
3 Blade set slightly deeper than timber thickness
4 Cutting with fence guide in position
5 Cutting across timber without fence guide
6 Length of timber clamped on as guide for cutting across large board
7 Wedge inserted into end of cut to prevent timber closing behind blade and overheating

5

6

7

Groove cutting Set the blade to the required depth and make a series of runs within the chosen width of the groove by fractionally adjusting the fence guide. Leave a thick sliver of timber standing between each run to ensure an accurate line to the groove; these can be cleaned out later with a sharp chisel. Any attempt to clean the groove by joining the saw cuts is likely to result in the fence slipping from the line, leaving a ragged groove.

Grooves can be undercut in dovetail fashion by using an angled saw as already described.

Taking precautions

Always wear protective spectacles when using a saw. Flying sawdust can be irritating and dangerous to the eyes.

The cutting action of the teeth on a circular saw blade is in an upward direction, so always lay material with a decorative finish with the decorative surface face down – especially when cutting decorative laminates and veneer facings – or you will rip up the decorative surface.

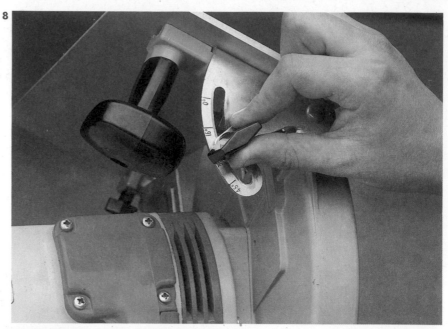

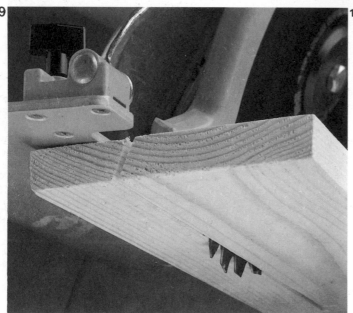

8 Selecting required angle before cutting
9 Blade set deeper than timber thickness for angle cutting
10 Making series of runs if cutting out groove
11 Cleaning out groove with sharp chisel

Jig saws

You can use the power jig saw, available either as a purpose-built unit or as an attachment to an electric drill, to cut a wide range of materials accurately. Interchangeable blades make it suitable for use on softwood and hardwood, man-made boards such as chipboard, plywood or blockboard, steel and other ferrous metals and non-ferrous ones such as copper and aluminium. It is ideal for complicated cutting jobs, but can also be used for straightforward sawing work.

The jig saw attachment works best with a two-speed or multi-speed drill. If you only have a single-speed drill, it is better to buy an integral jig saw unit. Some units have a two-speed control switch incorporated into the trigger switch; use the high speed for wood and laminated boards and the low speed for work with plastics and thin sheet metal. The same applies to jig saw attachments.

Cutting blades
At high speed the jig saw blade travels up and down at over 3200 strokes per minute, which places it under considerable stress; so you must check the blade is sharp and in good working order. Discard

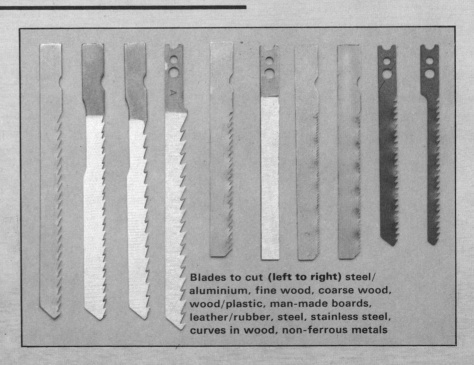

Blades to cut **(left to right)** steel/
aluminium, **fine wood, coarse wood,
wood/plastic, man-made boards,
leather/rubber, steel, stainless steel,
curves in wood, non-ferrous metals**

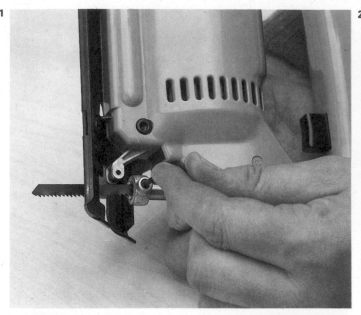

Working with a jig saw
1 Fitting blade with an
Allen key
2 Cutting decorative face
along adhesive tape
3 Cutting laminate placed
between hardboard offcuts
4 Cutting at an angle
along timber

worn blades since they are too hard to be re-sharpened. The units and attachments are usually supplied with one general-purpose cutting blade, although a variety of blades is available. Coarse blades increase the speed of cutting through material, while finer blades cut less quickly but greatly reduce the risk of splintering.

Fitting blades Make sure the jig saw is disconnected from the mains before fitting a blade or making any other adjustment. The blade is secured in the chuck either by two screws locked by an L-shaped (Allen) key or by a slotted screw which you tighten with a screwdriver. You should insert the blade with the teeth facing forward, centre it in the chuck and tighten the screws against the blade, taking care not to overtighten them.

Using the saw
Check the unit or power drill is switched off before connecting it to the mains. For the best results, clamp the work to a bench or table. Mark the line to be cut on the surface of the material and guide the saw along the cutting line; a blower behind the blade directs air through a plastic tube to sweep

dust from the line so it is not obscured. Always grip the jig saw firmly and see the lead is kept well away from the blade. To obtain maximum efficiency press down on the sole of the saw but never force the blade forward. Make sure any large overhangs of cutting material are well supported or the blade may be gripped by the work as the saw nears the end of the cut. Always let the motor stop before removing a blade from an unfinished cut.

Decorative surfaces The cutting action is on the upward stroke and you should always work with the non-decorative face of the material on the top so any tearing that might occur does not spoil the work. When there are two decorative surfaces place the main one face down. To prevent splintering put adhesive tape over the cutting line or score along it with a sharp knife before sawing.

Preventing fusion Friction heat may cause materials such as vinyl plastic sheet to melt and fuse solidly behind the blade. To prevent this, place adhesive-backed paper over the cutting line and saw through it using a general-purpose blade. Don't remove the protective paper until the cutting is completed or you will scratch the surface.

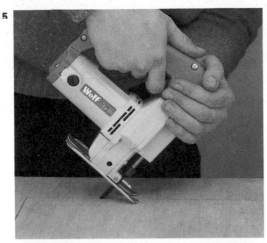

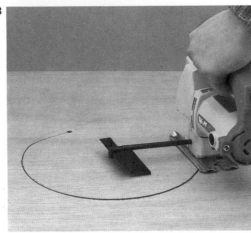

5 Cutting out a pocket
6 Using adjustable fence for narrow strip cutting
7 Cutting wide strip with batten as guide
8 Cutting out a circle with an adjustable fence. Scribe the required circle and mark its centre. Start the cut as for pocket cutting. Tap the centre spigot of the fence into the middle of the circle, place the fence over the spigot and insert the fence in the side of the saw until the length of the fence is the same as the radius of your circle. Tighten the adjusting screw to secure the fence, then cut out the circle

Padding To prevent chipping when cutting sheet laminates, tightly clamp a thin sheet of hardboard or plywood above and below the laminate at the cutting line. Clamp ferrous sheet and non-ferrous metals onto a backing of softwood or plywood to stop vibration and tearing.

Lubricants For metal and plastics spread a thin film of lubricant along the cutting line before sawing. It is important to use the right lubricant – cutting oil for steel, water or turpentine for aluminium and water for plastics. You can cut most other materials dry.

Warning Always wear protective spectacles when operating the jig saw. If the tool accidentally slips from the work area, don't attempt to catch it as the blade could easily tear your hand – it is wiser to sacrifice the blade. Never place the jig saw on the bench until the blade has stopped, then lay the tool on its side. Make sure it is placed on an uncluttered area when not in use and, when work is finished, store it away safely out of reach of children and animals. To keep it in smooth running order, lightly oil the lubricating points regularly.

Types of cut

The jig saw power tool is most effective when cutting intricate shapes and curves. Run it in from a starting point at the edge of the material and it will follow curved lines without effort. On some models you can tilt the shoe of the jig saw which enables you to cut angles up to 45 degrees.

Pocket cutting You can use this tool to cut a shape out of the middle of a piece of material, known as pocket cutting. The blade can be inserted in the middle of a panel without first having to drill a hole (though for thick material it is advisable to drill a pilot hole in the waste and saw out from this). First measure and clearly mark the surface to be cut, then tilt the saw forward so the rounded tips of the shoe rest on the work surface, but with the blade well clear of it. Switch on the power and move the saw in the tilted-up position until the blade is exactly over the point where you want to start cutting. Lower the rear of the shoe towards the work surface, keeping a firm pivoting pressure on the shoe tips with the blade exactly on the line. Never try to move the saw forward until the blade has cut through the material and the shoe comes to rest flat on the surface.

Although a rounded section may be cut in one operation, several cuts are needed for rectangular shapes. Use the saw along the full length of one side of the square or oblong to be cut and, with the motor still running, bring it back, curving it smoothly away from the first cut to work on the second side. Leave the waste piece in the corner to be cut out later. Repeat for the two remaining sides until most of the waste falls away, then reverse your working direction to complete the unfinished cuts and remove the corner pieces.

To cut a keyhole or other small opening, pass the saw backwards and forwards to take small pieces out of the material.

Straight cutting For accurate straight-line cutting, use the adjustable fence which locks into position with a small screw. If you are cutting widths wider than the adjustable fence, nail or clamp a straight batten at a suitable distance from the cutting line so the shoe of the jig saw runs along the batten to form the precise cutting line.

Abrasives and their uses

Abrasive papers, which are available in ranges varying from very coarse to very fine, have coatings such as granules of glass, emery, flint, aluminium oxide, silicon carbide and garnet. Sandpaper is a misleading term often given to glasspaper; abrasive papers are in fact used for 'sanding' or smoothing down a surface, but they do not contain sand. With all abrasive papers the procedure is to start with a coarse paper and work down through the finer grades until the required finish is achieved. A coarse abrasive will only give a coarse finish.

Backing paper

When using abrasives on any surface, there will be friction; this will increase with the coarseness of the abrasive you use. It is therefore important the backing paper holds together; as a general rule the backing is made thicker (or heavier) as the grit size increases. A larger grit size will mean increased friction and so a heavier backing is needed to prevent tearing.

The backing carries a number, or grit size, and also the simplified classification of, for example, fine, extra fine and medium. Low numbers indicate a coarse abrasive and high numbers correspond with fineness. Industrial users prefer to specify coarseness in terms of grit size; a typical range available in DIY shops is from grit size 40 (coarse) to 200 (fine or flour). Very hard abrasives such as silicon carbide paper come in the grit size range of 220 and 800 (fine and extra fine).

Cloth backing is used for greater flexibility, especially for heavy duty work and working metal. Fibre backing is used with industrial power sander discs because it holds its shape well when used at speed. Flexible foam sanding blocks come in various grit sizes; these are washable and avoid the need for a cork former (or sanding block).

Open coat This type of abrasive paper is made so the abrasive grains are separated by pre-set distances; this means only 50–70 percent of the paper is coated with abrasive, allowing abraded material to clear and preventing clogging.

Types of abrasive

Abrasives for use in the home can be classified as natural or man-made. Available in a wide variety of forms, each type has particular qualities which make it suitable for use on wood or metal or both.

Garnet

This is a natural abrasive of crushed semi-precious red stone. It has hard, sharp-cutting edges and is

1

2

fairly long-lasting, generating relatively little heat in action. Garnet is usually supplied on a paper backing in standard size sheets. It is a good, low-cost woodworking abrasive.

Emery
This is a black crystal abrasive with a slow cutting action which is quite short-lived. Emery, which is used to clean and polish metal, has cloth or paper backing and comes in standard size sheets.

Aluminium oxide
This is a man-made reddish brown abrasive which is both long-lasting and fast-cutting. It is very hard and sharp and is available either in standard size sheets, oblong sheets or on discs and drums for use with power tools. Aluminium oxide is used for removing paint from wood, for finishing wood and metal and for reclaiming old wood.

Silicon carbide (wet and dry)
This is a hard but brittle man-made abrasive used for refinishing car bodywork and for abrading paintwork to provide a key for repainting. It is used wet because the paint would clog it up if it were used dry. It can be used on soft metals such as aluminium and brass with excellent results, but should not be used on wood. Silicon carbide is available on a paper backing in standard size sheets.

Tungsten carbide
This is a very hard, sharp abrasive supplied on metal discs or metal sheets for use with power tools. It can abrade anything from wood to concrete and is generally used on hard materials which could not otherwise be abraded. It is long-lasting but expensive to use.

Crushed glass (glasspaper)
This is the most common and cheapest form of abrasive – it also has the poorest cutting power. Suitable for wood finishing, it is supplied in standard size sheets and must be stored in dry conditions.

1 The belt sander is used to abrade large areas where the finish is not crucial
2 An orbital sander will give a fine finish on a variety of surfaces without leaving score marks
3 Abrasive discs are made in various grades to fit flexible disc sanders
4 Types of abrasive paper: (**from top**) three grades of glasspaper; flour glasspaper; two grades of garnet paper; two grades of emery paper; three grades of silicon carbide paper

Wire abrasives

These include wire wool and wire wheels and cups (power drill attachments) and are used for general cleaning-up on a variety of surfaces. Wire wool is used for flattening coats of paint or varnish on metal and wood before applying a further coat. Wire wheels, brushes and cups can be used to remove paint, rust and grime. The cost of these products varies according to the type. They are durable, but prone to serious rusting.

Hand finishing

Where possible use abrasive paper with a cork or wood sanding block; this helps give an even finish since it holds the whole of the surface of the paper against the work. If you use the paper in the palm of your hand, it will only abrade the area where your hand is pressing. If you have to smooth down a shaped edge or a moulding, cut a matching shape block out of cork or wood and use the paper wrapped around it. To get the block to match the edge, cut it roughly to shape; put a piece of abrasive paper (rough side outwards) on the moulding and rub the block shape over it.

Finishing metal

Once the metal has been roughly shaped, select your abrasive and the type of backing – flexible (cloth) or paper. Work with an even pressure in straight lines along the length of the work. If the work is an irregular shape, the general rule is to work concave areas with convex formers and convex surfaces with the shoe-shine method.

A fine abrasive will give a smooth finish to a flat surface; but for an extra smooth surface, you can dye the surface with engineer's (Prussian) blue to highlight the imperfections and abrade the high spots until they are removed. On soft metals work through the grades of abrasive and give a final polish with a liquid abrasive or the finest grade of abrasive paper available.

Car bodywork Be very careful about preparation; clean the whole area with a wire brush, wire wool or a coarse abrasive. After filling the dent or scratch, a disc sander with either a tungsten carbide or aluminium oxide disc will remove the worst irregularities. An air-powered orbital sander with a wet silicon carbide attachment is even more effective. Finish the surface by hand with wet silicon carbide paper; work over the metal, paint and filler to achieve a smooth surface. Use a flat hand to work the paper in a circular motion on the convex surface to achieve an even finish all round You will need to use a former on concave surfaces.

Finishing wood

The finish you can give to wood can differ from a coat of paint to a premier finish on a fine piece of furniture. In all cases a basic minimum finish is required, the first few stages of which will be the same throughout.

If the wood is not planed – as in the case of basic construction work – you need only apply a preservative to it. Once you have planed and shaped other types of wood or joints in wood, abrasives are used to remove the irregularities. Use coarse or medium coarse grade garnet or aluminium oxide paper on hardwood.

Damp wood will not clean up to a good finish with any abrasive paper. Damp abrasive paper is useless, so always store it in a dry place. A cabinet scraper will give a fine finish on most surfaces and it may avoid the use of glasspaper altogether; use a

5 Wire wool for hand finishing
6 Wire wheel attachment for electric drill
7 Wire cup attachment for flexible disc sander
8 Sanding block
9 Wire brush

'mirror' shape former on irregular surfaces. Always work with the grain of wood, however difficult this may prove. If the paper gets clogged you may be able to clear it by running the back of the sheet over the edge of a bench – this will also make the paper more flexible and less likely to tear.

Once you have worked through the grades of paper, you can use flour glasspaper to give an overall smooth finish. To do this you need to raise the wood fibres by dampening the surface with a sponge and sanding as the wood begins to dry out. Repeat this process until a smooth, almost shiny surface has been achieved.

Avoid buying poor quality wood if you intend to give it a premier finish; sticky resin on the surface of pine, for example, will hinder finishing and may break through again after the timber is finished. If you do use such pine, scrape the resin off with a cabinet scraper.

Power finishing

This is simply the process of hand finishing speeded up. Use hand finishing when a slow approach is needed, such as on fine furniture, and power finishing when working by hand would consume needless time and effort.

Power tools are run off the domestic electricity supply but should never be run off a lighting circuit. Most power tools are double insulated, which makes them safe in all conditions except where it is very damp.

Warning Ordinary glasspaper is not suitable for power sanding because the bonding agent used is not strong enough to withstand the harsh sanding action; close-grained glasspaper will soon clog and stop abrading. Don't use cheap sanding discs.

Flexible disc sander

This power drill attachment is widely used for rough preparatory work on surfaces including wood, plastic and glass fibre. A rubber backing disc (or pad) either fits into the chuck of the drill or screws into the drill spindle when the chuck has been removed; the screw-in version is more secure and easier to handle. The disc fits into the pad by means of a centre locknut and plate; the pad allows flexibility to work around corners and other awkward areas.

This type of sander will not, however, give a very fine finish because the disc tends to dig into the surface of the work. A ball-joint disc is available which will give good finishing power; it does not dig into the work because the drill can be tilted without tilting the disc itself.

Use the disc at an angle to prevent score marks; angle the drill slightly to the right and away from the work, move it from right to left and hold the handle on the side of the drill to counteract its downward motion. Start with a coarse grit paper and work through to fine grade for finishing; a hand finish here will give a very fine surface, or you can use an orbital sander with fine abrasive paper.

If you use a disc sander to remove old paintwork, the paint may melt and clog the disc. Use tungsten carbide to alleviate the worst of this problem. Alternatively use a flap wheel, a power-drill attachment consisting of a large number of abrasive leaves arranged in the shape of a wheel. It will remove paint on wood or metal without clogging or scoring.

Orbital sander

This type, sometimes known as a finishing sander, is available as an integral unit or as an attachment.

10 Rubber backing disc for flexible disc sander
11 Ball joint attachment for flexible disc sander
12 Drum attachment for electric drill
13 Tungsten carbide abrasive disc

A guide to abrasives and their uses

Job	Abrasive	Method
Cleaning brickwork	Wire brush or tungsten carbide	Power disc sander or by hand
Finishing metal	Emery or aluminium oxide, then liquid abrasive	By hand
Finishing polyurethane varnish	Silicon carbide	By hand
Finishing wood	Aluminium oxide or garnet or wire, then glasspaper or fine garnet	Power tool (disc sander/belt sander/drum sander/orbital sander) and/or by hand
Paint removal (car)	Aluminium oxide or silicon carbide	Power disc sander or orbital sander or drum sander and/or by hand
Paint removal (metal)	Aluminium oxide or tungsten carbide or wire	Power disc sander or orbital sander and/or by hand
Paint removal (wood)	Aluminium oxide or tungsten carbide	Power disc sander or flap wheel or drum sander and/or by hand
Reclaiming old wood	Aluminium oxide or tungsten carbide (on tough work)	Power disc sander or orbital sander or drum sander and/or by hand
Refinishing car bodywork	Silicon carbide	Non-electrical orbital sander (unless used dry), then by hand
Rubbing down concrete	Reinforced silicon carbide disc	Power disc sander
Rust removal (metal/car)	Wire brush	Power tool and/or by hand

The advantage of an integral unit is it is always ready for use and does not need to be set up – you may also get slightly improved performance. It consists of a motor housed inside a moulded case and fitted with a pistol-grip handle; a second handle may be screwed into the case, if you want to hold it with both hands, and the trigger can be locked into the 'On' position. The integral unit and the attachment both employ the same method of operation and fitting of the abrasive pad.

The sander consists of a sponge rubber pad with an abrasive sheet fitted over it. The pad revolves in circles covering an area about 5mm ($\frac{3}{16}$in) in excess of the size of the pad. The high speed orbital action removes high spots from every angle and gives a fine finish. Abrasive paper is available in pad-size sheets in various grades or you can cut out standard size sheets into pad size (half or one third a standard sheet) for economy. The sheet fits over the platen (or base) and is locked in at each end of a sprocketed wheel at the front and back of the platen.

The advantage of the orbital sander is that it leaves no marks. It can be used on a wide variety of surfaces, especially on bare wood (sanding with the grain); it is practical for wood finishing, polishing and buffing (using a lambswool pad) and removing rust (with an aluminium oxide or tungsten carbide abrasive).

To clean up wood, you will have to use medium to fine glasspaper by hand. You can soak the wood to raise the grain; allow it to dry slightly before sanding. Finish with fine, then flour, glasspaper by hand. On close-grained wood you will achieve a fine finish with an orbital sander without the aid of the wetting technique or hand-sanding.

When you have two pieces of wood joined at right-angles, the orbital sander is the only device which can be used without sanding against the grain of one of the pieces; on concave surfaces use the 'toe' of the sander. During sanding, wood powder will form and get forced into the abrasive paper; this is not a problem and will, in fact, help the sanding action.

The orbital sander is an invaluable tool when decorating, since it can take the hard work out of the preparation of woodwork and sanding down between paint coats. The sander can also be used to rub down filled cracks or holes in wood or plaster.

Belt sander

This self-powered unit is more expensive than the other types of sander. An electric motor drives two rollers which rotate an abrasive belt; the belt is available ready made, in various grades, and is fitted to the sander with the rollers in the slack position.

Always move the sander forwards and remember to keep a firm grip to prevent it running away. Move it from one side to another across the surface of the work, straight with the grain, at a 45 degree angle to the surface. It gives a high quality finish, but does tend to leave tiny grooves. For a fine finish you will need to use an orbital sander afterwards – or finish by hand.

The belt sander is used in semi-industrial work where a perfect finish is not too important. You can hire it for jobs in the home if you have a large area to work, such as a floor or staircase.

Drum sander An attachment for a power drill, this comprises a foam drum onto which is fixed a cloth abrasive belt. It gives the same effect as a belt sander, but at a lower cost. If used along the grain of wood, it can be very useful for reclaiming old timber, although fine finishing by hand or with an orbital sander will normally be necessary in these circumstances.

Power saw benches

A hand-held power saw can be awkward to handle with precision, particularly on long pieces of unsupported timber. In the wrong hands it can even be dangerous. For cutting timber safely, accurately and quickly, it is best to have the power saw firmly anchored and supported. Power saw benches and saw table attachments are manufactured for the purpose. While many people will prefer to mount all their attachments semi-permanently on a fixed work bench, there are clear advantages in the mobility of the bench illustrated here, which can be moved easily from job to job. Perhaps more importantly, this type of bench is considerably cheaper than the traditional timber workbench.

Before buying a particular bench, consider carefully what other facilities the bench offers. A workbench can, for example, hold your timber securely for handsaw cutting, and can support a range of vices. Moreover, there is usually provision for a tool storage well, which every handyman knows is a great time saver. One important point to consider before you buy is where you are going to store the bench itself! The great virtue of the modern systems is their collapsible design. The benches can normally be either folded or simply dismantled by removal of keypegs or screws. Make sure your dealer supplies printed instructions on bench assembly if you have any doubts. If in time you feel the need for a proper fixed bench, your mobile power saw bench will not be wasted, for work on *The DIY Tool Guide* workbench project will be greatly simplified by your original power saw bench, which should prove an invaluable investment.

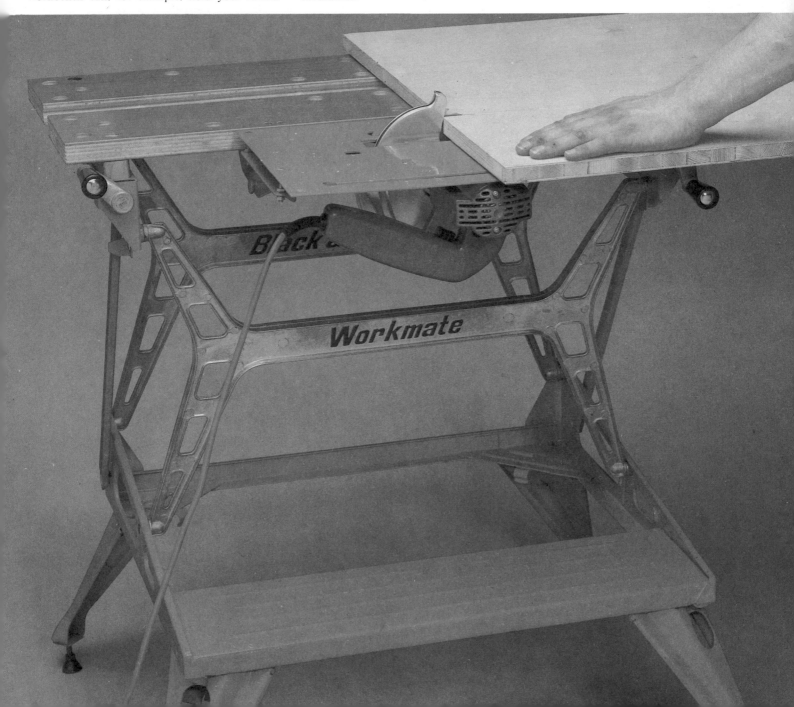

A fixed bench saw is the ultimate refinement in any home workshop, but power saws of this type are expensive and require considerable space. The alternative is to use a saw bench or saw table attachment, which can be fitted with either a separate portable power saw unit or an electric drill with a saw attachment. The great advantage of having a mounted saw is that both hands are left free for handling the material to be cut.

Power tool manufacturers make saw benches and attachments to suit their drills and saw units, so choose the one recommended for your particular drill or unit. The range includes floor-standing models, portable folding benches and saw tables which can be mounted on a bench. A rigidly mounted saw table is the first requirement for safe sawing, so allow for the table legs to be screwed down to the surface where you plan to work – particularly important with small tables.

Nearly all saw tables have facilities for fixing fences and guides such as those supplied with the Workmate saw table.

Workmate saw table

Because the Workmate bench is portable, sawing jobs can be tackled anywhere inside or out of doors. The saw table is quickly assembled onto it by means of a mounting bracket bolted under the jaws of the Workmate on the side with handles. As it does not interfere with other work done on the Workmate, the bracket can be left permanently in position.

The saw table is clipped onto the bracket and brought flush with the jaws by means of adjusting screws. Once this adjustment has been made, the saw is clipped into the underside of the table. Any saw unit or attachment from the Black & Decker range will fit.

Even when the saw is fixed in position, the table remains firmly in place. The jaws of the bench itself provide an extra working surface, which is useful when you are feeding widths of timber or boards across the saw blade. The assembly remains stable while the saw is running, even when a long piece of timber is being ripped through.

Previous page Saw bench attachments are available to fit the Black and Decker Workmate WM 625

1 Fixing mounting bracket to workbench
2 Fitting saw bench assembly to mounting bracket on workbench
3 Cutting strip off blockboard sheet using integral rip fence
4 Cutting blockboard using supplementary rip fence

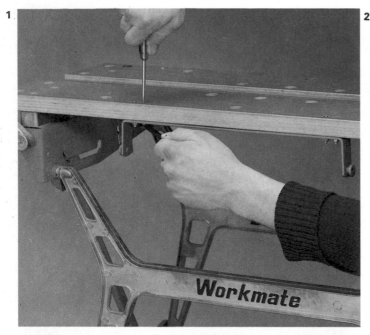

Saw table fences

Three useful fences are supplied with the saw table attachment: the integral rip fence, the supplementary rip fence and the mitre guide.

Integral rip fence Can be used as a guide when cutting through long pieces of timber.

Supplementary rip fence Fits into the Workmate jaws and allows a wider cut to be made, enabling planks to be cut across the grain.

Mitre guide Useful for accurate angle cutting or mitring. It fits into a slot on the saw table and is held by a wing nut. The angle is set as required and the guide is moved forward down the slot to feed the timber across the blade while maintaining the correct angle.

Once all the necessary adjustments have been made, the power saw can be connected to the main supply. A red plastic handle grip is supplied to lock the switch of the saw in the 'on' position.

Using a saw table

Always start the saw and get it running at maximum speed before feeding timber to the blade; switch off the power only when the cutting is complete. This will reduce stress and wear on the blade and prevent premature blunting of the teeth.

When feeding timber to the saw blade, use a V-shaped piece of wood to push the work forward and keep pressure on it during cutting. To feed large boards across the blade, remove fences to allow the boards to lie flat on the table.

Remove any nails from the timber before attempting to cut with a power saw and never feed green, freshly cut timber across a saw table: only a tree saw should be used to cut wet timber.

An electric saw tends to disperse dust over a wide area, so always wear protective spectacles and, when working inside, try to confine the work to a well ventilated workshop or room which is shut off from the rest of the house.

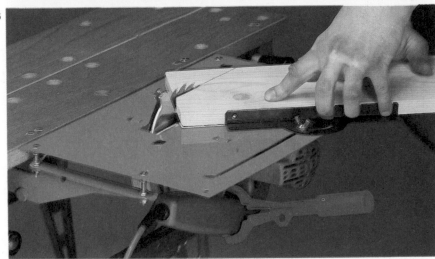

5 Cutting across grain of softwood plank
6 Angle cutting
7 Lock-on fork used to hold switch in 'on' position or for switching off quickly in an emergency
8 Jig used in conjunction with rip fence to make long tapered cuts in boards and planks. To ensure accuracy of cut, one arm of jig is marked off in 10mm graduations; if, for example, 1 in 10 taper is required, set jig arms 10mm apart at tenth mark from hinge and lock them into position
9 Tapered cutting with jig; place ungraduated arm against rip fence on saw bench, rest timber on other arm and feed timber into saw blade
10 Using batten to push board along at end of cut to prevent hands getting too close to saw

Tools to make yourself

A major driving force behind most of us who embark on DIY work is a desire to improve our surroundings, whether by building a much-needed cupboard, making some extra furniture or just fixing that rotten window frame. Few of us buy the necessary tools with any intention of making more tools, but that is precisely what we suggest you do, and for good reasons. Using tools to make tools was a basic principle of this country's industrial revolution, which brought about significant profits to the successful. Your own personal industrial revolution can be a very profitable enterprise, albeit on a smaller scale. The profit will show itself in both money saved and knowledge gained in how to handle your tools to best advantage.

Shop-bought, manufactured versions of the tools and equipment, for which this section of *The DIY Tool Guide* gives detailed plans, can be very expensive. Sash cramps, for example, are pricey tools, and for certain jobs there is no substitute. Moreover, a single sash cramp is often not enough for work on long pieces of timber. Our design uses not expensive metal but those scrap pieces of wood so often left over after a woodworking job.

If the home-made sash cramp is a cheap alternative to an expensive manufactured item, making other woodworking aids can be simpler than finding them in shops or continually borrowing them.

The jig for a power saw bench has many virtues. It is cheap, useful and, above all, it can contribute to your safety at work on a circular saw moving at high speed, where any slips can be dangerous. The tool belt is another aid to safety. Up a ladder or on the roof, you need hands to hold the tools and hands to do the work; this well-designed tool belt will make many jobs a bit easier.

The major project in this part of *The DIY Tool Guide* is the workbench. Anyone who has laboured through the years without the benefit of a workbench, carrying work from kitchen table to spare chair in search of a support for his work will realise the potential benefits of a purpose-built workbench. However, the tempting manufactured items in the shops are usually too expensive to be contemplated by the average handyman. The solution is at hand, in your own tool kit. For one last time you will risk gouging marks in the best dining table as you build yourself a highly attractive and functional workbench, to professional standards.

Several hints on making inexpensive yet practical substitute tools have already been given in *The DIY Tool Guide*. Most have been very simple, requiring little technical skill to achieve a successful end product. While by no means beyond the abilities of the average handyman, the projects on the following pages are more demanding than the home-made items suggested in our basic tool kit, where no woodworking skills were required.

These projects will require an understanding of elementary plans which will stand you in good stead for further woodworking projects, whether you intend to follow ready-drawn plans or to design your own furniture and fittings. Each item also demands accurate cutting, vital for a proper job at this level, and it is useful to learn on offcuts such as these used in the sash cramp project before inaccuracy on an expensive piece of wood causes an expensive waste on a major project.

True to the principle of *The DIY Tool Guide*, these home-made tools are all money-savers, they are all useful and primarily, they are all fun to make, offering a real sense of achievement in having created something truly useful with your own hands, which is the major pleasure of DIY.

Making a sash cramp

Sash cramps are useful for many carpentry jobs, but they are expensive to buy and often you will need more than one. This design does the same job as proprietary makes, will cost you next to nothing to make and provides another good opportunity to use up pieces of scrap wood.

Cutting list for softwood & hardwood

Description	Key	Quantity	Dimensions
Base (softwood)	A	1	1200 × 66 × 44mm
Fixed block	B	1	100 × 66 × 44mm
Moving block	C	1	125 × 66 × 44mm
Wedge (to shape)	D	1	275 × 50 × 20mm
Dowel rod	E	2	80 × 15mm diameter

stage 1

Measure and cut with a panel saw all the pieces of timber and the two lengths of dowel to the dimensions shown (**see cutting list**) and smooth all cut edges with medium fine, then fine, glasspaper.
Mark out and drill the two 15mm diameter holes at the angle shown in the moving block C (**see assembly diagram**). Using C as a jig, drill all the 15mm diameter holes through the base A. Pour woodworking adhesive in the holes in the moving block C; fix dowels E in the required position and, when the adhesive has set, trim the dowels flush with the top face of C. Make sure you fix the dowels so the angle will be the right way round (**see assembly diagram**) and

check C can be fitted into all the paired holes drilled in A.

stage 2

Mark the tapers (they taper in two planes) onto the fixed block B to the dimensions shown (**see 1**). Cut the tapers with a tenon saw and smooth over with a block plane and fine glasspaper. Drill four 6mm diameter clearance holes in B (**see 1**) and countersink them on the longer (upper) face to take No 12 screws. Hold B on A in the required position and mark with a bradawl through the clearance holes in B onto A. Drill 3mm pilot holes at these points, apply adhesive to the bottom face of B and fix it firmly in position, making sure you have the tapers the right way round (**see assembly diagram**), with No 12 countersunk screws 75mm long. Wipe off excess adhesive with a clean dampened cloth.
Mark out the tapers (they taper in two planes) on the wedge D to the dimensions shown (**see 2**). These tapers will fit into the tapers on the fixed block B, so make sure you have marked them out correctly by lining D up with B to see if the lines on it are parallel with the tapers cut on B.
Cut the wedge D to the required dimensions with a panel saw (**see 2**) and plane the edge, which will meet with the fixed block B, with a block plane.
Smooth all surfaces with medium fine, then fine, glasspaper and apply two coats of clear matt polyurethane lacquer, allowing the first to dry thoroughly.
In use, always insert pieces of scrap softwood between the moving block and wedge and the work piece to prevent bruising the timber.

Assembly diagram
(dimensions in millimetres)

○ holes 15 diameter

● countersunk holes 7 diameter

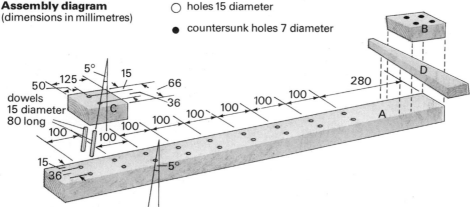

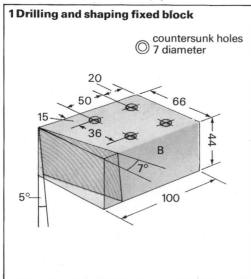

1 Drilling and shaping fixed block

countersunk holes
◎ 7 diameter

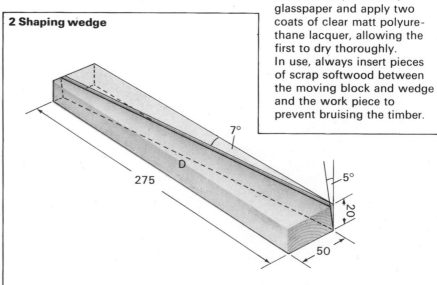

2 Shaping wedge

Making a jig

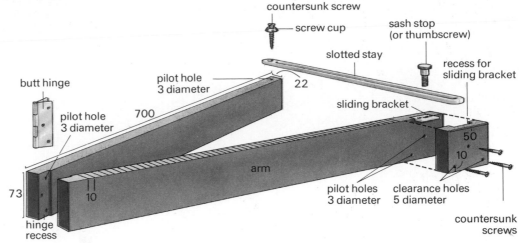

This jig is used as a guide to cut wedge-shaped pieces of timber on a saw bench. It should be made from 73 × 22mm ramin or a similar close grain hardwood.

stage 1

Measure and mark out the cutting lines for the three components across the width of the timber (**see assembly diagram**). Cut them squarely to size with a panel saw and smooth the cut edges with medium fine, then fine, glasspaper, slightly rounding off all sharp corners and edges. At one end of each arm mark the required length and depth of the recess for the hinge being used and cut out the waste between the lines with a 12mm chisel. Place one leaf of the hinge, so the knuckle lies just clear of the timber, in one of the recesses and mark with a bradawl through the holes onto the timber. Remove the hinge and drill 3mm pilot holes at these points. Screw one leaf of the hinge into one of the recesses with No 8 countersunk screws 12mm long. Fix the other leaf of the hinge in the recess on the second arm in the same way.

stage 2

Drill three 5mm clearance holes in the stop, one in the middle and the other two about 10mm up from the bottom edge (**see assembly diagram**). Countersink the holes to take No 8 screws. Hold the stop in the required position on one of the arms (**see assembly diagram**) and mark with a bradawl through the clearance holes in the stop onto the arm. Drill 3mm pilot holes at these points and glue and screw the stop firmly in position with No 8 countersunk screws 38mm long.

stage 3

Place the slotted stay in a vice and cut off the fixing bracket with a hacksaw (**see 1**).
With a 12mm chisel cut a recess for the sliding bracket in the stop and arm so the top edge of the sliding bracket is flush with the top edge of the timber (**see 2**). Push the bracket into this recess and mark with a bradawl through the holes onto the timber. Drill 3mm holes at these points and

screw the bracket firmly in position with countersunk screws 12mm long (and of the correct gauge for the bracket you are using). Drill a 3mm pilot hole in the other arm (**see 3**) and screw the slotted stay in position placing a screw cup or washer between the screw head and the stay.
If you cannot obtain a stay of this type improvise by hammering a bolt instead of the sliding bracket into one arm and secure it with a wing nut. Drill a hole

slightly smaller than the bolt you are using and hammer the bolt (with the head sawn off) into this hole so it protrudes by about 15mm. Slip the slotted stay over the bolt and secure it with the wing nut. Screw the other end of the stay to the other arm as before.
Draw lines squarely across the top edge of the arm from the hinge to the stop at 10mm intervals exactly.

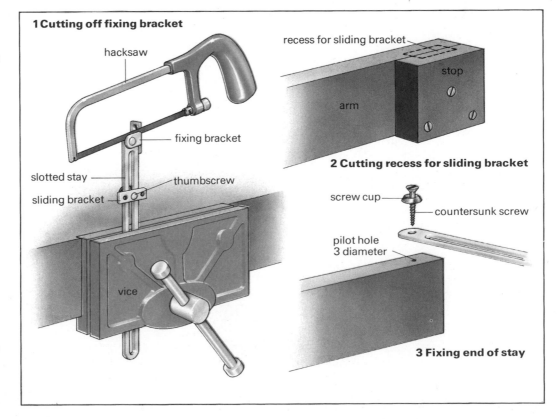

1 Cutting off fixing bracket

hacksaw

fixing bracket

slotted stay

sliding bracket

thumbscrew

vice

recess for sliding bracket

arm

stop

2 Cutting recess for sliding bracket

screw cup

countersunk screw

pilot hole 3 diameter

3 Fixing end of stay

Making a workbench

There are many proprietary workbenches on the market, ranging from simple, plain work surfaces to the craftsman's bench which incorporates a variety of holding devices and storage facilities. These do, however, tend to be expensive and you may prefer to save money by making a bench yourself.

Whether you buy or make a workbench, the frame must be rigid and the top flat, solid and free of bounce so your work is adequately supported. For woodworking, the bench should be free-standing to enable you to pull it out to the middle of the workshop or garage when handling large pieces of timber. When a bench is to be used solely for metalwork or as a mounting for a workshop machine (such as a grindstone or drill stand), it is better to fix it permanently against a wall to ensure the structure is stable.

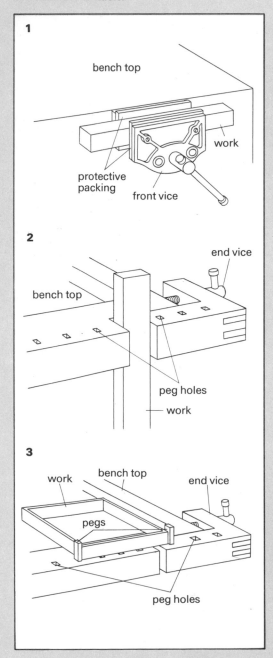

Dimensions The height of the bench should be about 760–840mm (30–33in) or at about the same height as your knuckles are from the floor when you are standing with your arms held straight at your sides. This height will enable you to work comfortably – and safely – when hammering, sawing, chiselling or doing other jobs; it is also convenient for intricate jobs since you can sit down to work. The bench top should be about 1200–1500mm (or 48–60in) long and up to 900mm (or 36in) wide, or as space in the workshop allows.

Proprietary workbenches
Traditionally workbenches are made with a sturdy, table-like framework, using 75×50mm (3×2in) timber for the main construction. Hardwood (usually beech) is commonly used, but pine and other softwoods are suitable. The end frames are usually made with glued and dowelled joints and are securely fixed to the long rails with mortised and draw-bolted joints. Many proprietary benches have tops of solid or three-layer laminated hardwood (again usually beech) and they are between 460 and 760mm (18 and 30in) wide.

Some benches come fitted with shelves and cupboards; on others it is possible to fit your own storage facilities. However, these do make it difficult to sit comfortably at the bench.
Dual-purpose wood and metalwork bench This type has a swing-over flap at each end; with wood and metalworking vices mounted on each flap, you can quickly convert the bench to either craft.
Multi-purpose benches These are fitted with front and end vices to give extremely versatile systems of clamping. The front vice is used like a conventional woodworker's vice to hold timber horizontally for planing, sawing, cutting mortises and drilling; the end vice is designed to take large and small timbers and is usually used for holding wood vertically when shaping, forming tenons etc. The end vice has a series of holes which match with other holes in the fixed part of the bench and these provide a third method of holding timber – a bench dog system. Square steel pegs, or dogs, fit into the holes and, when the end vice is tightened, enable large timbers and assemblies to be securely held.

Some benches have vice clamps, which are used in the same way as bench holdfasts to hold down timber on the worktop, and a deadman – a device which is secured in the end vice and used in conjunction with the vice clamp to hold long lengths of timber, doors and frames up to 3m (or 10ft). There is a special type of workbench, basically made of metal with a plywood top. The bench incorporates three vices and holes for bench dogs so a large number of different holding tasks can be accomplished.

If space is restricted, it is a good idea to choose a foldaway, portable bench such as the Black and Decker Workmate.

Home-made workbenches
Although you will not be able to make your own workbench for less than the price of the most basic Workmate, a home-made bench can have the advantage of storage facilities and a larger work

Top Combined wood and metalwork bench
Above Bench with integral end vice; the front vice is an optional extra
1 Front vice detail
2 End vice detail
3 Dog clamp system detail
4a Two pieces of chipboard screwed together form a simple worktop. Make the top narrower than the bottom to provide a tool well, but fix a batten at the back to stop tools falling off
4b This assembly will provide a firm supporting framework for the top.
Inset Detail of the angled mortise and tenon joint which secures the bracing to the legs. The timber sizes given are finished sizes

surface, as well as being made to your own requirements. A home made workbench is described on the following pages. If you do not want to go to the expense, you can easily make a work surface to fix to a wall or to sit on top of an old table.

A good way to make a tough worktop is to use two pieces of 18mm (¾in) chipboard screwed together from the underside. When the surface becomes worn, it is a simple matter to remove the screws and refix the top piece upside down. For a metalwork or mechanic's bench, a laminate-covered top is useful because it is easily cleaned; alternatively the top can be covered with thick linoleum, vinyl or sheet metal to protect the surface from oil, grease and scuffing.

Make the top piece slightly narrower than the bottom to form a shallow tool well at the back of the bench. This is handy for keeping small tools – such as pencils, squares and rules – out of the way when they are not in use. The well should have triangular fillets at each end so sawdust and wood shavings can be easily swept out; fix a batten at the back to prevent anything falling off.

If the structure is to be fixed to a wall, screw a sturdy supporting framework, made from 50 × 50 mm (2 × 2in) timber, to the underside. Use halving joints to make the framework and include cross-pieces for extra strength. Legs, made from 75 × 75 mm (3 × 3in) timber should be fixed to the front two corners of the main frame using wood dowels and angle brackets. Fix the back bearer of the frame to the wall with screws and wallplugs and brace the legs with 50 × 38mm (2 × 1½in) timbers, fixed with mortise and tenon joints.

If the worktop is to be mounted on an old table, screw through the underside of the table into it. Ideally your worktop and table should be the same size, but in any case the work surface should not overlap the top of the table.

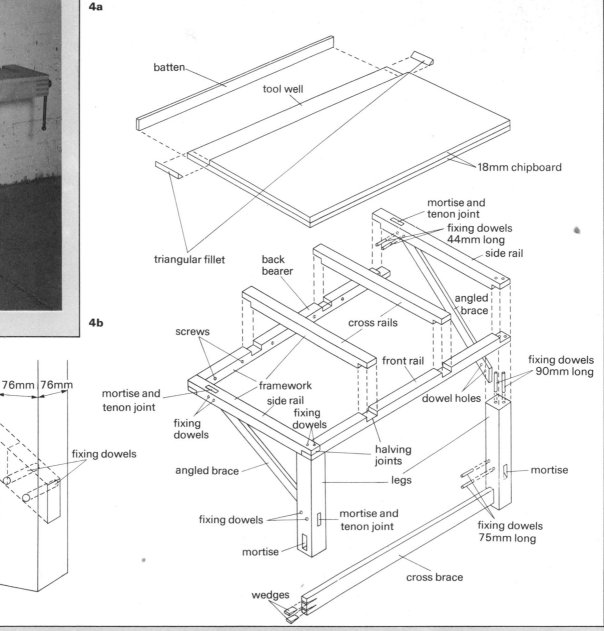

The workbench frame and top

This workbench is a very strong and rigid structure with facilities to cope with most carpentry needs. It has a well at the back, so tools in use will not clutter up the worktop, and plenty of storage space. Both vices are included in the cost of materials. One real advantage of this particular workbench lies in the fact that it can be dismantled should you ever want to move it.

stage 1

Measure and cut all the pieces of timber according to the dimensions shown with a fine-tooth panel saw (**see cutting lists**). To avoid confusion later on, label each part with the appropriate letter.

Measure and mark out the tenons at one end of all four legs A, at both ends of the bottom cross rails B to the dimensions shown (**see 1**) and at both ends of the long rails D (**see 2**). Cut all these

tenons squarely and accurately with a tenon saw. Measure and mark out the mortises in the legs A and the top cross rails C (**see 1**) and the tapered mortises to take the pegs H inside the tenons in the long rails D (**see 2**). The mortises in C, and those in A which hold the bottom cross rail B, are slightly dovetailed to take wedges to ensure really strong joints. Chop out the mortises with a sharp chisel. Cut the four pegs H to the required shape (**see 3**) and smooth the cut edges with medium fine, then fine, glasspaper. Assemble the frame without adhesive to check all the rails fit together squarely and trim any joints which are too tight.

Take the frame apart and rub all the softwood pieces smooth with medium fine, then fine, glasspaper. Give them all a final rub over with flour glasspaper, apply woodworking adhesive to the tenons at both ends of one of the bottom cross rails B and

Tools and materials

timber (see cutting lists)
measuring tape, pencil and try square, marking gauge
sharp trimming knife, metal straight-edge
fine-tooth panel saw, tenon saw, hacksaw, coping or jig saw
medium fine, fine and flour glasspaper
hammer, mallet, box or socket spanner
screwdriver, bradawl, countersink bit (for wood and metal)
fine flat file, 20 and 25mm chisels, block plane
electric drill, 2, 4, 5, 6, 9, 12 and 18mm bits, 25mm flat bit
three sash cramps, jig or drill press
woodworking vice (for front vice)
one 400mm vice screw, nut and bracket to fit (for end vice)
woodworking adhesive and clean cloth
No 6 countersunk screws 25mm long and 6mm long spacing
   washers to fit
No 10 brass countersunk screws 19, 32, 50 and 75mm long
12mm long panel pins
coach screws 100 and 125mm long and washers to fit
one brass lock and catch plate, two barrel bolts
four 50mm brass butt hinges and 9mm screws to fit
300mm of plastic or metal curtain track (for end vice runner)
300mm of 12 × 3mm aluminium section (for end vice slide)
250mm of 12mm diameter dowel (for two support pegs)

Assembly diagram

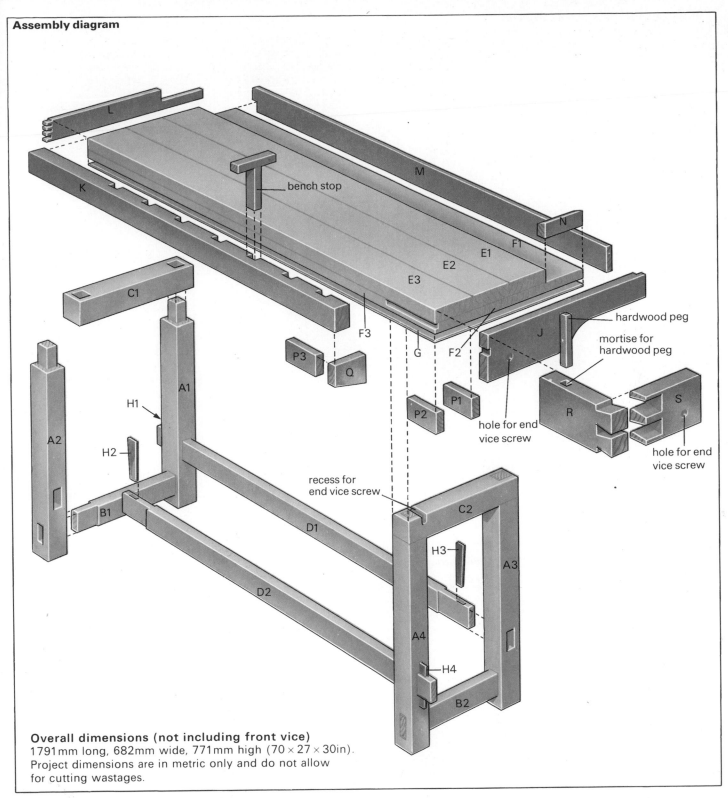

bench stop

hardwood peg

mortise for
hardwood peg

hole for end
vice screw

hole for end
vice screw

recess for
end vice screw

L

K

M

N

E1

F1

E2

E3

F3

G

F2

J

P3

Q

C1

A1

H1

A2

H2

B1

P1

P2

D1

D2

R

S

C2

H3

A3

A4

H4

B2

Overall dimensions (not including front vice)
1791mm long, 682mm wide, 771mm high (70 × 27 × 30in).
Project dimensions are in metric only and do not allow
for cutting wastages.

fix it to two of the legs A,
ramming wedges into the
mortise and tenon joints with
a mallet for strength. Wipe off
all excess adhesive with a
clean dampened cloth.
Apply adhesive to the tenons
at the top of these two legs
and fix on one of the top
cross rails C, ramming wedges
into the joints with a mallet
as before. Wipe off all excess

adhesive and trim off any
protruding wedges with a
sharp chisel. Assemble the
other half of the frame in the
same way.

stage 2
Drill all the 5mm diameter
clearance holes in the base
planks F according to the
dimensions shown (**see 4**)

and countersink them to take
No 10 screws. Rub smooth
all surfaces of the top planks
E and base planks F with
medium fine glasspaper; apply
adhesive to both side edges
of one of the top planks and
butt the other two against it
on a flat surface, cramping
the planks together with
three sash-cramps until the
adhesive has set. Make sure

all edges remain flush when
the cramps are tight.
When the adhesive in the top
planks has set hard, spread
adhesive over their bottom
faces and lay the base planks
F on them in the required
position (**see 4 and 5**). Fix
them firmly down with the
50mm long No 10
countersunk screws, making
sure the base planks butt

Cutting list for softwood & plywood

Description	Key	Quantity	Dimensions
Legs	A	4	695 × 73 × 73mm
Bottom cross rails	B	2	455 × 73 × 44mm
Top cross rails	C	2	455 × 73 × 73mm
Long rails	D	2	1574 × 73 × 44mm
Top planks	E	3	1674 × 149 × 44mm
Base planks	F	3	1674 × 200 × 29mm
Top underside cladding (plywood)	G	1	1674 × 600 × 3mm

Cutting list for hardwood

Description	Key	Quantity	Dimensions
Pegs	H	4	140 × 33 × 16mm
Right facing	J	1	618 × 140 × 35mm
Front facing	K	1	1486 × 76 × 64mm
Left facing	L	1	633 × 76 × 18mm
Back facing	M	1	1707 × 76 × 18mm
Tool-well block	N	1	153 × 44 × 35mm
Strengthening blocks	P	3	133 × 64 × 35mm
Vice front	Q	1	128 × 98 × 35mm
Vice block	R	1	305 × 140 × 64mm
Vice back	S	1	210 × 140 × 64mm

tightly together. Instead of drilling pilot holes, place the fixing screws in the previously drilled clearance holes in the base planks and tap them with a hammer to get them started. Make certain all these screws are fully countersunk and wipe off excess adhesive.

Lay the top underside cladding G on the bottom face of the base planks so all edges are flush (**see 5**) and fix it down with the 12mm long panel pins, spacing the pins at about 100mm intervals over the plywood.

Plan and elevations
(dimensions in millimetres)

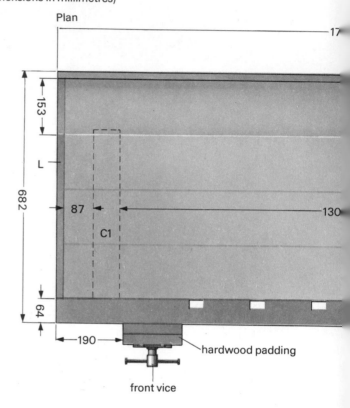

Plan

hardwood padding

front vice

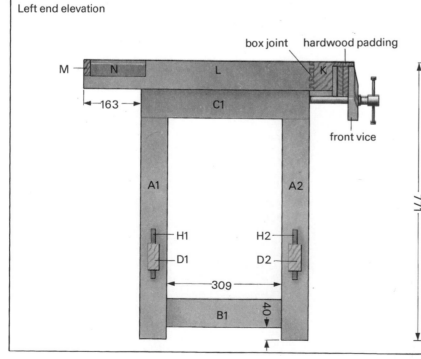

Left end elevation

box joint   hardwood padding

front vice

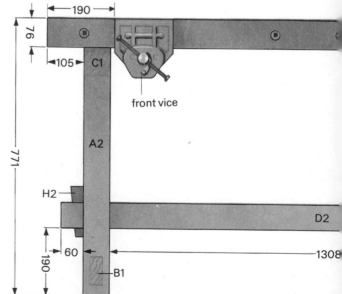

Front elevation

front vice

stage 3

Mark out the shaping lines, the rebate and the positions of the 9mm clearance holes on the right facing J according to the dimensions shown (**see 6**). At each point drill a 25mm diameter counterbore hole 12mm deep with a flat bit to take the coach screw heads and drill a 9mm diameter clearance hole through the centre of each one. Drill the 25mm diameter hole to take the end vice screw at the dimensions shown (**see 6**). Cut the curved shape with a coping or jig saw and the rebate

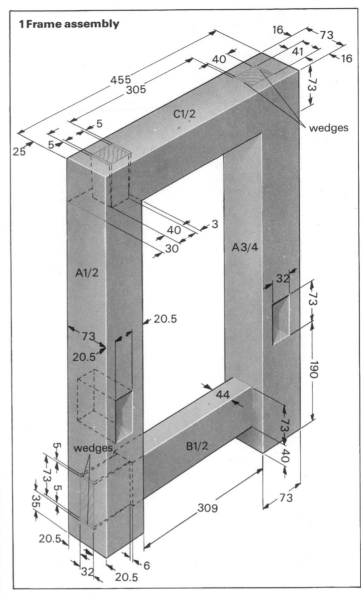

1 Frame assembly

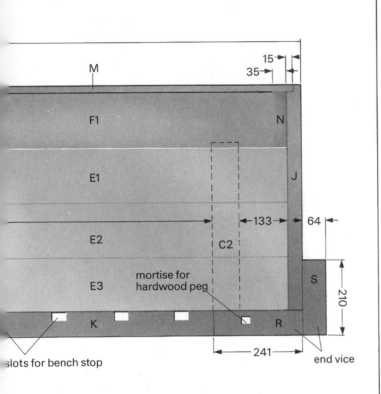

mortise for hardwood peg

slots for bench stop

end vice

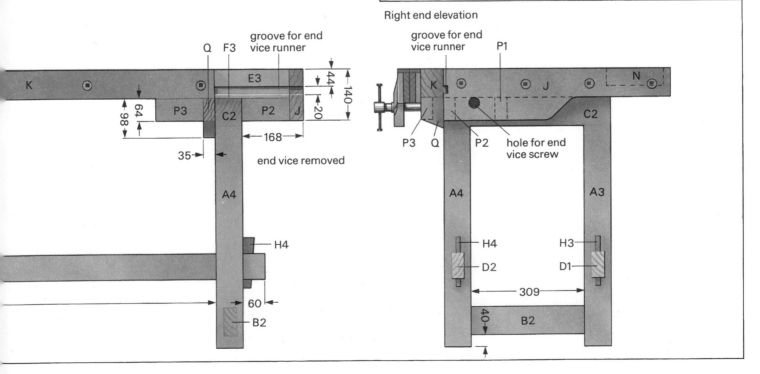

Right end elevation

groove for end vice runner

end vice removed

groove for end vice runner

hole for end vice screw

2 Long rail detail

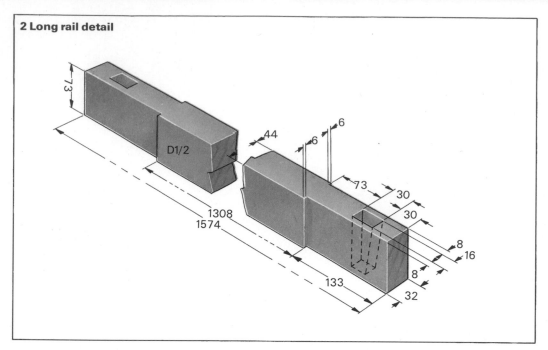

3 Shaping pegs

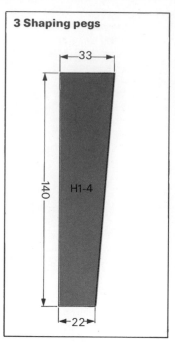

4 Base planks drilling plan

+ countersunk hole 5 diameter

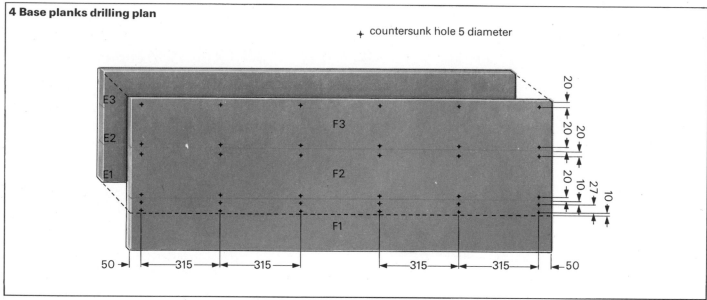

with a tenon saw.
Mark out the seven slots in the front facing K according to the dimensions shown (**see 7**). To form each slot, make two cuts with a tenon saw to the required depth and chop out the waste from between the cut lines with a 25mm chisel; smooth the inside with a fine flat file.
Mark out and cut the box joint in the front facing and drill the six 25mm diameter counterbore holes 12mm deep as before according to the dimensions shown (**see 7**). Drill a 9mm diameter clearance hole through the centre of each counterbore hole.
Cut the rebate at one end of the left facing L and the box

joint at the other end according to the dimensions shown (**see 8**). Fit the box joints on the front and left facings together without adhesive to try for fit; if the tenons on the box joints fit together too tightly, trim them as necessary with a flat file. If they are too loose, you will have to pack the gaps with pieces of scrap wood when you are fixing the facings to the assembled bench top.
Drill the 5mm diameter clearance holes in the left facing at the dimensions shown (**see 8**) and countersink them to take No 10 screws.
Hold the right facing J in the required position against the

bench top so the top and front edges of the facing are flush with the top and front edges of the top planks E (**see 9**). Mark with a coach screw through the clearance holes in the facing onto the top planks. Drill 6mm pilot holes at these points, apply adhesive to the fixing edge of the bench top and fix the right facing firmly in position with the 100mm long coach screws, placing washers between the coach screw heads and the timber. Drive the coach screws firmly home with a box spanner and wipe off all excess adhesive.
Mark out the 9mm deep recess to take the vice runner in the right facing J and the base planks F according to

the dimensions shown (**see 9**). Chop out the waste with a 20mm chisel and smooth the inside of the recess with a flat file.
Cut the plastic or metal curtain runner with a hacksaw to 270mm long and, at about 50mm intervals, drill 4mm diameter countersunk clearance holes to take No 6 screws. Fix it in position in the recess with the 25mm long countersunk screws (**see 9 inset**).
Glue and screw the front facing K firmly in position (**see plan**) so the top edge of K is flush with the top face of the top planks E, using the 125mm long coach screws. Glue and screw the left facing firmly in position

5 Top assembly

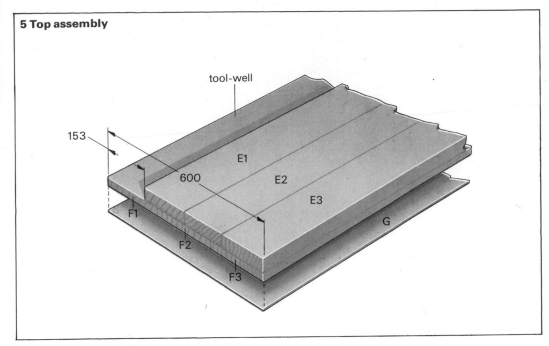

tool-well

153

E1

600

E2

E3

F1

F2

F3

G

6 Right facing detail

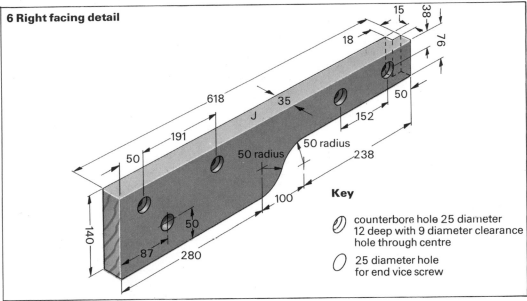

15

38

18

76

618

35

50

191

152

50

50 radius

50 radius

238

140

50

100

87

280

Key

⬭ counterbore hole 25 diameter
12 deep with 9 diameter clearance
hole through centre

⬭ 25 diameter hole
for end vice screw

J

8 Left facing detail

Key

o countersunk clearance
hole 5 diameter

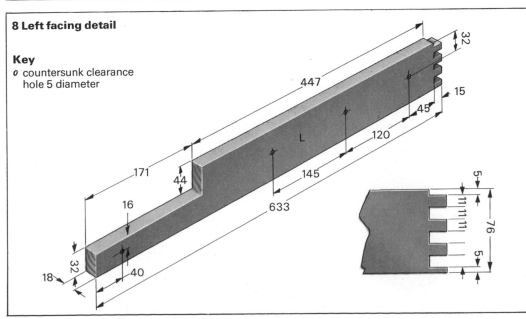

447

32

15

45

171

44

120

16

145

633

5

11 11 11

32

40

76

18

5

7 Front facing detail

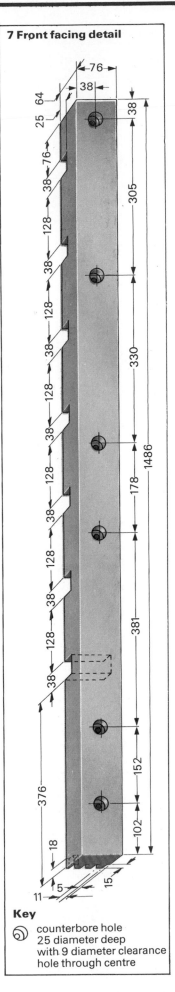

76

64

38

25

38

76

38

305

128

38

128

330

38

128

38

128

178

1486

38

128

381

38

128

38

376

152

18

102

5

11

15

Key

🌀 counterbore hole
25 diameter deep
with 9 diameter clearance
hole through centre

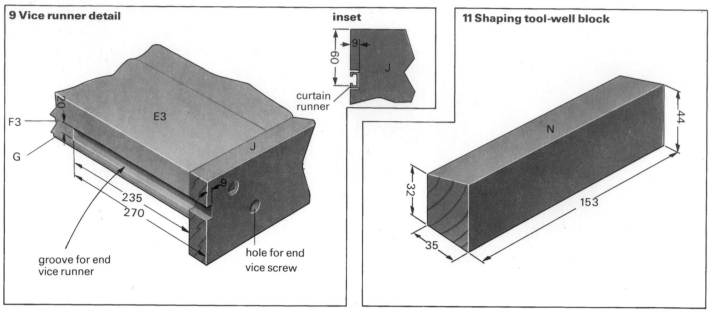

9 Vice runner detail

20
F3
G
E3
J
235
270
9
groove for end vice runner
hole for end vice screw

inset

60
9
J
curtain runner

11 Shaping tool-well block

N
44
32
35
153

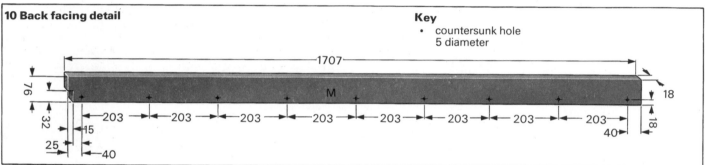

10 Back facing detail

Key
• countersunk hole 5 diameter

1707
76
M
18
32
203 — 203 — 203 — 203 — 203 — 203 — 203 — 203
15
25
40
40
18

using the 32mm long No 10 brass countersunk screws. Cut a small notch in one corner of the back facing M and drill all the 5mm diameter clearance holes in it according to the dimensions shown (**see 10**); countersink them to take No 10 screws. Glue and screw the back facing firmly in position with the 32mm long No 10 brass countersunk screws (**see left end elevation**).

Chamfer the tool-well block N to the dimensions shown (**see 11**) with a tenon saw or block plane and glue and screw it in position with a 100mm long coach screw through the previously drilled counterbored clearance hole in the right facing J. Wipe off excess adhesive.

stage 4

Drill two 5mm diameter clearance holes in the strengthening blocks P1 and P2 (**see 12**) and countersink them to a depth of 10mm. Glue and screw these two blocks to the underside of the bench top

just inside the right facing J (**see 12**) using 75mm long No 10 screws.

Drill two 25mm diameter counterbore holes, 12mm deep, in the other strengthening block at the dimensions shown (**see 12**) and drill a 9mm diameter clearance hole through the centre of each one. Cut the vice front Q to shape (**see 12 inset**) and drill a counterbore and clearance hole in it as before at the dimension shown (**see 12**). Hold it in the required position against the underside of the bench top and mark with a coach screw through Q onto the bench top. Drill a 6mm pilot hole at this point and glue and screw the vice front firmly in position with a 100mm long coach screw. Wipe off excess adhesive. Fix the other strengthening block P3 in position in the same way, making sure the front edge of P is flush with the front edge of the front facing K and that one end of P is butted hard against Q (**see 12**). Wipe off all excess adhesive.

Mark out and cut the dovetails on the vice block R and the vice back S according to the dimensions shown (**see 13**).

Mark out the mortise in the vice block R at the dimensions shown (**see 13**), drill an 18mm diameter hole through the marked rectangle to remove the bulk of the waste and finish off by making the edges square with a 20mm chisel.

Apply adhesive to the fixing edges of the dovetails and bring them together, tapping the joint with a mallet to ensure a tight fit. Leave the assembled end vice until the adhesive has set hard.

When all the adhesive has set, hold the end vice in the required position against the bench top (**see plan**) and mark with a pencil through the 25mm diameter hole (already drilled in the right facing J) onto the vice back S. Drill a 25mm diameter hole through the vice back at this point, using a jig or drill press to ensure the hole is straight. Pass the vice screw through this hole

and secure it by screwing into the vice back through the special bracket provided with the vice screw.

Cut a 270mm length of the 12mm wide aluminium section and smooth the ends with a fine flat file, slightly rounding the corners. Drill 4mm diameter holes at the dimensions shown (**see 13 insets**) and countersink them for No 6 screws. Fix the slide to the inside of the vice block R with the 25mm No 6 countersunk screws, placing spacer washers between the slide and the timber (**see 13 insets**). Fix the vice nut between the strengthening blocks P1 and P2 (**see 12**) on the inside of the right facing J so the hole in the nut lines up with the 25mm diameter hole drilled in J. Use as large fixing screws as as possible; the length and gauge of the screws will depend on the size of the vice nut. Slide the end vice into position, making sure the slide on the inside face of the vice block engages in the runner on the side edge of the bench top.

12 End vice fixing

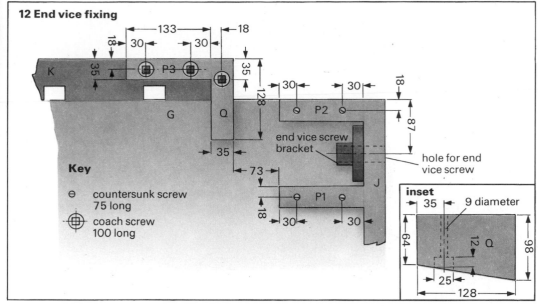

Key

⊖ countersunk screw
75 long

⊕ coach screw
100 long

end vice screw bracket

hole for end vice screw

inset

35 9 diameter

12 Q

25

128

64 98

13 Making end vice

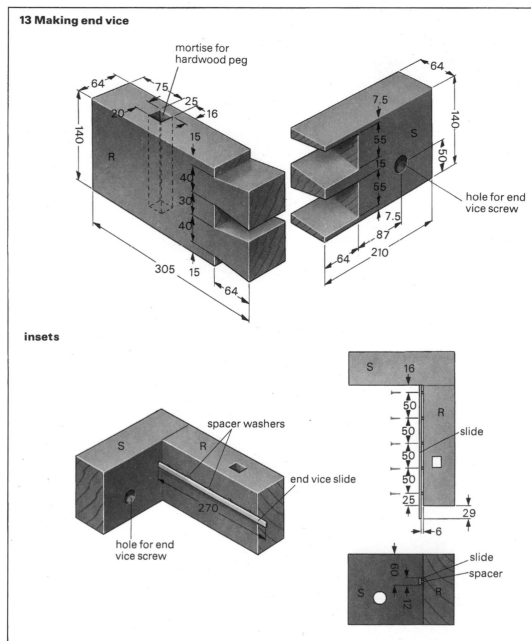

mortise for hardwood peg

hole for end vice screw

insets

spacer washers

end vice slide

hole for end vice screw

slide

slide
spacer

Assemble the frame, ramming the pegs firmly home inside the mortises in the long rails with a mallet. Place the top in the required position on the frame (**see front and side elevation**) and mark onto the top cross rail C2 where the vice screw for the end vice should pass through it. Cut a recess at this point with a coping saw so the top is resting firmly on the frame. Remove the top and drill a counterbore and clearance hole as before through the underside of both top cross rails C 120mm in from each end. Lift the top back in position on the frame and mark with a coach screw through the clearance holes in the cross rails onto the underside of the top. Remove the top and drill 6mm pilot holes at these points to a depth of not more than 60mm. Replace the top and screw through the top cross rails with the 125mm long coach screws; don't use adhesive or you will not be able to remove the top.
Using pieces of scrap hardwood you may have lying round your workshop, make a T-shaped bench stop to fit in the slots in the front facing K and a peg to fit inside the mortise in the vice block R (**see assembly diagram**). These must be a tight fit inside the slots (or mortise) so there is no movement when the work is gripped tightly.
You should also use some scrap hardwood or plywood to pad the front vice, but first mount the vice onto the front facing at the dimensions shown (**see front elevation**). Screw the padding in position in the vice, making sure the top of the padding will be flush with the top face of the bench top.

The workbench cupboard and drawers

The frame of the workbench is now complete. Accurate work will have paid dividends in terms of rigidity and strength. These qualities will be further enhanced by the making and insertion of the cupboards and drawers for tool storage, instructions for which now follow. These latter stages of the workbench project involve the addition to the outer structure of two large open compartments (one on each side), a lockable cupboard in the centre and a strong drawer.

Cutting list for plywood

Description	Key	Quantity	Dimensions
Sides	A	2	420 × 414 × 12mm
Dividers	B	2	420 × 402 × 12mm
Base	C	1	1308 × 414 × 12mm
Back	D	1	484 × 420 × 12mm
Drawer sides	E	2	390 × 86 × 12mm
Drawer front and back	F	2	432 × 86 × 12mm
Drawer front facing	G	1	456 × 123 × 12mm
Drawer base	H	1	456 × 390 × 12mm
Cupboard doors	J	2	273 × 229 × 12mm

Cutting list for softwood

Description	Key	Quantity	Dimensions
Bottom drawer runners	K	2	358 × 22 × 22mm
Top drawer runners	L	2	390 × 22 × 22mm
Brace batten	M	1	460 × 44 × 16mm
Peg rails	N	2	505 × 73 × 22mm

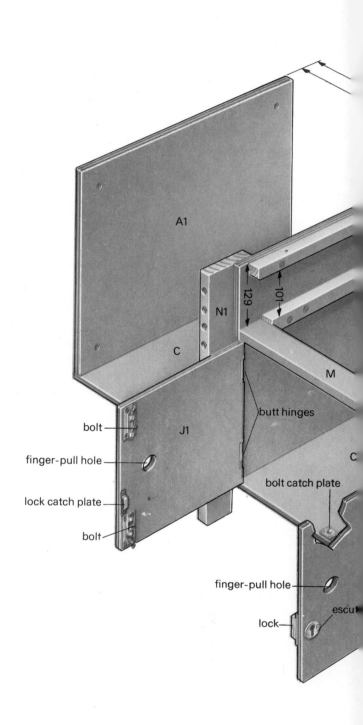

stage 6

Measure and mark out all the cutting lines on the sheet of plywood according to the dimensions shown (**see cutting list and cutting plan**). Score along these lines through the surface veneer with a sharp trimming knife held against a metal straight-edge. Cut all the plywood pieces to size with a fine-tooth panel saw, keeping where possible to the waste side of the line to avoid damaging the surface veneer. Cut all the softwood pieces with a tenon saw to the dimensions shown (**see cutting list**). Rub smooth all surfaces of all the cut pieces of timber with medium fine, then fine, glasspaper and label each part with the appropriate letter.

Drill all the 5mm diameter clearance holes in the bottom and top drawer runners K and L and countersink them to take No 10 screws (**see 14**).

Apply adhesive to the fixing edge of each runner and fix them to the dividers B at the dimensions shown (**see cupboard assembly**), using 32mm long No 10 screws. Wipe off excess adhesive with a clean dampened cloth. Drill twelve 5mm diameter clearance holes in the base C at the dimensions shown (**see 15**) and countersink them to take No 10 screws. Hold each divider B, one at a time, squarely against the base (**see cupboard assembly**) and mark with a bradawl through the clearance holes in the base onto the dividers. Drill 2mm pilot holes at these points and fix both dividers in position with the 32mm long No 10 screws. Don't use adhesive to fix the dividers; it is not necessary and you would otherwise not be able to take the cupboard apart.

Drill eight 5mm diameter clearance holes in the back D at the dimensions shown (**see 16**) and countersink them to take No 10 screws. Hold D in the required position against the base and dividers and mark with a bradawl through the clearance holes in the back D onto both dividers, making absolutely certain the dividers remain squarely fixed to the base. Drill 2mm pilot holes at these points and fix the back in position with the 32mm long No 10 screws; don't use adhesive. Hold the brace batten M in the required position between the two dividers B so the lower face of M is flush with the lower face of the bottom drawer runners K; mark onto the outside face of the dividers where to drill the four clearance holes (two on each) for the fixing screws. Drill 5mm diameter clearance holes at these points and countersink them to take No 10 screws. Fix the batten in position with the 32mm long No 10 screws; don't use adhesive.

stage 7

Remove the top of the workbench by undoing the four coach screws and check the wedges are firmly home in the mortises in the long rails. Position the base C (with the dividers and back attached) so the edges of the base are flush with the edges of the long rails. Mark with a bradawl through the clearance holes in the base onto the long rails. Drill 2mm pilot holes at these points and fix the base in position with the 32mm long No 10 screws; don't use adhesive. Drill all the 5mm diameter clearance holes in the sides A at the dimensions shown (**see 17a and 17b**) and countersink them to take No 10 screws. Mark out and cut the shape in the top front corner of the side A2 according to the dimensions shown (**see 17b**), making sure the countersunk holes are on the inside face. Smooth the cut edges with medium fine, then fine, glasspaper.

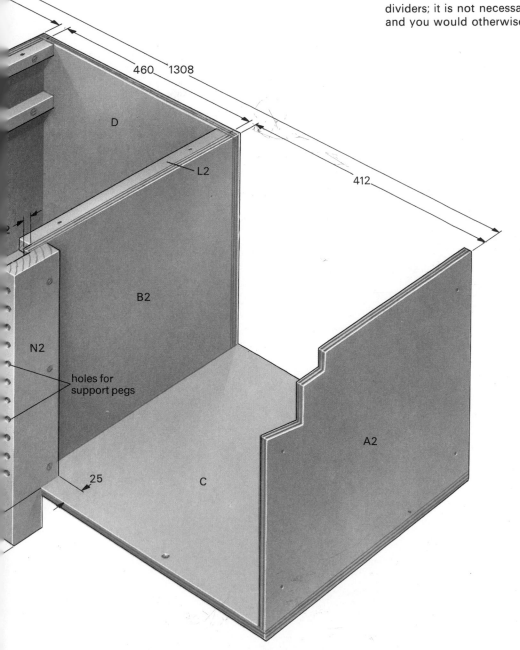

Cutting plan for plywood

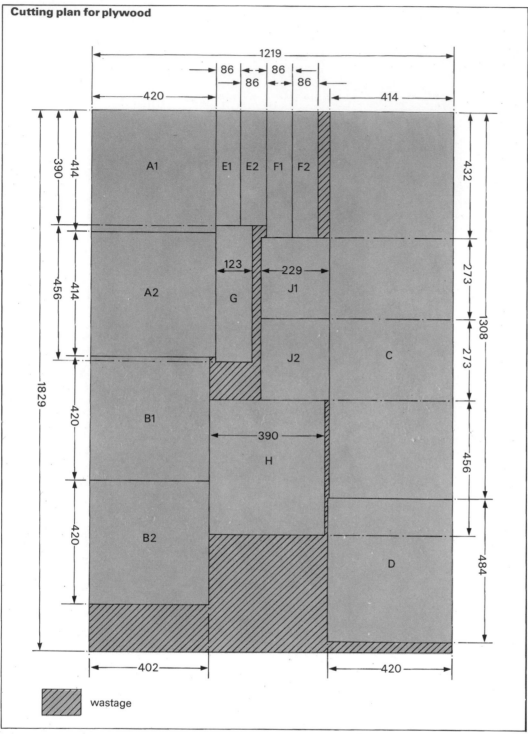

wastage

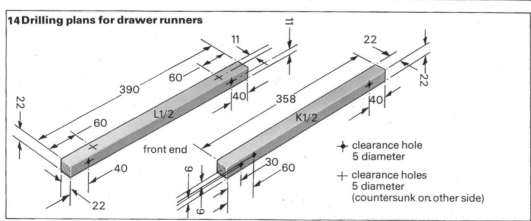

14 Drilling plans for drawer runners

11

11

22

390

60

60

L1/2

40

22

22

358

22

40

K1/2

front end

6

6

30

60

+ clearance hole
5 diameter

+ clearance holes
5 diameter
(countersunk on other side)

40

22

1219

86

86

86

86

420

414

414

390

456

414

1829

420

420

123

G

229

J1

J2

A1

A2

B1

B2

E1 E2 F1 F2

390

H

C

D

432

1308

273

273

456

484

402

420

Place the sides A in the required position inside the rest of the assembly (**see cupboard assembly**) and mark with a bradawl through the clearance holes in the sides onto the legs. Drill 2mm pilot holes at these points and fix the sides in position with the 32mm long No 10 screws; don't use adhesive. Drill three 5mm diameter clearance holes in both peg rails N at the dimensions shown (**see 18**) and countersink them on opposite faces to take No 10 screws. Mark out and cut the rebate with a tenon saw (**see 18**) and smooth the cut edges with medium fine, then fine, glasspaper. Check both rails are identical in size and clamp them together (rebates downwards) in a vice. Mark out the heights of all the peg holes across both rails using a try square, spacing the holes equally but stopping 120mm from the bottom ends (**see 18**). This will ensure the pegs align when in use. Drill all the 12mm diameter holes 50mm deep (**see 18**). Hold both rails N in the required position (**see cupboard assembly**) and mark with a bradawl through the clearance holes in the rails onto the dividers B. Drill 2mm pilot holes at these points and fix the rails in position with the 32mm long No 10 screws. Cut the 12mm diameter dowel in half and slightly chamfer all ends to form the two support pegs.

stage 8

Drill all the 5mm diameter clearance holes in the drawer base H according to the dimensions shown (**see 19**) and countersink them to take No 10 screws. Drill all the 5mm clearance holes in the drawer sides E and front F2 according to the dimensions shown (**see 20a and 20b**) and countersink them to take No 10 screws. Hold the sides in the required position on the drawer base (**see 21**) so all edges are flush; mark with a bradawl through the clearance holes in the base onto the sides. Drill 2mm pilot holes at these points, apply adhesive to the fixing edge of E1 and E2 and fix them firmly and squarely in

15 Drilling plan for base

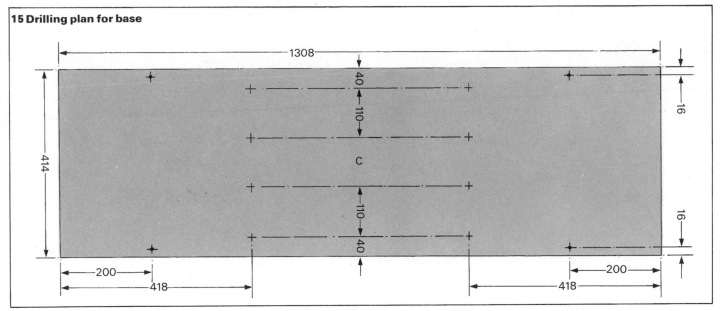

16 Drilling plan for back

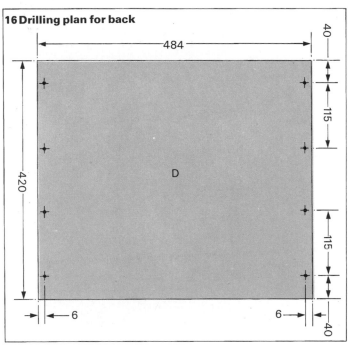

position with the 32mm long No 10 screws. Wipe off excess adhesive. Fix the drawer back and front F1 and F2 in the same way, except this time you must also screw through the sides into F1 and F2. The countersunk holes in F2 should face inwards.

Hold the drawer front facing G in the required position against the drawer assembly (**see 21**), making certain the side edges are flush and the top edge protrudes exactly 22mm above the top edge of the drawer front F2 and sides E. Mark with a bradawl through the clearance holes in F2 onto G and drill 2mm pilot holes at these points; drill to no more than 6mm deep to ensure the drill bit does not come out the other side.

Apply adhesive to the front face of the drawer front and fix the drawer front facing firmly in position with the 19mm long No 10 screws. Wipe off excess adhesive and leave to set.

When all the adhesive in the assembled drawer has set hard, drill a 25mm diameter finger-pull hole through the drawer front facing and the drawer front at the dimensions shown (**see 21**), making sure to clamp a piece of scrap wood to the back face of the drawer front so the drill bit will not tear off surface veneer as it bursts through the other side.

17 Drilling and shaping plans for sides

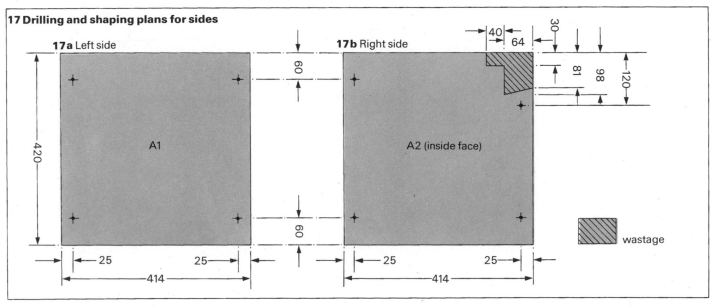

18 Drilling and shaping plan for peg rails

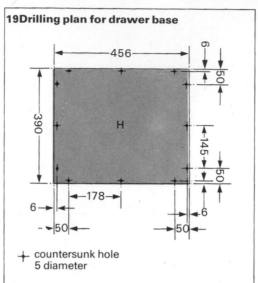

73

175
50

505

N2

35

25

85

25

22

48

+ countersunk hole
5 diameter
(N1 countersunk
on other face)

⊕ hole for peg
12 diameter, 50 deep

stage 9

Drill a 25mm diameter finger-pull hole in both cupboard doors J at the dimensions shown (**see 22**), placing a piece of scrap wood under the drilling area as before. Fix a lock to one of the doors, following manufacturer's instructions, and fix the catch plate to the other door (**see 22**). Screw two barrel bolts to the door with the catch plate fixed to it (**see 22**). The lock and bolts enable you to store dangerous or valuable tools out of the way of children.

Mark out the required positions of the two hinges on each door (**see 22**) and cut recesses for the thickness of the closed hinges in the edge of both doors. Screw one leaf of each hinge into the recesses and screw the other leaves to the inside

19 Drilling plan for drawer base

456

6

50

390

H

145

50

6

178

6

50

50

+ countersunk hole
5 diameter

20 Drilling plans for drawer sides and front

20a Sides

390

12

43

86

E1/2

6

6

12

20b Front

432

25

86

F2

50

166

50

25

21 Drawer assembly

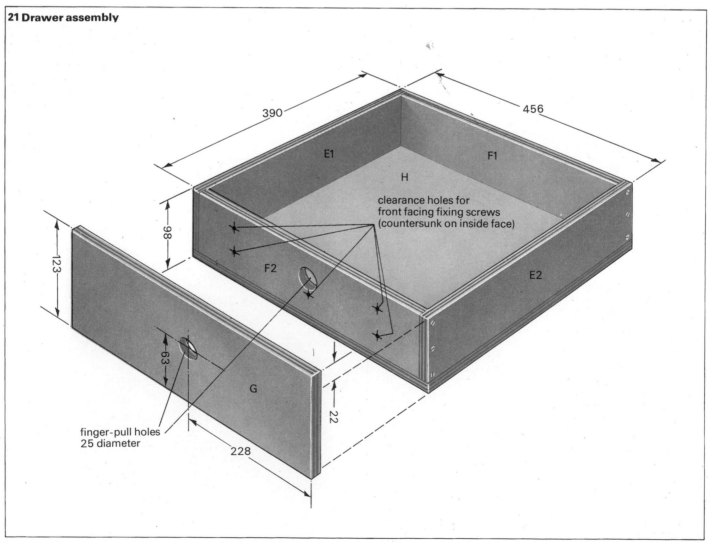

390

456

E1

F1

H

clearance holes for
front facing fixing screws
(countersunk on inside face)

98

123

F2

E2

63

G

22

finger-pull holes
25 diameter

228

face of the dividers B, using 9mm long brass countersunk screws of the correct gauge for the hinges. Close both doors and mark onto the cupboard base C and the brace batten M where the barrel bolts will enter; drill holes of the correct diameter at these points to a depth of 6mm. If the barrel bolts have catch plates, screw them in place over the drilled holes. Replace the workbench top (don't screw it down) and mark with a bradawl through the clearance holes in the top drawer runners L onto the bottom planks. Remove the top and drill 2mm diameter pilot holes 28mm deep at these points. Fix the top back in position with the four coach screws and screw through L1 and L2 with 50mm long No 10 screws.

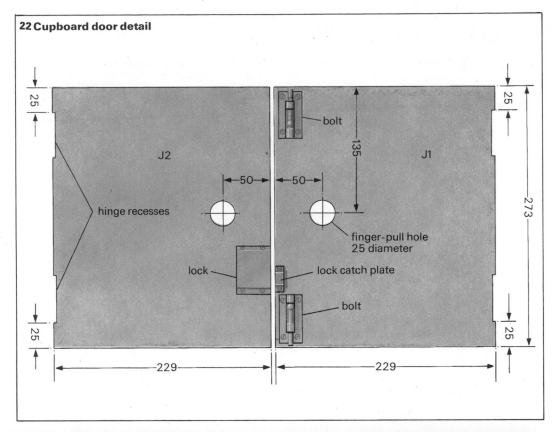

22 Cupboard door detail

J2

hinge recesses

J1

bolt

135

50 · 50

finger-pull hole
25 diameter

lock

lock catch plate

bolt

25 · 25 · 273 · 25 · 25

229 · 229

Mounting a vice

A most useful addition to a workbench is a woodworking vice, the principal requirement of which is that it grips over the largest possible area. Some ready-made benches incorporate large vices, but often you will have to fix your own; the size and type you choose depends on the type of work.

Woodworking vices
Some woodworking vices clamp onto a workbench and can be removed as necessary. These surface-mounted vices are less effective than the flush-mounted type since they have narrower and shallower jaws and are difficult to use because they hold the work above the level of the bench. It is advisable, if possible, to mount any vice permanently below the bench top so it does not protrude above the surface.

Clamp-on vice This type of woodworking vice is useful if your workbench is used for other purposes; when not in use the vice may be removed quickly and stored out of the way. Usually the vice is rested over the edge of the bench and the screw clamp is tightened beneath. Put a piece of scrap timber between the underside of the bench and the swivel screw to prevent marking the bench.

The main disadvantage with this type of vice is its lack of stability, although some models do have bolt holes in their base plates so the vice may be permanently placed if desired. There is, however, a loss of stability with all clamp-on types because they do not hold the work flush with the bench; this is especially true if the work is quite long.

Bench-mounted vice The ideal type is the permanent woodworking vice, the method of fixing varying with the model and size you choose. The vice should always be mounted near a bench leg for stability.

Usually the rear jaw of the vice is recessed into the bench edge and the body of the vice screwed to the underside of the bench, using 50mm (2in) coach screws through pieces of packing timber. Cut a recess in the front edge of the bench and fit the rear jaw of the vice flush with the edge. Screw the vice into position and fix an edging strip, about 22mm ($\frac{7}{8}$in) thick, along the bench edge. Alternatively you can cut a deeper and longer recess in the bench, fit the vice and fix the edging strip into the recess with countersunk screws.

The opening width of the jaws is not greatly reduced and the vice will offer a wide, flat area for holding long work. Don't cut too deeply into the underside of the bench since this will weaken it. The vice should have drilled holes in the front jaw to accept replaceable protective facings of hardwood or plywood; these should be lipped over the top of the jaw to protect the work and give a flush surface with the bench.

Metalwork vices
These vices have clamp-on, permanent or semi-permanent variations. There are many types and sizes of metalwork vice, most of which incorporate caps made of soft metal to prevent the work being damaged by the jaws.

Clamp-on vice The main disadvantage of this type of vice is its lack of stability. It is suitable for light work, where there is a limited amount of work

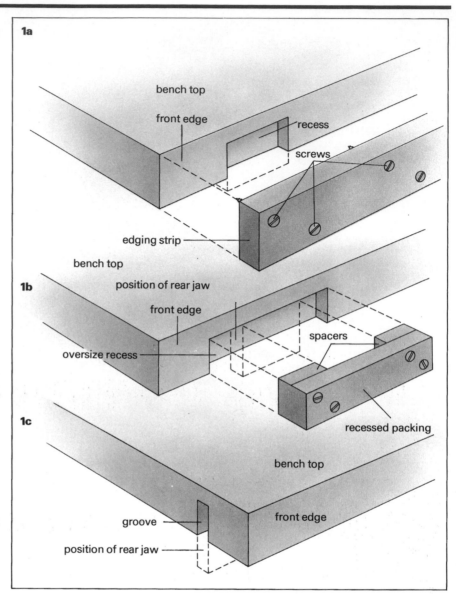

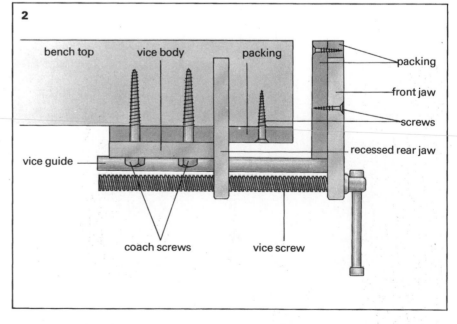

Mounting woodwork vice:
1a In front edge cut recess of same length and thickness as jaw of vice; cover with edging strip. **1b** Or cut oversize recess in front edge; use spacers of same thickness as rear jaw fitted each end of packing. **1c** Or cut in underside groove of same thickness and length as rear jaw. **2** Screw body through packing to underside; fit front packing to lie flush with bench top.
Mounting metalwork vice: **3** Screw body to bench top with rear jaw in line with front edge; or bolt through chipboard and hardwood block (**inset**). **4** Screw semi-permanent vice to T-block; or use bolt and recess heads (**inset**)

space available or in cases when the amount of metalwork you do does not justify the expense of a larger vice.

Bench-mounted vice A permanent metalworking vice is easy to mount. If the bench is made of thick timber, use three 50mm (2in) coach screws to fix the vice to the bench; if the bench top is chipboard, drill through the top and mount the vice through its fixing holes with three stout nuts and bolts. To increase rigidity on thin chipboard, fix through a piece of timber (ideally hardwood), about 19mm (¾in) thick, placed underneath the top. Mount the vice so the fixed rear jaw is in line with the front edge of the bench; this means you can use the vice to hold long pieces of work in the vertical plane.

It is best to mount the vice immediately above a bench leg; this gives stability and leaves most of the bench top clear so large sheets of metal can be easily handled. Some vices are swivel-based; fix these by drilling one hole through the bench for the swivel base stud and wing nut. For extra stability fix the swivel baseplate down onto the bench with three coach screws or nuts and bolts as before.

Semi-permanent vice This type is ideal when you

use a woodworking bench for metalwork from time to time. The vice is mounted on a T-shaped block, which has a vertical leg gripped in the jaws of a woodworking vice or Workmate bench. The vice allows secure mounting and flexibility; the mounting block may be turned through 180 degrees to allow the jaw slide to be used as a forward facing mini anvil. The whole vice and mounting can be removed from the bench quickly and stored away.

Make the mounting block from 50mm (2in) thick timber, large enough to take the baseplate of the vice. Fix the vertical leg securely to the top piece, using PVA woodworking adhesive and stout screws. Fix the vice to the block with 50mm (2in) coach screws or use nuts and bolts, with the heads of the bolts countersunk into the base of the block. The leg of the block should run from front to back when held in an end vice and from side to side when held in a front vice.

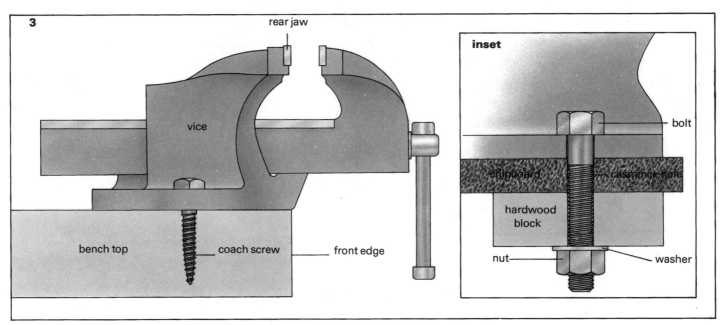

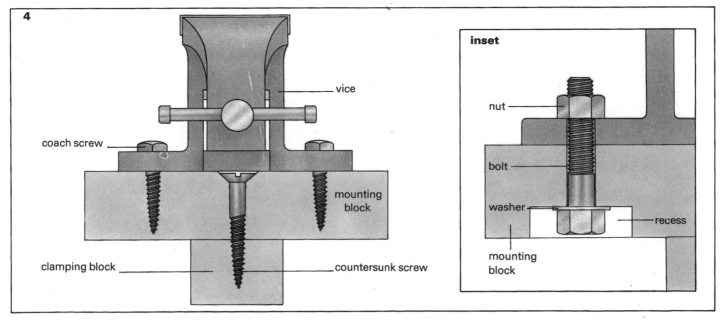

Making a tool belt

stage 1

To make the nail bag, cut a rectangle of canvas measuring 460 × 180mm and cut two 460mm lengths of the binding tape. Fold the lengths of binding over the two long edges of the canvas and pin and stitch them in position. Bind one of the short edges, turning under 10mm at each end before folding over the edge. Pin and stitch in position (**see 1**) and oversew the ends.

At the unbound end, measure in 10mm and fold over the canvas; measure 65mm from this fold and make another fold to form a wide loop. With the unbound edge on the inside, pin and sew the loop down (**see 2**).

Lay the canvas down with the loop on the underside, measure 165mm in from the other end (bound) and fold over to the top side to form the pocket (**see 3**).

Plan (dimensions in millimetres)

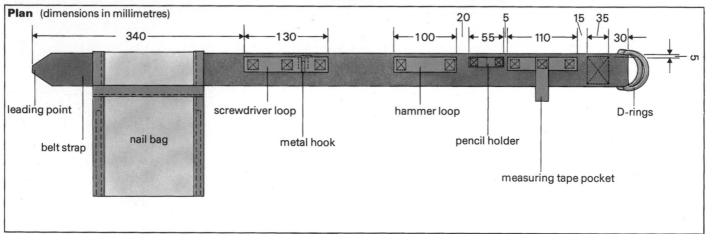

leading point · belt strap · nail bag · screwdriver loop · metal hook · hammer loop · pencil holder · measuring tape pocket · D-rings

---

1 Binding edges of nail bag

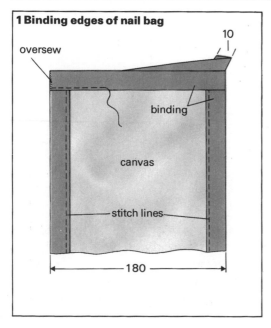

oversew · 10 · binding · canvas · stitch lines · 180

2 Making loop for nail bag

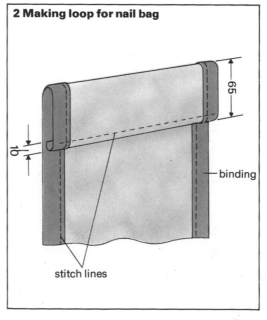

65 · 10 · binding · stitch lines

Tools and materials

measuring tape, thread
scissors, old kitchen knife
needles, pins, tailor's chalk
490 × 180mm of strong
  canvas
1.2m of 35mm wide binding
  tape
your waist measurement and
  an extra 225mm of 50mm
  wide man-made fibre
  webbing tape
285mm of 25mm wide man-
  made fibre webbing tape
250mm of 16mm wide man-
  made fibre webbing tape
55mm of 12mm wide elastic
two 50mm D-rings
one wire coat hanger or
  225mm of strong, ductile
  garden wire
vice or two pairs of pliers
hacksaw and fine emery paper

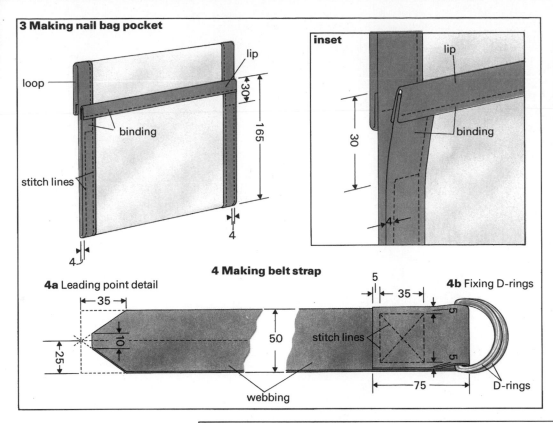

3 Making nail bag pocket

loop

lip

30

165

binding

stitch lines

4

4

inset

lip

30

binding

4

4 Making belt strap

4a Leading point detail

35

10

25

webbing

5

35

50

stitch lines

4b Fixing D-rings

5

5

75

D-rings

stage 3

To make the measuring tape pocket, cut the 16mm wide webbing into one 135mm length and one 110mm length with a hot knife as before. Sew them together at right-angles at the dimensions shown (**see 5a**) so the 135mm length forms the cross-bar and the 110mm length forms the upright. Place the belt strap face down with the D-rings on the left. Measure 70mm in from the melted end of the fold securing the D-rings, place the centre of the bottom end of the measuring tape pocket at this point and stitch it to the belt strap (**see 5b**), making sure the pocket is upside down; make the stitch lines into a crossed rectangle according to the dimensions shown (**see 5b**).
With the belt face up, stitch the ends of the cross-bar to the belt strap at the

Pin the two sides together and stitch them with strong thread 4mm in from the edges of the pocket, starting from the bottom and stopping 30mm from the lip (**see 3**). Stitch across the width of the binding 30mm down from the lip to join the two stitch lines together at each side of the pocket (**see 3 inset**).

stage 2

To make the belt strap, add 225mm to your waist measurement and cut the 50mm webbing tape to this length. At one end of this, mark out the leading point according to the dimensions shown (**see 4a**) and then cut it to shape with a hot knife. The knife is easily heated by blowtorch or in a cooker flame. Cutting it in this way is not dangerous, providing you are careful; it melts the man-made fibres so they bind together and will not fray. Melt the other end of the webbing in the same way and pass this end through the two D-rings (**see 4b**). Stitch down a 75mm fold, placing the stitch lines at the dimensions shown (**see 4b**); the crossed rectangle stitching will give extra strength to the belt strap.

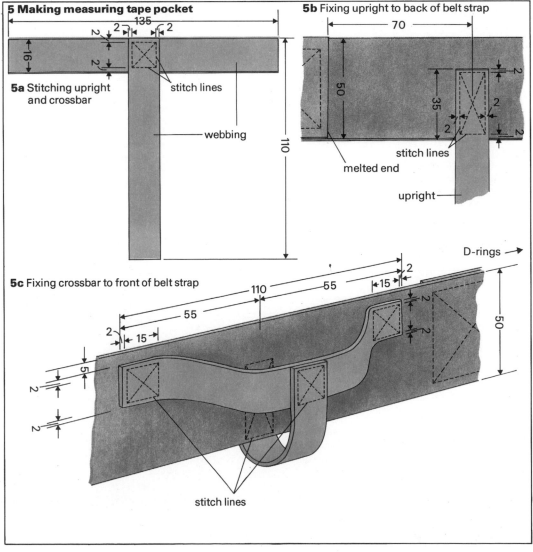

5 Making measuring tape pocket

135

2

2

2

2

16

5a Stitching upright and crossbar

stitch lines

webbing

110

5b Fixing upright to back of belt strap

70

50

35

2

2

2

2

stitch lines

melted end

upright

5c Fixing crossbar to front of belt strap

110

55

15

2

55

2

15

5

2

2

stitch lines

D-rings →

2

2

2

50

6 Making pencil holder

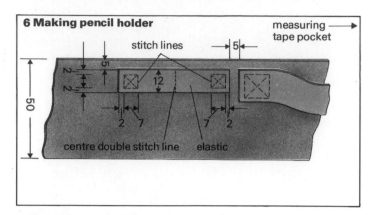

stitch lines

measuring tape pocket

centre double stitch line   elastic

7 Making hammer loop

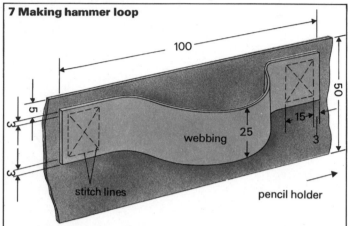

webbing

stitch lines

pencil holder

dimensions shown; make the stitch lines into a crossed rectangle as before (**see 5c**).

stage 4

To make the pencil holder, stitch the 55mm length of the elastic to the belt strap; make the stitch lines into a crossed rectangle at both ends of the elastic at the dimensions shown (**see 6**).

Double-stitch the middle of the elastic to the belt strap to form a loop at both sides of the stitch line; these loops will take pencils and pens of almost any diameter.

To make the hammer loop, cut a 130mm length of the 25mm wide webbing with a hot knife as before. Stitch this length of webbing to the belt strap at the dimensions shown (**see plan**), making the stitch lines into crossed rectangles (**see 7**).

stage 5

You can make the metal hook out of a wire coat-hanger or some strong, ductile garden wire. Using a vice or two pairs of pliers, bend the wire to the required shape according to the sequence

shown (**see 8a–g**).

When you have bent the wire into shape, cut off any excess with a pair of pliers or a hacksaw and smooth the cut ends with a fine flat file. If you use pliers to bend the wire, smooth over any indentations left by the jaws with fine emery paper.

To make the screwdriver loop and wire hook holder, cut a 150mm length of the 25mm wide webbing with a hot knife as before. Stitch this webbing to the belt strap at the dimensions shown (**see plan**), making two crossed rectangles at the dimensions shown (**see 9**). Make the screwdriver loop by stitching another crossed rectangle at the dimensions shown (**see 9**). Push the wire hook in position and secure it by making two stitch lines just inside the upright parts of the hook (**see 9**).

Slide the pointed end of the belt strap through the loop in the nail bag; it is easily removable so you can wash it.

The belt is fastened by threading the leading point of the belt strap through the D-rings according to the sequence shown (**see 10**).

8 Making metal hook

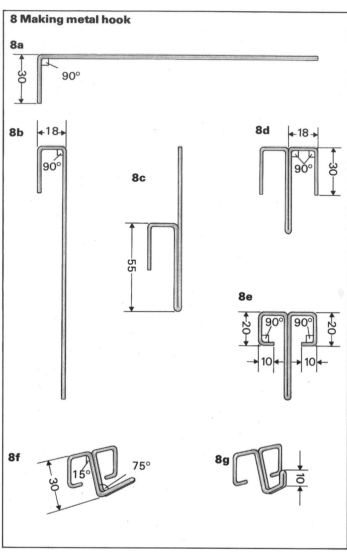

8a   30   90°

8b   18   90°

8c   55

8d   18   90°   30

8e   90°   90°   20   20   10   10

8f   30   15°   75°

8g   10

9 Making screwdriver loop

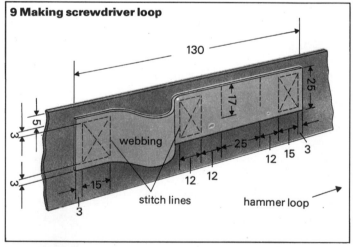

130   25   5   3   17   3   webbing   25   15   3   12   12   12   15   3   stitch lines   hammer loop

10 Fastening belt

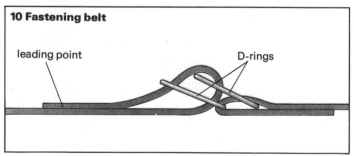

leading point   D-rings

Fixing and fastening

Owning the right tools is of crucial importance to the handyman, but it is not enough in itself to guarantee a good job. Good tools cannot be employed to their full potential on poor quality materials. Obviously, the better the wood you work with, the more satisfactory the finished job will be, but more basic elements also influence the quality of your work. The right additional hardware is vital. Care in selecting the right equipment will pay off both in the strength and the visual appeal of the project. For this reason we devote the following part of *The DIY Tool Guide* to an examination of some of the most fundamental, but often misunderstood jobs which every handyman must tackle. Almost without exception, DIY jobs around the home will involve the use of nails, screws or wall-fixing devices. With this knowledge in mind, we offer a comprehensive guide to the hidden complexities of these three basic techniques.

Everyone knows how to use a hammer and a nail, but costly projects can be damaged or weakened by using the wrong hammer with the wrong nail. While an unsuitably heavy hammer can easily bruise timber on a delicate project, the wood can equally easily be split by an ill-chosen nail. To solve the problem of selection, we illustrate and describe the many special nails on the market, and suggest some ingenious yet simple techniques for fixing nails without damage to either wood or fingers!

The variety of nails is more than matched by the wide choice of screws. There are special screws designed to cope with specific jobs, from fixing burglar-proof devices to attaching wall mirrors. We outline the choice, explain the much-used 'glue and screw' technique and show how to approach the often difficult task of gaining a strong screw fixing in the end grain of wood. Of course a clean fixing is not possible without the correct screwdriver for the particular screw. The tip of the screwdriver blade must fit the screw head perfectly if damage to screw or surrounding timber is to be avoided.

Securing a strong fixing into a wall will often be impossible without the aid of a suitable wall plug, toggle or bolt. Even such apparently insuperable problems as a plasterboard or hardboard wall can provide adequate support in combination with the right device. *The DIY Tool Guide* survey of fixing and fastening devices will prove particularly useful in selecting the right aid. It gathers in one place a wide range of plugs and bolts, some of which are generally familiar only to the professional but all of which are available to the home handyman. Our analysis of the most effective method for using each device, together with a chart matching fixings to the individual materials most often encountered, should provide the means of fixing even the heaviest objects securely to the wall.

Screws and screwing

Screws are available in a variety of sizes and finishes – including steel, stainless steel, brass, chromium plated, black japanned and sherardized – and screw heads are either slotted, or cross slot – called Supadriv or Pozidriv. (You may come across Phillips screws in some of the fittings around the home, although these are no longer made.) Screws are bought by quantity, unlike nails which are bought by weight.

Countersunk The most common screw used in woodwork. The flat head tapers towards the shank allowing it to be driven slightly below, or flush with, the work surface.

Round head To hold in place fittings which have not been drilled with countersunk holes. These decorative screws are used where they have to be left exposed.

Raised head These can only be countersunk to the rim, so the head still protrudes above the work surface. Mostly used with fittings which have been drilled with countersunk holes.

Dome head For mirror and fascia fixings. The head is flat and should be countersunk. It has a threaded hole in the middle of the slot into which a decorative cap can be fixed.

Clutch head The specially shaped head makes it impossible to remove the screw. Suitable for fitting locks and other burglar-proof devices.

Self-tapping For sheet metal fixings. They cut their own thread when driven into a small pilot hole and are available with round, raised or flat heads.

Coach For heavy duty fixings. The head is bolt-shaped so the screws have to be fixed into the work with a spanner.

Dowel A double-ended screw for dowelling together two pieces of timber. The screw has a thread at both ends and a shank in the middle. Drive half of the screw into one piece of timber using a pair of pliers on the shank and then twist the other piece of timber onto the screw.

Chipboard The large thread profile gives a stronger grip in chipboard than an ordinary screw and the thread continues right up to the head.

Screw hooks and eyes Most hooks and eyes can be bought either plain or shouldered, in shapes and sizes to suit the job in hand.

Screw sizes
The size of a screw is measured in two dimensions – the overall length from head to point and the diameter of the shank (gauge). Most woodworking screws range from gauge Nos 4–14 and their length varies from 9–152mm ($\frac{3}{8}$–6in).

You must have all the necessary details available when buying screws – quantity, gauge, finish, type and length. For example you might ask for ten No 8 brass countersunk screws 38mm ($1\frac{1}{2}$in) long.

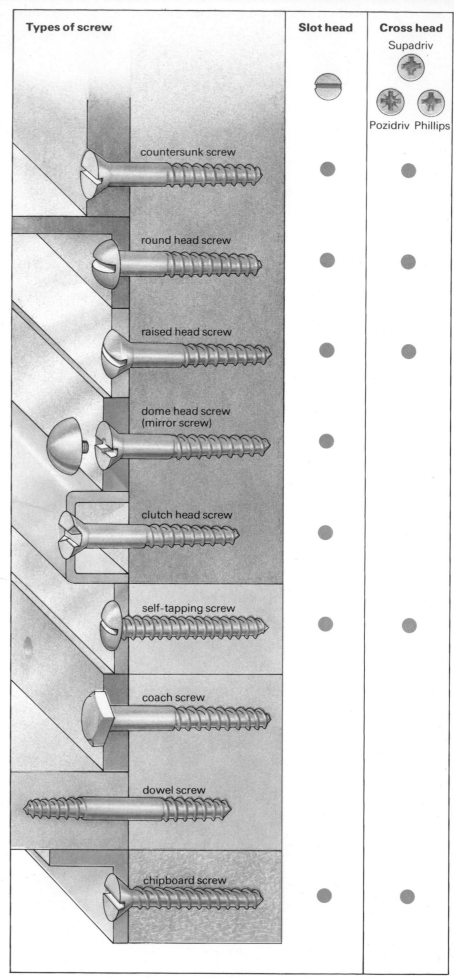

Types of screw | **Slot head** | **Cross head** (Supadriv, Pozidriv, Phillips)

- countersunk screw
- round head screw
- raised head screw
- dome head screw (mirror screw)
- clutch head screw
- self-tapping screw
- coach screw
- dowel screw
- chipboard screw

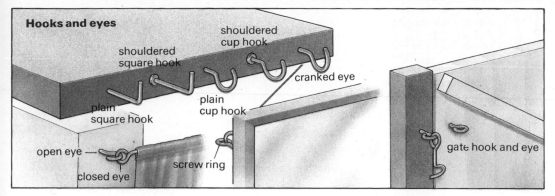

Hooks and eyes

shouldered
square hook

shouldered
cup hook

cranked eye

plain
cup hook

plain
square hook

gate hook and eye

open eye —

closed eye

screw ring

How to use screws

When joining two pieces of timber together, drill a clearance hole through the first piece so the shank of the screw can be passed through it. Drill a pilot hole (you can make some holes with a bradawl) in the second piece of timber; this hole should be slightly smaller in diameter than the threaded part of the screw. Pilot holes are especially important when using hardwoods to prevent splitting.

When using countersunk screws, countersink the clearance hole to take the head of the screw. This is done with a countersink bit which can easily be fitted into an electric or hand drill. There is a countersink bit with a handle which saves time as you do not have to insert it in the drill chuck. Use a bit with two cutting edges for softwoods and a multi-edged bit when countersinking into hardwoods.

Guide to clearance and pilot holes

Screw gauge	Clearance hole	Pilot for hardwood	Pilot for softwood
No 4	3mm ($\frac{1}{8}$in)	2mm ($\frac{5}{64}$in)	bradawl
No 6	4mm ($\frac{5}{32}$in)	2mm ($\frac{5}{64}$in)	bradawl
No 8	5mm ($\frac{3}{16}$in)	3mm ($\frac{1}{8}$in)	2mm ($\frac{5}{64}$in)
No 10	5mm ($\frac{3}{16}$in)	3mm ($\frac{1}{8}$in)	2mm ($\frac{5}{64}$in)
No 12	6mm ($\frac{1}{4}$in)	4mm ($\frac{5}{32}$in)	3mm ($\frac{1}{8}$in)
No 14	6mm ($\frac{1}{4}$in)	5mm ($\frac{3}{16}$in)	4mm ($\frac{5}{32}$in)

End grain Screws, like nails, do not provide a strong fixing when driven into the end grain of wood. The joint can be strengthened by inserting a dowel across the grain so screws driven through the end grain will penetrate the dowel.

Gluing and screwing This term is used when you need to strengthen a joint by gluing as well as screwing. Apply a coating of woodworking adhesive to one face of the timber pieces to be joined. Screw the two pieces together while the adhesive is still wet and wipe off with a clean dampened cloth any excess that squeezes out. Leave the adhesive to dry for 8–12 hours.

Washers, cups and sockets Washers are mostly used with round head screws to provide extra pressure at the fixing point. Screw cups are used when screwing into thin materials where countersinking would weaken the fixing. Sockets allow the screw to lie flush with the work surface and also give a decorative finish to the fixing.

Warning Steel screws will eventually rust if covered with a water-based filler or emulsion paint and cause brown patches to spread across the paint surface after application. To prevent this, use noncorroding screws or make certain any steel screws are primed with a rust-preventative metal primer before proceeding with any decoration, the effect of which could otherwise be spoiled.

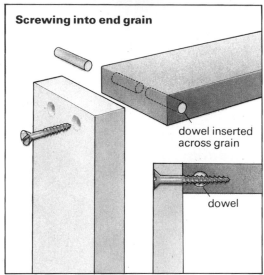

Screwing into end grain

dowel inserted
across grain

dowel

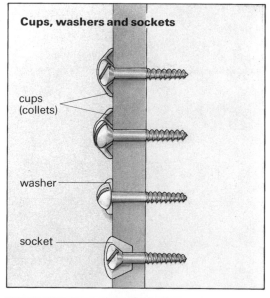

Cups, washers and sockets

cups
(collets)

washer

socket

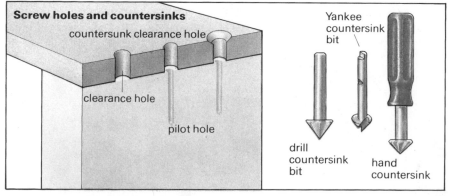

Screw holes and countersinks

countersunk clearance hole

Yankee
countersink
bit

clearance hole

pilot hole

drill
countersink
bit

hand
countersink

Nails and nailing

Nails provide the quickest and easiest method of fixing or joining together pieces of wood. Nailed joints will be considerably strengthened by also applying woodworking adhesive. A wide range of nails is available, so make sure you use the right type and size of nail for the job you have to do.

Types of nails
Nails and tacks are available in small quantity packs, but it is usually cheaper to buy them by weight. The number in any given weight will obviously depend on the size of the nail.

Round wire nails These large round head nails are mostly used for rough carpentry where appearance is not important but strength is essential. They are inclined to split a piece of wood. Sizes from 20–150mm (¾–6in).

Oval wire nails Most suitable for joinery work where appearance is important since they can easily be punched below the surface. They are less likely to split the wood if driven in with the longer sides parallel to the grain. Sizes from 12–150mm (½–6in).

Round or lost head nails Stronger than oval wire nails, they can easily be punched below the surface of the wood. Sizes from 12–150mm (½–6in).

Cut clasp nails Rectangular in section, they are difficult to remove and provide a very strong fixing in wood and pre-drilled masonry. Sizes from 25–150mm (1–6in).

Cut floor brads Also rectangular, they have an L-shaped head and are nearly always used for nailing floorboards to joists. Sizes from 12–150mm (½–6in).

Panel pins Round lightweight nails used for delicate cabinet work and for fixing small mouldings into place. They can easily be punched below the surface. Sizes from 12–50mm (½–2in).

Veneer pins Very small type of panel pin.

Hardboard nails These have a diamond-shaped head which is virtually hidden when hammered into hardboard. Sizes from 9–38mm (⅜–1½in).

Clout nails Most are galvanized for use outside. Particularly suitable for nailing down roof felt as the large round head on these nails holds the felt firmly in position without tearing it. Sizes from 12–50mm (½–2in).

Masonry nails Toughened round nails which can be hammered into brick, breeze block and most types of masonry. Different gauges are available and lengths are from 19–100mm (¾–4in).

Tacks Used for nailing carpets to floorboards or stretching fabric onto wood. They have very sharp points and large round flat heads. Sizes from 19–32mm (¾–1¼in).

Sprigs Similar to tacks but without heads. They are used mainly to hold glass in window frames before applying putty which covers them up. Sizes from 12–19mm (½–¾in).

Upholstery nails Available in chrome, brass and other metallic finishes, they are used as a secondary fixing with tacks. The dome head gives a decorative finish when nailing chair coverings into place. Various head sizes are available.

Staples U-shaped round wire nails with two points to hold lengths of wire in position. Some staples have an insulated lining for fixing flex and electric cable.

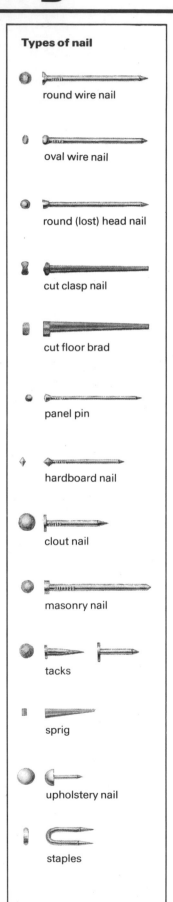

Types of nail

round wire nail

oval wire nail

round (lost) head nail

cut clasp nail

cut floor brad

panel pin

hardboard nail

clout nail

masonry nail

tacks

sprig

upholstery nail

staples

Nailing methods
When joining two pieces of wood, the length of the nails used should be just under twice the thickness of the thinner piece of wood. Where possible nail through the thinner piece into the thicker piece in any joint and drive the nail in at a slight angle, where you can, to increase the strength of the joint. Always nail on a firm surface; if nailing unsupported wood, hold a heavy block behind it.

Preventing wood splits Nails easily cause both hardwoods and softwoods to split, especially near the end of a length. To avoid splits in hardwoods, for each nail drill a pilot hole slightly smaller in diameter than the nail. This also applies to chipboard and plywood.

Softwoods offer little resistance to nails but are still liable to split. Don't drive in nails close together in the same line of grain and always try to use oval nails with the longer sides parallel to the grain. It is also worth slightly blunting the point of the nail before hammering it into the wood and, if possible, cutting lengths of wood oversize so nails do not have to be driven in close to the end; you can trim the wood after fixing.

Clench nailing When joining two pieces of wood together the strongest bond will be made by clench nailing, preferably using round wire nails. Space the nails up to 12mm (½in) apart and drive them through the wood from either side, leaving at least 25mm (1in) showing through the other side. Bend over the projecting end of each nail with a hammer and drive right into the wood.

Angle nailing Any nail driven at an angle into the wood will give a stronger grip than if driven in at right-angles to the surface. You will achieve the strongest joint by driving one nail at a 45 degree angle to the wood and a second nail at the same angle from the opposite direction.

Using small nails and pins You may have difficulty in starting off panel and veneer pins, especially if you have large fingers. To prevent bruising your fingers, use the flat pein side of the head of a cross pein or pin hammer to strike the pin. Once it is secured, use the round striking face to drive it home. You can also hold the pin with thin long-reach pliers or push it through a thin piece of card and hold it until the pin grips enough to need no further support. Remove the piece of card before driving the pin home.

Hidden or secret nailing With certain decorative woodworking jobs, lift up a sliver of wood with a sharp chisel and nail through underneath this, punching the nail below the surface. Use small oval or lost head nails. Glue the sliver of wood back into position with woodworking adhesive and rub over the area with fine glasspaper; the marks will barely be visible.

There is another method of secret nailing, useful when laying tongue and groove floorboards (and securing tongue and groove joints). Hammer the nail into the tongue at a 45 degree angle so it goes through the board (not through the other side of the tongue) and into the fixing surface. The nail will be concealed by the groove in the next board.

The easiest and quickest method of hiding a nail is to punch it below the surface and fill the hole with cellulose filler or plastic wood.

Nail punch A steel, pencil-like implement about 100mm (4in) long which enables you to sink pin and nail heads below the surface without damage whereas a hammer head would bruise the work on the last few blows. The punch should be of the same diameter as the head of the nail.

Using a nail punch Hammer the nail until it lies just proud of the surface. Place the tapered end of the punch on the nail head and strike it with a hammer until the head sinks below the surface. Fill the hole to give a smooth finish.

Warning Iron nails will rust easily if covered with a water-based filler and emulsion paint, causing brown patches to spread across the painted surface. Either use galvanized nails or make sure any iron nails are thoroughly treated with a rust-resistant metal primer before continuing decoration.

Gluing and pinning Apply a thick layer of wood-working adhesive to both faces to be joined. Select the appropriate nails or pins for the job and nail the two pieces of wood together while the adhesive is still wet. Wipe off any excess adhesive with a clean dampened cloth and leave to dry for up to 12 hours. Gluing and pinning gives a strong joint even when the fixing faces of two pieces of wood are quite small.

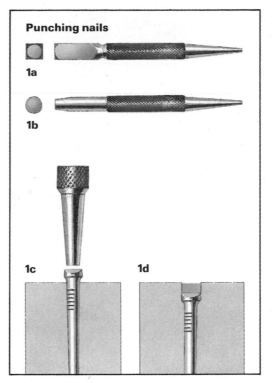

Punching nails

1a

1b

1c   **1d**

1a Square-headed nail punch
1b Round-headed nail punch
1c Nail proud of surface,
1d Nail below surface
2 Nail through thin to thick
3a To avoid splitting wood, don't hammer nails into the same line of grain; (inset) keep flat side of oval wire nail parallel to grain
3b cut timber overlength and then saw off waste
4 Clench nailing
5 Angle nailing
6a Start panel pin with a cross pein hammer
6b Alternatively hold panel pin with piece of card
7a Chisel up sliver of wood and hammer nail in underneath (inset). Nail hidden when sliver is glued back in position
7b With tongue and groove boards hammer nail through tongue at an angle so that nail is hidden when next board is put in position

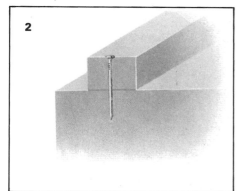

2

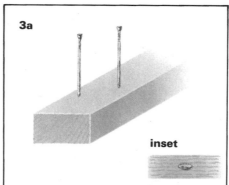

3a

inset

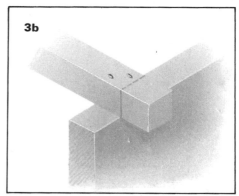

3b

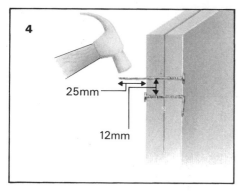

4

25mm

12mm

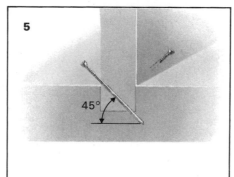

5

45°

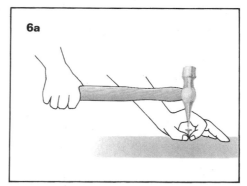

6a

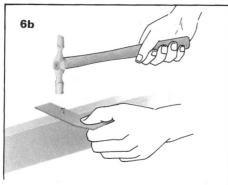

6b

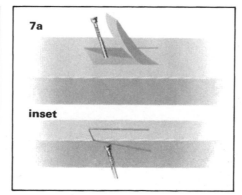

7a

inset

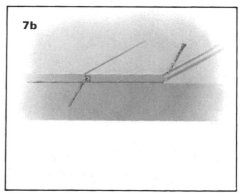

7b

Fixing it to stay up

The correct fixing method depends not only on the construction of the wall but also on the weight and nature of the object to be supported.

There are two basic types of wall – solid (brick or block built) or hollow partition. From the point of view of wall fixings cavity construction can be regarded as solid brickwork. If you tap the surface of your wall you will get either a solid or hollow response depending on the construction. Remember where a thick plaster coating is applied to brickwork it is important to get your fixing securely into the brickwork for maximum support. Hollow types consist of sheets of plasterboard or laths and plaster fixed to a timber framework and are mainly used for partitioning.

Decide exactly where you want to place the fitment on the wall and then mark the fixing holes accordingly. Drill holes in the fitment first, if not already made. Don't attempt to fix heavy items on partition walls unless you can drill into the framework of the partition.

Drilling into a wall

For this job you will need a tungsten carbide-tipped masonry drill bit fitted into the chuck of an electric or hand drill. The tough carbide tip ensures a long life for the drill bit even with the rapid wear and tear involved in drilling masonry. If your drill has more than one speed, operate it as slowly as possible.

If you find a section is extremely hard, such as a concrete lintel above a door or window, you may need a hammer action electric drill or a drill fitted with a hammer attachment. The hammer drill bit is driven into the wall by turning and hammering simultaneously.

If a power or hand drill is not available then a hole can be made with a jumping bit (such as the Rawldrill or Stardrill) and a club hammer (a heavy duty hammer with a large striking face).

Rawldrill Used for punching holes in all types of masonry. This bit is made from a high quality steel for toughness and durability. The bit is fitted into a special holder through its tapered shank; it is fluted so that debris from the hole is cleared out as work progresses.

Fit a bit of the correct diameter into the tool holder. Mark clearly with a pencil where the hole is to be made, place the bit on the mark and gently tap the holder with a hammer. Turn the holder slightly between blows and continue until you reach the required depth. Use the special ejector tool to remove the bit from the holder.

1 Nylon wall plugs with helical wings (Fischer type GB)
2 Nylon collapsible anchors (Fischer type NA)
3,4 Spring toggles with hook or washer (Fischer types KDH3 and KD3)
5,6 Spring toggles (Rawlplug)
7,8 Gravity toggles (Rawlplug)
9 Fibre wall plugs (Rawlplug)

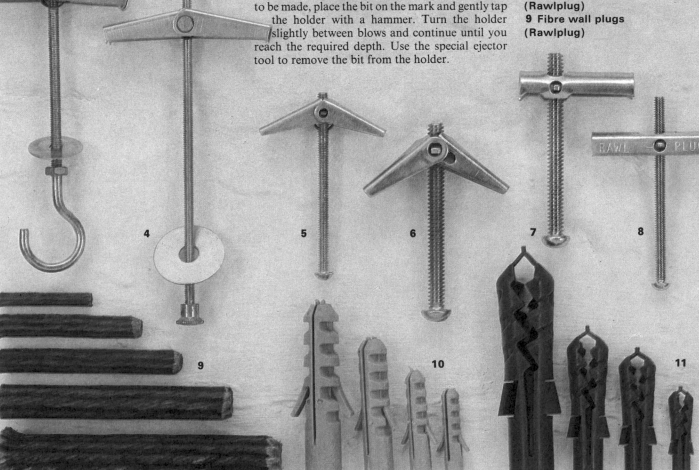

112

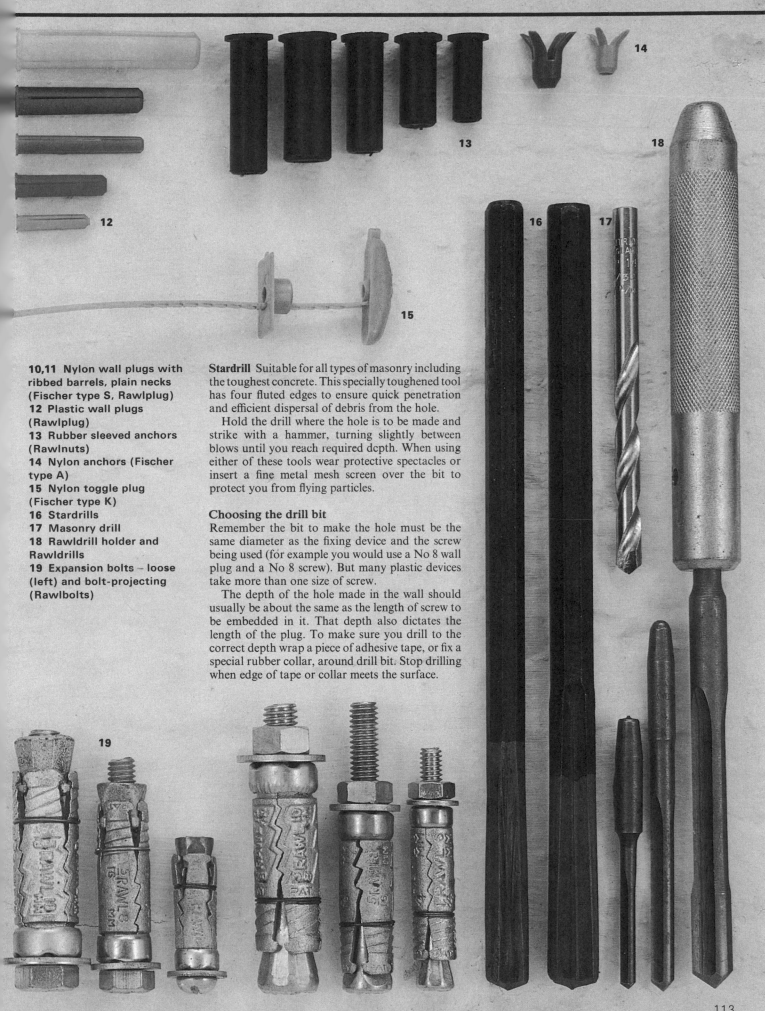

10,11 Nylon wall plugs with ribbed barrels, plain necks (Fischer type S, Rawlplug)
12 Plastic wall plugs (Rawlplug)
13 Rubber sleeved anchors (Rawlnuts)
14 Nylon anchors (Fischer type A)
15 Nylon toggle plug (Fischer type K)
16 Stardrills
17 Masonry drill
18 Rawldrill holder and Rawldrills
19 Expansion bolts – loose (left) and bolt-projecting (Rawlbolts)

Stardrill Suitable for all types of masonry including the toughest concrete. This specially toughened tool has four fluted edges to ensure quick penetration and efficient dispersal of debris from the hole.

Hold the drill where the hole is to be made and strike with a hammer, turning slightly between blows until you reach required depth. When using either of these tools wear protective spectacles or insert a fine metal mesh screen over the bit to protect you from flying particles.

Choosing the drill bit
Remember the bit to make the hole must be the same diameter as the fixing device and the screw being used (for example you would use a No 8 wall plug and a No 8 screw). But many plastic devices take more than one size of screw.

The depth of the hole made in the wall should usually be about the same as the length of screw to be embedded in it. That depth also dictates the length of the plug. To make sure you drill to the correct depth wrap a piece of adhesive tape, or fix a special rubber collar, around drill bit. Stop drilling when edge of tape or collar meets the surface.

Types of wall fixings and how to use them

Situation	Type of fixing	How to use
Masonry, brickwork and concrete	**Plastic wall plugs** (Rawlplug) The variety of plug lengths available makes these convenient when large number of fixings has to be made. The plug is tapered internally to centre screw correctly, making it easier to use than fibre plug. The range is coded in seven colours, each taking variety of screws. (To fit screws Nos 4–20)	Drill hole to same depth as wall plug. Push plug into hole, slip screw through fitment into plug and tighten.

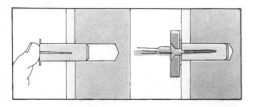

	Fibre wall plugs (Rawlplug) Screws can be withdrawn and replaced if necessary without removing plugs. Cut to exact length as required. (Range to fit screws Nos 6–26; coach screws 6mm/¼in and 12mm/½in diameter)	Drill hole and insert plug to just below wall surface. Turn screw into plug up to shank and then withdraw it. The plug expands to fit hole tightly making it easier to find centre of plug when fixing fitment into place and to drive screw home firmly. Note that plug should be as long as threaded part of screw.

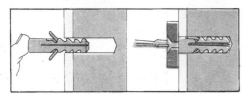

	Nylon wall plugs with ribbed barrel and plain neck (Fischer type S; Rawlplug) Ribbed barrel gives really tight fit. Each plug takes variety of screws, also shank of screw. (Fischer plugs fit screws Nos 2–14; Rawlplug Nos 6–18)	Drill hole slightly deeper than wall plug being used. Push plug into hole, slip screw through fitment into plug and tighten.

| **Soft materials, such as lightweight building blocks** | **Nylon wall plugs with ribbed barrel and plain neck** (Fischer type S; Rawlplug) As for **Masonry etc.** | Drill hole slightly deeper than wall plug being used. Push plug into hole, slip screw through fitment into plug and tighten. |

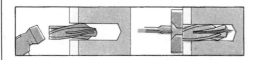

	Nylon wall plugs with helical wings (Fischer type GB) The helical wings grip contours of hole, giving very strong fixing. (To fit screws Nos 10–18)	Drill hole of same diameter as plug body. Overall diameter of plug will be twice drill hole, so you must hammer plug into wall. Slip screw through fitment into plug and tighten.

| **Irregular or oversize holes** | **Compound fillers** (Rawlplastic; Screwfix) These compounds come in powder form in small cans | Moisten sufficient amount of powder with water and ram into hole either with special tool (often provided with filler) or any flat piece of metal about same size as hole. When filler is still moist make indentation with sharp tool where screw is to go. |

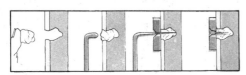

| **High temperature areas** | **Fibre wall plugs** (Rawlplug) As for **Masonry etc.** | Drill hole and insert plug to just below wall surface. Turn screw into plug up to shank and then withdraw it. The plug expands to fit hole tightly making it easier to find centre of plug when fixing fitment into place and to drive screw home firmly. The plug should be as long as threaded part of screw. |

	Expansion bolts (Rawlbolts) Projecting type (when bolt cannot be removed) is suitable when fixture can be suspended before being screwed into place. With loose type, fixing bolt can be removed at any time. The anchoring unit comprises shield with expander nut. Loose type allows bolt to be inserted after shield is in place	Drill required hole. If using projecting type insert it, position fitment on bolt end and tighten nut. With loose type, insert shield and position fitment over it; pass bolt or stud through fitment into shield and tighten.

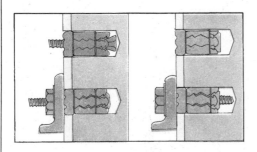

Types of wall fixings and how to use them

Situation	Type of fixing	How to use
Extra hard walls 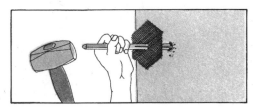	**Nylon wall plugs with ribbed barrel and plain neck** (Fischer type S; Rawlplug) As for **Masonry etc.**	Drill hole slightly deeper than wall plug being used. Push plug into hole, slip screw through fitment into plug and tighten. You cannot make hole with a standard hand drill when surface is very hard. Use jumping bit (Rawldrill; Stardrill) or hammer drill to make hole. You must wear protective spectacles or insert fine metal mesh screen over drill bit to protect you from flying particles.

Situation	Type of fixing	How to use
Plasterboard, hardboard, lath and plaster 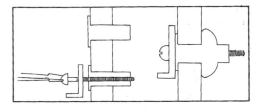	**Rubber-sleeved anchors** (Rawlnut) Used in thin, cavity walls and especially useful in thin sheets of metal or plastic because fixing is vibration-proof. When screw is tightened, rubber sleeve is compressed against reverse side of wall. The anchor will remain in place if retaining screw removed. (Variety of sizes available; screws supplied with anchors)	Drill hole of same diameter as rubber sleeve and insert anchor until flange touches wall surface. Slip screw through fitment into anchor and tighten.
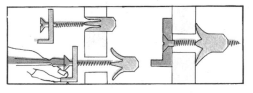	**Nylon anchors** (Fischer type A) Very useful when cavity in hollow wall is particularly small. If screw is removed anchor is lost. The screw should be at least equal in length to thickness of fitment plus thickness of wallboard and length of anchor. (Three anchor sizes to fit screws Nos 6, 8 and 10)	Drill required hole. Insert screw through fitment into anchor, with two or three turns only, before pushing it through hole into wall cavity. Pull fitment towards you to compress anchor tongue against wall and tighten screw at same time.
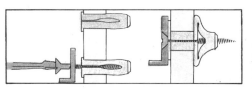	**Nylon collapsible anchors** (Fischer Rivet Anchor type NA) As screw is tightened, body expands; device remains in place if screw is removed. (Four sizes to fit screws Nos 6, 8 and 10)	Drill required hole and push anchor through until flange touches wall surface. Slip screw through fitment into anchor and tighten.
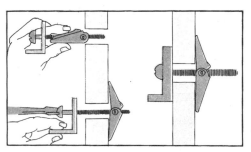	**Spring toggles** (Fischer types KD3 and KDH3; Rawlplug) Metal thread screw and two spring-loaded metal arms which spread load over wide area on reverse side of wall cavity. Toggle is lost if screw removed. (One size of each Fischer type and either metal thread screw or hook supplied. Three sizes of Rawlplug type, with or without screws)	Drill hole just big enough to allow toggle to be passed through with its spring-loaded arms squeezed together. Pass fixing screw through fitment into toggle. Push toggle through hole until arms spring apart, pull fitment towards you and tighten screw.
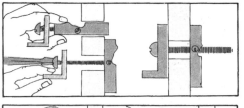	**Gravity toggles** (Rawlplug) When toggle is passed through hole, bar drops down at right-angles to fixing screw. The toggle is lost if screw is removed. These can only be used when fixing to vertical surfaces. (Three sizes, with or without screws)	Drill hole just big enough to allow toggle to be passed through when bar is parallel to fixing screw. Pass fixing screw through fitment into toggle and push toggle through hole until bar drops. Pull fitment towards you and tighten screw until fitment is firm.
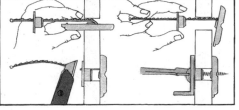	**Nylon toggle plugs** (Fischer type K and KH) The notched nylon strip makes it possible to use device on any thickness of wall or board as plugs are easily adjusted. The toggle remains in place if screw is removed. (Toggle 32mm/1¼in or 57mm/2¼in long, both take No 8 screw)	Drill required hole so toggle collar fits neatly into it with flange touching surface of wall. Push toggle through hole, fit collar in place and pull notched nylon strip towards you until device is tightly in place. Cut off any surplus from strip. Slip screw through fitment and collar into toggle and tighten.

Tool care

It is easy to make good resolutions about tool care, and even easier to forget them at the end of a hard day's work. When we finish a difficult job which has taken far longer than we hoped and expected, it is tempting in our exhausted state to leave the tools lying scattered over the floor, dirty and unprotected, forgotten until they are needed once again. In such moments, when all we can think of is our own thirst and fatigue, it really is worth taking a few moments to clean the tools down and return them to their proper place. Their useful life will be extended by good care, and future work will be far more pleasurable if it is not automatically preceded by a lengthy period devoted to repairing damage during improper storage.

The first priority is a place to store the tools, which will ideally be by hanging them on the wall from purpose-built racks and hooks. It is not recommended to store cutting tools loose in a tool box. However, there are times when such a practice is unavoidable, for example when you need to transport a selection of tools to a work site remote from the workroom. In such circumstances, the blades should all be protected to prevent damage to both cutting edges and unwary fingers. While special plastic caps are manufactured to protect the delicate cutting edge of a chisel, you can prevent accidents with a saw by covering the blade with a slotted piece of waste timber, which can easily be held in place by a rubber band.

The tips on the following page give the do's and don'ts of basic tool care. They are followed by more detailed information on the sharpening of chisels, planes, gouges and saws.

Chisels and gouges need frequent careful sharpening if their efficiency is not to be impaired, and few people should find the elementary instructions too difficult to follow. New equipment has recently come on the market putting traditionally awkward sharpening jobs within the scope of the amateur handyman. However, should the prospect of sharpening and setting a saw prove too daunting, it is not necessary to resign yourself to using a blunt saw. Local tool shops will, in many cases, operate an inexpensive sharpening and resetting service. Alternatively, the manufacturers may be able to offer advice on any problems.

Manufacturers' servicing arrangements are particularly significant where power tools are concerned. The major manufacturers should all operate servicing networks, but it is advisable to check out the arrangements before you buy an expensive tool. Basic servicing of an electric drill is not difficult, as can be seen from the annotated diagram in this section of *The DIY Tool Guide*. However, it may prove wise to use the manufacturer's expertise for sharpening circular saw blades, which must be kept sharp. Blunt blades can lead to overloading of the power tool's motor, a relatively costly replacement.

Throughout *The DIY Tool Guide* we have stressed the value of buying the best tools you can afford. In all probability your tool kit now represents a sizeable financial investment. It is only sensible to protect your assets, and since the techniques of tool care are not complex, it should not prove difficult to make lifelong friends of your best tools, provided you treat them with the respect they deserve.

Care of electric drills

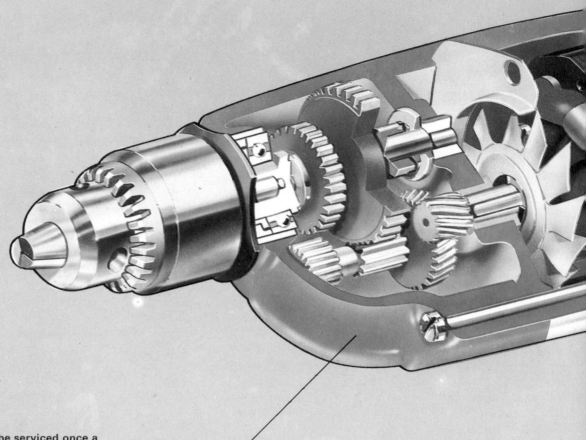

Your electric drill should be serviced once a year by a local dealer or manufacturer, or by yourself. Always check the terms of a current guarantee, however, as this might be invalidated by home servicing or repairs. The service involves removing the motor, clearing away all dust in the drill and lubricating the gear wheels, bearings and brushes. If you tackle this job yourself, the golden rule is always to remove the plug from the socket before attempting any adjustments, maintenance or repair work.

One and two-part casings
With this type you can usually pull away the gearbox and chuck assembly from the front of the body by releasing the retaining screws. Take off the cover at the back of the body to reach the brushes and rear bearing. Remove the brushes before carefully levering out the end plate to withdraw the motor. On certain drills the casing will open down the middle when you release the retaining screws. Some screws may be longer than others, so note their positions. You will be able to wipe out most of the dust with a clean lint-free rag. Use a small stiff brush (not a wire one as this would scratch the commutator) when cleaning the more intricate parts.

Fitting new switch
Replace a faulty switch by removing the hand grip cover and releasing the switch retaining screw. Disconnect the leads and position the new switch, making sure you refit the leads to the same terminals as for the old unit. Tighten retaining screw and replace cover.

Removing dust
Drill motors collect large amounts of dust because of the work they do. If air vents clog up, the motor will overheat and dust will eventually get into the working parts, causing excessive wear. Every few months hold the smallest nozzle attachment you have on your vacuum cleaner over the ventilation slots and suck out as much dust as possible.

Lubricating bearings
The gear wheels and ball-bearing races in the drill must be packed with a high melting-point grease. Use light oil for bush-type bearings, where the shaft runs in a plain collar of phosphor-bronze. If there is a felt pad, soak in oil.

Bearing types
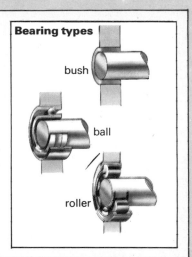

bush

ball

roller

Carbon brushes
Replace any carbon brushes that are worn down close to their spring seats. Clean brushes with white spirit, but note their positions when removing. Check when replacing that they slide in their housings.

Renewing flex
If the flex wears or a core breaks so no power reaches the switch, the flex must be renewed. Remove the hand grip cover by releasing the retaining screws, undo the flex clamp (similar to that on a plug) and disconnect the leads from the switch. These may be held with terminal screws or clamped. Fit the new flex with the leads in the same positions as the old ones. Check the flex is tightly clamped and replace the cover.

Basic items
vacuum cleaner, small nozzle attachment
screwdriver, clean lint-free rag
small stiff brush (not wire)
high melting point grease
light oil, white spirit

equipment

Sharpening planes, chisels and gouges

When you look at a plane, chisel or gouge blade, you will see two angles form the cutting edge. This edge is sharpened to a 30 degree angle and the long ground face slopes back more gradually at about a 25 degree angle.

Oilstone

The honed edge is kept razor sharp by rubbing on an oilstone; these are expensive and must be looked after carefully. They are usually 50mm (2in) wide and 25mm (1in) thick; some are 150mm (6in) long, but a 200mm (8in) stone is better because it allows you to make a longer stroke.

Oilstones are available in coarse, medium and fine grades. There are also combination stones which are usually fine on one side and medium on the other. Coarse grade stones are required only when the edge of the plane or chisel blade is badly chipped and large amounts of metal have to be removed. The medium grade is used to get the blade ready for the final honing and the fine grade to give the final cutting edge.

Planes and chisels

Keep the oilstone in a box and put a few drops of light oil on it each time before use. Hold the blade at a 30 degree angle to the oilstone and, keeping the angle constant, work the blade backwards and forwards over the entire surface of the stone.

Keep rubbing until a feather-edge burr builds up on the flat side of the blade. With practice you will be able to do this freehand, holding the handle with one hand and maintaining pressure on the blade with the other. But at first you will find it much easier to keep the blade steady if you use a honing guide.

2

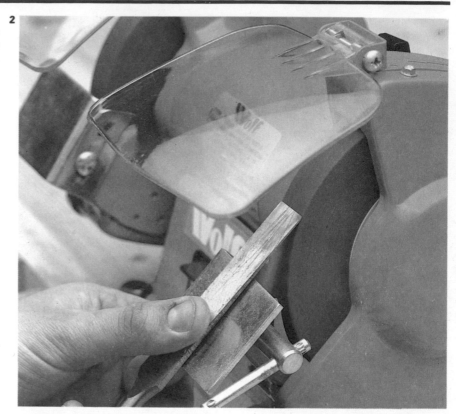

3

4

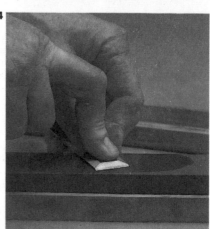

1

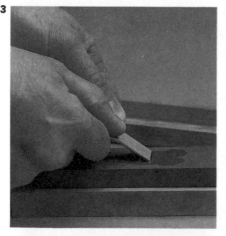

5

6

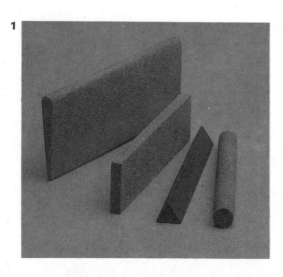

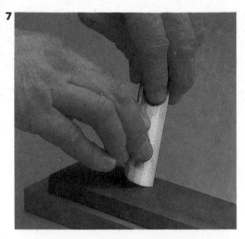

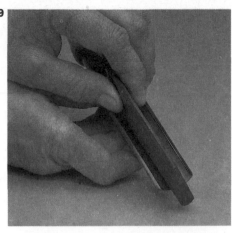

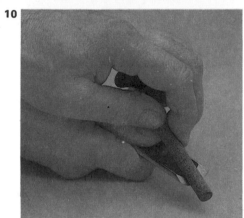

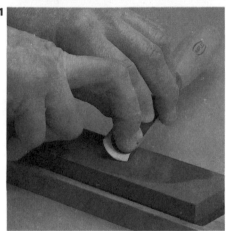

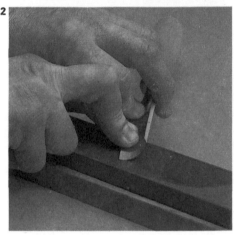

1 Slipstones come in various shapes; use a cylindrical or tapered one for sharpening gouges. 2 Use a grindstone wheel to restore a square edge and 25 degree grinding angle on a chisel or plane blade, then restore the 30 degree cutting edge on a slipstone. 3 When sharpening a chisel or plane blade hold it at an angle of 30 degrees on the oilstone and rub it back and forth. 4 Once a burr has built up, hone the flat side, keeping it flat on the oilstone, until the burr wears thin and turns to the bevelled side. 5 A honing guide may be used to maintain the 30 degree angle; use the screw at the side to adjust to the required angle. 6 Move the honing guide back and forth along the oilstone. 7 & 8 Hone the angled side of a firmer gouge with a sideways twisting action. 9 Use a slipstone to remove the burr from the inside edge of a firmer gouge. 10 To sharpen a scribing gouge first rub the inside edge with a slipstone. 11 & 12 Rub the outside edge of a scribing gouge on an oilstone

Turn the blade over and hold it flat on the oilstone until the burr wears thin and turns back to the bevelled side. Using less pressure each time, continue honing each side of the blade in turn (occasionally wiping the edge clean with a rag) until the burr wears off, leaving a razor-sharp edge.

It is most important for the oilstone to be absolutely flat otherwise the chisel or plane blade will not have a true, straight edge. From time to time lay the edge of a steel rule across the stone to check it is still flat. If it is seriously mis-shapen, buy a new stone. Slight irregularities can be removed by grinding the stone with water and carborundum (sold for gem engraving and polishing) on a piece of float glass. Always keep your stone clean.

Warning Use only float glass here as this is manufactured to ensure a true flat surface; sheet glass will have slight imperfections and the surface will not be sufficiently flat.

Gouges

The principle of sharpening a gouge is the same as that for a chisel or plane; a burr is built up on the cutting edge and worked until it drops off. But the method of rubbing is different and a slipstone is used in addition to an oilstone. A slipstone is smaller than an oilstone and is made in different shapes. The one used for sharpening gouges has its long edges rounded and is tapered to give two different radii. A cylindrical one may also be used. Keep it in its own box to protect it from dust.

Firmer gouge

Build up a burr on the inside edge by rubbing the angled side of the blade on an oilstone, holding the

blade at 30 degrees to the stone. Use a sideways twisting action to ensure even contact with the stone along the length of the edge. When you have built up a burr on the inside, return it by rubbing a slipstone forward and back along the inside edge parallel to the blade. Repeat this two-step procedure until the burr drops off, leaving a razor-sharp edge.

Scribing gouge

Sharpen a scribing gouge in the same way as a firmer gouge but reverse the sequence. First build up a burr on the inside edge by rubbing a slipstone to and fro on the cutting edge, holding the stone at a 30 degree angle to the blade. When you have built up the burr, return it by rubbing the outside edge on the oilstone; hold the blade flat on the stone and twist it from side to side with a gentle rocking motion.

Grinding blades

If the blade of a chisel or plane is seriously chipped or badly worn, you can regrind it yourself on a grindstone wheel to restore a square edge and the 25 degree grinding angle. Regrinding a gouge is more difficult and we recommend you take it to your tool supplier.

Don't let the blade overheat; hold it only lightly against the grindstone, pointing against the direction of rotation of the wheel, and occasionally dip it in water. On no account must the cutting edge turn blue; if it does, this indicates the blade has lost its hardness.

After regrinding, restore the 30 degree cutting edge by honing the blade on an oilstone.

Sharpening saws

Saw sharpener

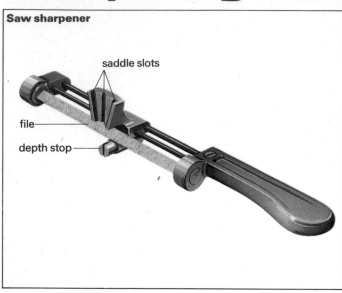

saddle slots

file

depth stop

Above Saw sharpener maintains correct depth of teeth and gives accurate filing angle (Eclipse 38 saw sharpener)

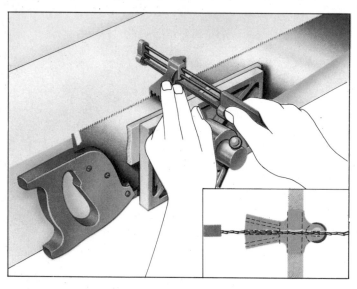

Above For rip saw, set file angle to correct tooth shape and follow sharpening procedure as for cross-cut saw but use only middle saddle slot of sharpener and file teeth consecutively rather than alternately

Right Release ridged anvil screw on saw set, press and turn until anvil number in line with hammer corresponds to number of points per 25mm (1in) on saw. Squeeze handles to grip anvil and tighten ridged anvil screw

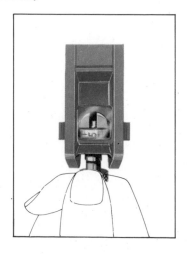

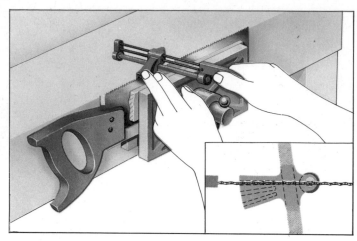

Above Set file angle for required tooth shape for cross-cut or tenon saw. Clamp saw between pieces of hardboard in vice. Run fine flat file over tops of teeth to give equal height. Mark gullet of one tooth set towards you about 20mm ($\frac{3}{4}$in) from handle end of saw. Place file in marked gullet with top saddle slot and depth stop straddling teeth (inset). File every alternate tooth with three or four strokes. Return to handle end of saw and place file in gullet next to marked gullet with bottom saddle slot and depth stop straddling teeth. File alternate teeth as before

Saw set

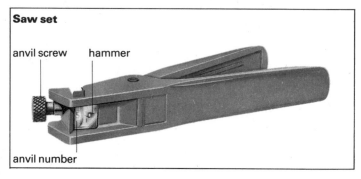

anvil screw   hammer

anvil number

Above After sharpening, teeth must be set to ensure clean, easy cut. Saw set will guarantee every tooth tip is accurately bent out on either side of blade (Eclipse saw set)

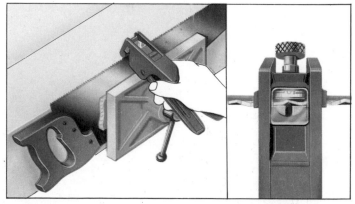

Above Clamp saw pieces of hardboard in vice and mark first tooth set away from you. Place head of saw set over saw so tooth to be set is directly in line with hammer (inset). Gently squeeze handles together to set tip of tooth, release handles and lift saw set clear. Set every alternate tooth, turn saw round and set remaining teeth

Care of basic tools

Steel measuring tape

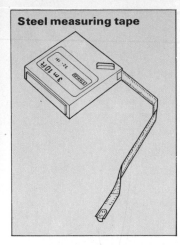

DON'T leave steel measuring tape extended, especially with blade on edge, on workbench or floor in case something falls onto it; damaged tape will be virtually useless

Saw

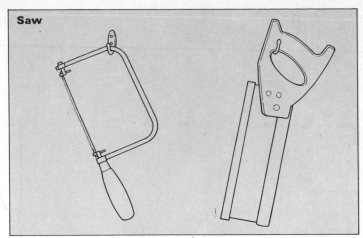

DO hang up saws by handle or frame when not in use and put blade guard over cutting edge; if left lying about teeth may get damaged. Lightly oil blade to prevent rust. Sharpen teeth, or replace blade, regularly.

Electric drill

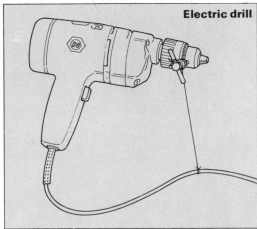

DO tie chuck of electric drill to lead with string, but allow enough length to turn key without having to untie it. Service drill regularly as worn parts will impair efficiency.

Hammer

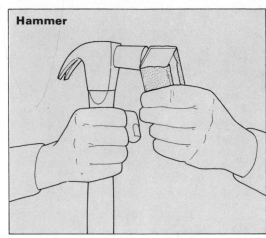

DO keep hammer heads clean and free of any traces of adhesive; rub hammer face squarely with fine glasspaper round block of wood. Bang loose heads back into place and/or use wedging pins.

Chisel

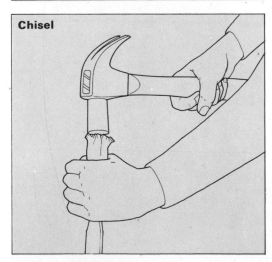

DON'T use hammer on wood-handled chisels; side of hammer head can be used on plastic handles. Ideally use mallet to prevent damaging handle. Never use chisel as screwdriver or you will ruin edge. Maintain good cutting edge by regular sharpening.

DON'T use screwdrivers as levering devices or for raking, chipping or digging holes. If shafts are bent or blade ends not squarely cut they will not turn screws efficiently.

Screwdriver

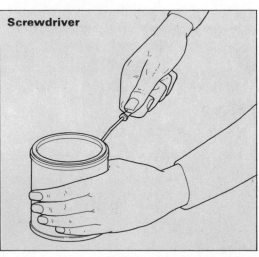

Plane

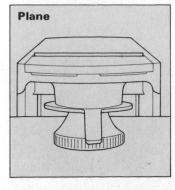

DO check plane blades are correctly adjusted. Hold bottom of plane squarely up to light; blade should be parallel to bottom so it cuts evenly across its full width

DO rest planes on their side to avoid damaging blade or bottom and keep regularly sharpened. After use, store in dry place to avoid rusting.

Plane

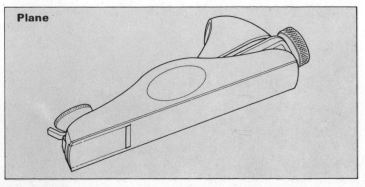

Appendix 1 Tool hire

A good tool kit should contain all the basic tools which the handyman might regularly require for a wide variety of jobs. It would, however, be a poor investment to buy those obscure and expensive tools and items of equipment needed for a one-off project; even if the tools are indispensable to the job in hand, they are not worth buying if you will rarely, if ever, need them again.

The tool hire trade has now expanded its services to the home handyman – one sector of building activity which has shown consistent growth in recent years. Most tools can be hired by the day, week or month and many hire shops have free catalogues and price lists. It is a good idea to acquire a catalogue before you need any tools, since advance knowledge of hire possibilities in your area could prevent an unnecessarily expensive purchase.

Price It is always worth studying the price lists published by hire contractors; weekly rates, for example, can represent excellent value, sometimes as little as twice the daily rate. To take full advantage of such concessions, arrange your work schedules around the cheap rates; for example, sand all the floors in the house at the same time, rather than having to hire the sander on several occasions. Special cheap weekend rates often operate from closing time on Saturday to Monday morning. Delivery and collection cost extra and it is sensible to book tools several days in advance, if possible, to avoid disappointment and delay to your work.

Tools available

The tools you are most likely to hire will be those for the one-off job and it is precisely these tools you are least familiar with. Reputable hire contractors are aware of the problems faced by the amateur needing specialist tools for the first time and many companies have produced printed instructions on using each hire tool. Whether printed instructions exist or not, all shops should be willing to give a demonstration of the tool in action. Such demonstrations are important because a visual display can be easier to understand than written instructions and you will be able to see the tool is in good working order; you will be asked to leave a sizeable deposit (perhaps the equivalent of three weeks' hire charge) when you take the tool home and you do not want to be liable for any earlier damage.

Tools can be hired for most of the jobs the ambitious handyman will tackle. Besides such general building aids as tarpaulins, ceiling props, surveying levels and sash cramps, there are such specific tools as tile cutters and damp-proofing injectors. Below is a list of the range of tools under job headings. Availability will vary around the country, so check with your local dealer before you make your plans.

Cleaning and carpeting Powerful versions of the familiar domestic carpet shampooer are available, together with floor scrubbers, vacuum cleaners and soil extractors. Tools for cutting and laying carpet are also for hire.

Concreting Concrete mixers, powered by petrol or electricity, can also be used for mixing plaster. Additional concreting equipment – wheelbarrows, spirit levels, shovels and pickaxes – can be hired together with a compactor, which is useful for compressing the foundations before concreting over.

Demolition Various demolition hammers and drills will save time when breaking up concrete or demolishing brickwork and masonry.

Drilling The full range of electric drills is available, although a two-speed drill is so useful it should be part of any basic tool kit. Special drills include an angle drill, for working in confined spaces such as between the floor joists; this is often necessary when rewiring.

Floor renovation The perfect hire tool is a powerful floor sander, used for sanding down and fine finishing of wood, cork or composition floors. Other tools polish marble, tiles and other flooring

Below: Well-appointed tool hire shops, like this one, have sprung up in recent years to meet a growing demand

surfaces. Edger discs are available to reach inaccessible areas.

Heating and lighting Heater blowers, powered by electricity or gas, speed drying-out processes as well as keeping you warm during extensive alterations to the home. Gas-powered floodlights and lanterns help you work at night on projects remote from a power supply.

Ladders and access aids It is essential to have the correct ladder for the job. In particular, roof ladders, platform steps and aluminium section ladders with ladder brackets are available to improve safety during work. Platforms, scaffolding and trestles are also available for hire.

Lifting and moving To prevent back damage putting an end to your DIY work, it is worth hiring trucks, trolleys, miniature cranes, winches and wheels to lift and move heavy items.

Painting and decorating Stripping old wallpaper off walls and ceilings is greatly simplified by hiring a steam wallpaper stripper, powered by gas or electricity. The machine also helps reduce damage to plaster during scraping. Folding tables for pasting, dust sheets and blow lamps can be hired, although these are useful items to own.

Sanding and planing Belt sanders can be hired to remove wood rapidly, while disc sanders are effective for sanding smaller areas of wood, plastic and metal. Orbital sanders are for fine finishing, but will not cope with heavy work. Laminate trimmers and planes can also be handy.

Sawing If you do not own a power saw and you have a large amount of cutting to do, the range of saws on hire can make the job infinitely less daunting. There are circular saws, jig-saws and chain saws. A saw bench can also be hired.

Spraying Sprayers are available suitable for loading with a variety of materials.

Plumbing A complete range of plumbing tools and equipment – from tube benders and pipe vices to pipe threaders, drain-clearing rods and drain pressure testers – can be hired.

Power Generators will provide electric power anywhere for lighting, powering tools and heating.

Appendix 2
Metric conversion charts

Imperial measurements are expressed below in yards, feet and inches rather than in decimals for convenience if converting with rulers or measuring tapes which do not include decimal readings.

Metric prefixes and abbreviations

The metre is used as an example below. The same prefixes apply to litres (l or lit) and grams (g). The abbreviation lit is used for litre when unqualified to avoid confusion with the numeral 1.

millimetre (mm)	0.001	one thousandth metre
centimetre (cm)	0.01	one hundredth metre
decimetre (dm)	0.1	one tenth metre
metre (m)	1	one metre
decametre (dam)	10	ten metres
hectometre (hm)	100	one hundred metres
kilometre (km)	1000	one thousand metres

Feet/metres

ft	in		m
3	3	**1**	0.30
6	7	**2**	0.61
9	10	**3**	0.91
13	1	**4**	1.22
16	5	**5**	1.52
19	8	**6**	1.83
23	0	**7**	2.13
26	3	**8**	2.44
29	6	**9**	2.74
32	10	**10**	3.05
65	7	**20**	6.10
98	5	**30**	9.14
131	3	**40**	12.19
164	0	**50**	15.24
196	10	**60**	18.29
229	8	**70**	21.34
262	6	**80**	24.38
295	3	**90**	27.43
328	1	**100**	30.48

Yards/metres

yd	ft	in		m
1	0	3	**1**	0.9
2	0	7	**2**	1.8
3	0	10	**3**	2.7
4	1	1	**4**	3.7
5	1	5	**5**	4.6
6	1	8	**6**	5.5
7	2	0	**7**	6.4
8	2	3	**8**	7.3
9	2	6	**9**	8.2
10	2	10	**10**	9.1
21	2	7	**20**	18.3
32	2	5	**30**	27.4
43	2	3	**40**	36.6
54	2	0	**50**	45.7
65	1	10	**60**	54.9
76	1	8	**70**	64.0
87	1	6	**80**	73.2
98	1	3	**90**	82.3
109	1	1	**100**	91.4

Length (linear measure)

Fractions of 1 inch in millimetres

Thirty-seconds, sixteenths, eighths, quarters and one half

in	mm
1/32	0.8
1/16	1.6
3/32	2.4
1/8	3.2
5/32	4.0
3/16	4.8
7/32	5.6
1/4	6.3
9/32	7.1
5/16	7.9
11/32	8.7
3/8	9.5
13/32	10.3
7/16	11.1
15/32	11.9
1/2	12.7
17/32	13.5
9/16	14.3
19/32	15.1
5/8	15.9
21/32	16.7
11/16	17.5
23/32	18.3
3/4	19.0
25/32	19.8
13/16	20.6
27/32	21.4
7/8	22.2
29/32	23.0
15/16	23.8
31/32	24.6
1 inch	25.4

Twelfths, sixths and thirds

in	mm
1/12	2.1
1/6	4.2
1/4	6.3
1/3	8.5
5/12	10.6
1/2	12.7
7/12	14.8
2/3	16.9
3/4	19.0
5/6	21.2
11/12	23.3
1 inch	25.4

Note

Find the Imperial figure you wish to convert in the **heavy** type central column and read off the metric equivalent in the right-hand column and vice versa.
For example:
10 inches = 254 millimetres and 10mm = 0.39in.

Conversion from inches is only taken up to 40 in the chart below, see next chart for continuation.

Inches/millimetres

in		mm
0.04	**1**	25.4
0.08	**2**	50.8
0.12	**3**	76.2
0.16	**4**	101.6
0.20	**5**	127.0
0.24	**6**	152.4
0.28	**7**	177.8
0.31	**8**	203.2
0.35	**9**	228.6
0.39	**10**	254.0
0.43	**11**	279.4
0.47	**12**	304.8
0.51	**13**	330.2
0.55	**14**	355.6
0.59	**15**	381.0
0.63	**16**	406.4
0.67	**17**	431.8
0.71	**18**	457.2
0.75	**19**	482.6
0.79	**20**	508.0
0.83	**21**	533.4
0.87	**22**	558.8
0.91	**23**	584.2
0.94	**24**	609.6
0.98	**25**	635.0
1.02	**26**	660.4
1.06	**27**	685.8
1.10	**28**	711.2
1.14	**29**	736.6
1.18	**30**	762.0
1.22	**31**	787.4
1.26	**32**	812.8
1.30	**33**	838.2
1.34	**34**	863.6
1.38	**35**	889.0
1.42	**36**	914.4
1.46	**37**	939.8
1.50	**38**	965.2
1.54	**39**	990.6
1.57	**40**	1016.0
1.97	**50**	
2.36	**60**	
2.76	**70**	
3.15	**80**	
3.54	**90**	
3.94	**100**	
7.87	**200**	
11.81	**300**	
15.75	**400**	
19.68	**500**	
23.62	**600**	
27.56	**700**	
31.50	**800**	
35.43	**900**	
39.37	**1000**	

Quick conversion factors – length

Terms are set out in full in the left-hand column except where clarification is necessary.

1 inch (in)	= 25.4mm/2.54cm
1 foot (ft)/12in	= 304.8mm/30.48cm/0.3048m
1 yard (yd)/3ft	= 914.4mm/91.44cm/0.9144m
1 mile (mi)/1760yd	= 1609.344m/1.609km
1 millimetre (mm)	= 0.0394in
1 centimetre (cm)/10mm	= 0.394in
1 metre (m)/100cm	= 39.37in/3.281ft/1.094yd
1 kilometre (km)/1000m	= 1093.6yd/0.6214mi

Quick conversion factors – area

1 square inch (sq in)	= 645.16sq mm/ 6.4516sq cm
1 square foot (sq ft)/144sq in	= 929.03sq cm
1 square yard (sq yd)/9sq ft	= 8361.3sq cm/ 0.8361sq m
1 acre (ac)/4840sq yd	= 4046.9sq m/0.4047ha
1 square mile (sq mi)640ac	= 259ha
1 square centimetre (sq cm)/ 100 square millimetre (sq mm)	= 0.155sq in
1 square metre (sq m)/ 10,000sq cm	= 10.764sq ft/1.196sq yd
1 are (a)/100sq m	= 119.60sq yd/0.0247ac
1 hectare (ha)/100a	= 2.471ac/0.00386sq mi

Quick conversion factors – volume

1 cubic inch (cu in)	= 16.3871cu cm
1 cubic foot (cu ft)/ 1728cu in	= 28.3168cu dm/0.0283cu m
1 cubic yard (cu yd)/ 27cu ft	= 0.7646cu m
1 cubic centimetre (cu cm)/ 1000 cubic millimetres (cu mm)	= 0.0610cu in
1 cubic decimetre (cu dm)/ 1000cu cm	= 61.024cu in/0.0353cu ft
1 cubic metre (cu m)/ 1000cu dm	= 35.3146cu ft/1.308cu yd
1cu cm	= 1 millilitre (ml)
1cu dm	= 1 litre (lit) See **Capacity**

Index

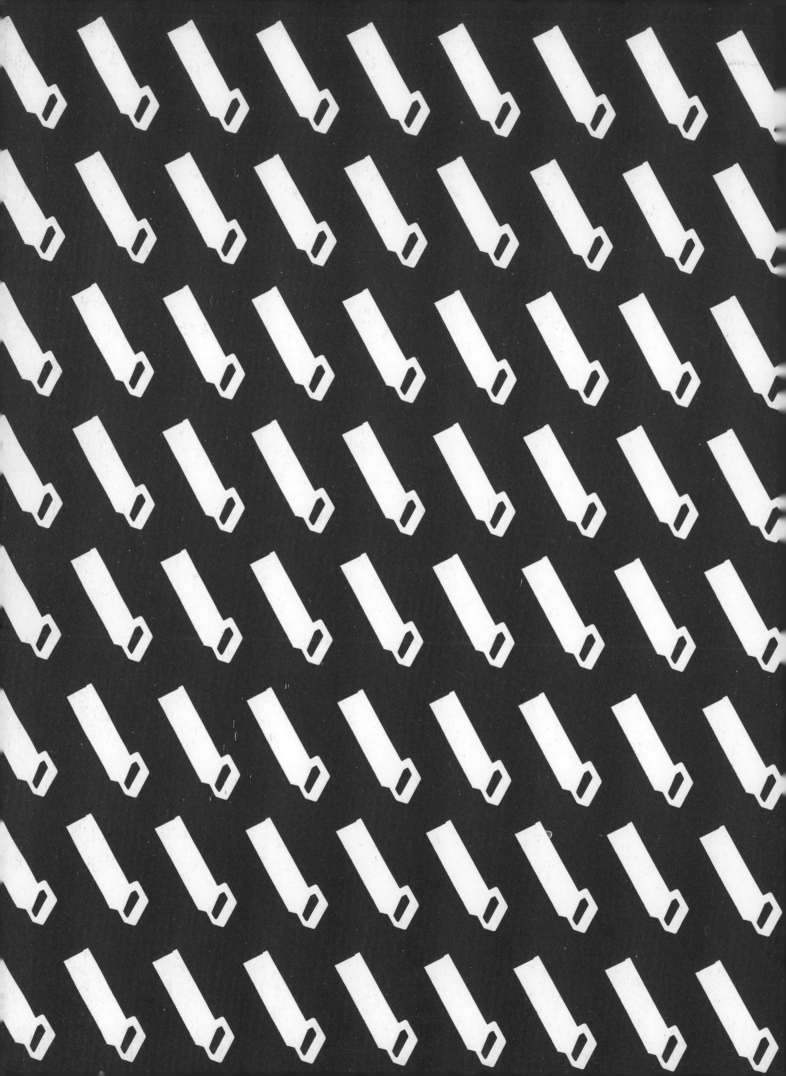